Claude de Passione

A novel of Romance, drama, and deceit

John H Gray

All rights reserved. In accordance with the U.S. Copyright Act of 1976, the scanning, uploading, and electronic sharing of any part of this book without permission of the publisher is unlawful piracy and theft of the author's intellectual property. If you would like to use material from the book (other than for review purposes), prior written permission must be obtained by contacting
thestory@myself.com
Thank you for your support of the author's rights

All characters and events in this book are fictitious. Any similarity to real persons, living or dead, is coincidental and not intended by the author.

Other works by the author:
Journey of Betrayals (2017)
Journey to Unknown Consequences (2018)

In Conjunction with Aruban Historian
And Author Mr. Dufi Kock

The Torpedo Incident at Eagle Beach (2009)
E.S. Antilla

ISBN 978-0-9952387-4-9

© Copyright registered (2018) John H Gray

Part 1

The Early Years

Chapter 1

Present day, Passion Fields Estate Winery, Napa Valley, California

Claude walked across the loose gravel driveway to the estate garage. The stones crunched beneath his feet as he walked through the brisk early morning air. He glanced around. No one else in the palatial home had yet arisen. Claude looked out over the expansive fields of the vineyard. Small pockets of misty cloud hung in the valleys. Already the early gentle summer temperatures were proving favorable to an excellent yield of the family's famous and acclaimed grape vines.

Claude opened the doors to the garage and walked to his favorite car. He loved his expensive and rare collection. He smiled to himself as he viewed his prize possession. The red Ferrari 250LM shone in the early sunlight that danced through the high windows of the garage.

Claude opened the driver's door and slid himself onto the luxurious black leather seat. He made sure the car was in neutral gear and cranked the key in the ignition. The Ferrari burst into life. The crackling of the exhausts of the high-performance car echoed across the vineyard and throughout the surrounding hills.

Claude eased the car into gear to start his drive from the northern California hills of Napa Valley to Sausalito. He was leaving to fetch Claire Waters, his girlfriend, for the special brunch he had planned at the Tides Restaurant in

Bodega Bay. Today he would give up the years of flamboyant bachelor life and finally propose marriage. Afterward, they would return to the mansion and announce the news to the surviving members of Claude's family. Claude felt a momentary pang of loss as he thought of his father Marquis Charles and the circumstances of his death. He wished the Marquis was still alive to be with him on his wedding day.

His family consisted of a younger brother, Philippe who was mentally deranged and functioned with the capabilities of a five-year-old. His sister, Catherine had become deeply religious and joined the order of the Carmelite nuns after a disastrous affair with the local mayor.

Claude feared the reaction of his domineering mother. He firmly believed she was the one responsible for the playboy life he had lived and his many affairs. He wondered if her actions had caused him to look for different qualities in the hundreds of women he had dated and been intimate with. He smiled to himself as he recalled those days. He remembered the affairs with the divorcees, the bored married wives and the emotionally deprived girls looking for easy street. He wondered how he had escaped unscathed.

He pulled away from the garage and drove slowly down the estate's long eucalyptus-lined driveway. Already, the scent from the eucalyptus filled the air. Claude loved his life in Napa Valley. The life he had lived in France seemed long ago and without the richness his life provided him here in California.

As Claude was about to pull out onto the highway he spotted the beat up old grey Ford F-150 pickup truck hurtling toward him. At the gate, he braked, turned off the car's ignition and waited.

The old pickup slowed and braked sharply. Loose gravel and stones flew from the locked front wheels. The driver's door flew open.

"Claude, mate. Where are you off to so bloody early this morning? Crikey mate, its bloody Sunday."

Claude smiled to himself. Barry Jones, the Australian he had partnered with as his main vintner for their California vineyards had a heart of gold beneath that rough and tumble veneer.

"Well, Barry. I am driving down to Sausalito to pick up Claire and bring her back here. Today I have something special planned. Soon it will be the end of my days as a bachelor."

"Struth mate. You bloody French guys will do anything to get a Sheila. Take it from me that you will regret that decision sooner than later. Anyway, good luck with it all. I've got to go attend to the early crop picking. The migrant workers should be arriving anytime now. Don't go getting lost in that fancy car of yours. It sure is bait for the highway patrol guys to chase after you and write you some nasty tickets."

Claude thanked Barry and after restarting the Ferrari pulled out onto the highway and around Barry's beat up old truck. He had offered Barry a fine new truck but, like Barry, it did n't fit the mold of Barry's character. Claude laughed out loud and accelerated away and over the rolling hills toward Interstate highway 80 that lead to Sausalito and over the Golden Gate Bridge to San Francisco. He was looking forward to the early drive alone during which he could rehearse the proposal he intended to deliver later that day the Claire.

He pulled onto the freeway some fifteen minutes later and settled in for the two hour drive. He was in no hurry. The traffic was light at that time of the morning. Light fog patches required him to occasionally slow and use caution.

As he approached the ramp to turn off to Sausalito, the fog thickened. It was a typical San Francisco Bay morning for that time of year.

He wound down the steep hill to the docks that lined the shore. He drove along the narrow road until he reached the pale yellow 3 story house in which Claire shared an apartment with her sister.

Claude pulled the Ferrari into the driveway and eased himself out of the driver's seat. He walked to the front door and rang the bell. He had no sooner pressed the button for the bell when Claire threw the door open. She was dressed in a pair of white capris which were set off with a bright pink blouse. She embraced Claude and smacked a huge wet kiss on his cheek.

Claude was happy and returned the passion right there on the doorstep.

"Are you packed and ready for the week? I have several trips planned for us and we will visit some of our neighbor's vineyards."

Claire motioned to the suitcase that sat behind her against the wall. Claude reached past her and picked up the case. It weighed a ton.

"Ma Chérie. What do you have in there? I will need to take up weight lifting if you continue to pack like this."

"Claude. You exaggerate." She laughed. "Maybe it contains a surprise for you. Come, let us go. I can't wait to get away from the city and up to Bodega Bay."

In their happy and light-hearted mood, they could never have foreseen the fate that awaited them.

Chapter 2

15 years earlier

**Le Chateau Bon Chance,
Bordeaux District, France**

The wealthy and aristocratic de Passioné family was renowned for their wines and extravagant lifestyle. Claude de Passioné was born into a life of luxury and privilege. There was nothing he wanted that wasn't provided to him. He attended private schools and socialized with some of Europe's most elite and available debutants.

The Marquis de Passioné and his wife, The Marchioness were noble descendants whose ancestors had been able to retain their wealth through France's troubled times. While he was still relatively young, The Marquis had taken over and expanded the family's wine growing and distribution business. The business had flourished under his stewardship and soon additional vineyards in France, Spain, and Germany were added. The Marquis longed to acquire a vineyard in California to produce white wines that would complement the famous reds produced at his other vineyards.

The Marquis was concerned. He had spent hours with Claude teaching him about the business, yet he showed little interest in it. That night, The Marquis, whose name was Charles, called to his wife, Marie-France to join him in the salon to discuss Claude's future.

"My dear Marie-France, what are we to do with that boy. He is more interested in cars and aircraft, and now girls, than assuming a role here with me. I am distressed. He is high spirited and I fear that he will find himself in trouble before long. He is spending more time away from the Chateau and has been drawing large sums of money from his account. Something must be done."

Marie-France sat quietly while thinking. "Charles he is a young boy who is quickly developing into a man. These things you worry about are normal. Remember when you were his age. I recall the stories of some particularly naughty things you were involved in."

The Marquis smiled as he remembered the wild escapades of his youth. Vivid in his mind was his first true love affair when he was sixteen. His parents caught him and the neighbor's girl in the wine cellars where the vintage wines were kept. That was the very first time that Charles had heard or learned the meaning of the word "castration."

"Yes you are correct but we need to prepare him for life. I would like to see him receive an excellent education at The Sorbonne in the Latin Quarter of Paris. We own several pensions there and could establish him in residence. It is only a five-hour drive and we must learn to trust him. I am eager that we get him educated and well-groomed to take over the estates. I want him to develop an interest in business and hopefully, assume a role in the operations before finally taking them over when I retire."

Marie-France nodded her agreement. "Let me speak to him. I will ensure that the boy listens and co-operates. "

The Marquis considered this. Since Claude's birth, she had dominated every aspect of his life. At times he believed she spoke and treated their six King Charles Cavalier Spaniels better than Claude who would be unable to argue this with his domineering mother. Charles was convinced that Marie-France's control over their son was a major cause in the lack of interest in the family and the business. To send Claude away to The Sorbonne in Paris would get him out from her constant criticism and let him develop and find his way.

"Yes. I will agree with you speaking to Claude and convincing him of this idea."

"I will have a lunch with him tomorrow. It will be done."

Chapter 3

The Lunch

Marie-France dispatched a manservant to fetch Claude for the lunch which was to be served in the sunroom. It was a beautiful day. Sun streamed in the windows and highlighted the Lily of the Valley that was organized in elaborate vases on the buffet beneath the window. Beyond the window was a view over the sweeping gardens. A profuse explosion of bright color stretched down toward the private tennis courts.

She became impatient as she sat waiting for Claude's arrival. Little did she realize that the servant was having trouble getting Claude to open his door. Inside Claude was preoccupied with the latest French girlie magazine.

"Young sir. You must open up and hurry. The Marchioness Marie-France is awaiting you for lunch."

"The old bitch can just wait. I am busy. Go tell her I will be there soon."

Claude's resentment for his mother was common knowledge amongst the staff.
"What shall I tell her to explain your tardiness?"
"Tell her I am bathing at present. Now go."

Thirty minutes passed before Claude descended the stairs to the foyer and walked to the sunroom. He opened the door and walked briskly into the room.

Marie-France let out a gasp.

"What is that you are wearing? It looks abominable."

"They are now all the fashion in England. They are stovepipe jeans and this is my rocker jacket."

Marie-France was aghast.

She turned to the Marquis.

"Charles, do something. I refuse to have any member of the de Passioné family be seen wearing such trash."

"My dear, he is young. He will wear the fashions that his friends do. Besides, I have to leave now. I have meetings in Paris. It will be late when I arrive there. I will be spending the night in Paris and maybe tomorrow night."

Claude eyed his father. He knew that the Marquis had more on his mind than business. He had become aware of his father's philandering.

The Marquis arose from the chaise lounge and crossed over to Marie-France. He took her hand and with a slight bow bent to kiss her hand.

Claude looked on in disgust. His father looked across at him and their eyes momentarily locked. Claude averted his eyes and walked toward the table which was set with fine tableware and several decanters of wine. As the Marquis left the room, he reached for a handcrafted goblet and clumsily poured himself a cabernet.

"Mother, would you care for wine?"

"Yes, I will take a sauterne."

Claude poured the golden liquid into a tall wine glass and placed it on the small side table beside her.

"Now we must talk about some matters that are concerning your father and I. Years are passing and it is time for you to make some decisions for your future. We are not always going to be here for you. So far you are my biggest disappointment. You have access to everything but show no interest in any career. All you care about are stupid cars, motorbikes, airplanes and of course, girls. Trust me on this. One of those girls is going to hurt you and disgrace our family. You seem to have a natural ability to pick up the trashiest ones. All come from the gutters with the pig swill and urine of working drunks. You show no ambition to work and excel at anything. Unless you change and change soon, we will advise our lawyers and notaries to remove you entirely from any family inheritance. Tell me of one achievement you have had in the past year, besides getting into trouble with the law."

Claude bit his lip in an attempt to control his temper and the inevitable vocal outburst that would follow. He had never disclosed the reason for the vicious fight he had started. His pride had been wounded then and now it was happening again. He thought back to the night and the gathering of local boys at the local park. It was when they started talking about his mother and her insatiable desire for young boys that Claude had lost it. It was when the Lemieux brothers boasted that they had lost their virginity with her when they were fifteen and seventeen that sent Claude into a frenzy. He had grabbed a rock from the ground and caved in Jacques Lemieux skull. Jacques was now a vegetable in the Bordeaux Home for Imbeciles. The learned medical opinion was that he would never regain his mental faculties.

It was a known fact that Marie-France fancied young men and played hard when the Marquis was away.

Claude knew it was true. He had watched the constant procession of anonymous young men who arrived and disappeared into the Chateau. On one occasion he had asked the Marchioness about them. Her reply did not convince him. He refused to believe anyone required that many therapeutic massages, even though she had injured her back several years earlier.

"Mother, you insult me. I have great ambition and desires. They are just not the same as yours or fathers."

Marie-France scowled at him.

"How dare you contradict me? Tell me one positive thing you have achieved alone."
Claude thought back through the past couple of years. He had to admit that nothing had been achieved. Before he had become a teenager his life had been full of sports and

friends. Now he was a loner who reflected on his life when alone in his room. His friends had all gone after the fight and the ensuing problems that had occurred for all the boys.

Marie-France glared at him.

"Why couldn't I have had a son of whom I could be proud?"

Claude felt the empty feeling creep back into him as he started to slip back into his undiagnosed depression.

"If only she knew why I fought. It was for her. I cannot tell her why" he thought.

"Claude there may be a nice solution for all of us. I spoke to your father. We believe you have reached an age and a point in your life where it is best for you to receive a higher education and this will mean leaving our home to take up residence at the university. Your father has made inquiries for you to attend the Sorbonne in Paris."

Claude could not believe what he was hearing. Finally, he had the opportunity to escape from her and his father who was making those constant business trips. He jumped at the chance.

"I would love that. I will make you both proud."

"Good. Now come and we will have lunch."

The servants arrived with Salade Niçoise that was followed by a dessert of lemon mousse.

They ate in silence. Claude was deep in thought. Silently he was thrilled with the prospect of his new independent life away from the Marchioness.

Chapter 4

The next weeks were filled with trips to the Sorbonne in Paris and submitting paperwork for admission, along with selecting the appropriate courses.

Throughout the process, Marie-France pushed her agenda at Claude. He resisted and eventually selected a combination of entry courses that were essential for an arts and business career. He was careful to select a few that could be dropped and substituted for business-related courses, should he wish to change programs.

Once his academic objectives were established Marie-France took control of selecting which pension he would live in and with whom. Claude was counting the days until the courses commenced and she and her interfering were gone. He intended to have a huge party with his fellow renters to celebrate the start of the year. Silently, his celebration was to be free of the Marquis and the Marchioness and their perverse and controlling lives.

He shared the pension with two young brothers from the fishing village of Collioure near the Spanish border. The brothers, Jean and Henri Beaulieu shared a common goal to become doctors, but each specializing in a different discipline. Their upbringing in the village of Collioure had resulted in them both developing extreme and outgoing boisterous personalities. Claude took an immediate liking to them. He could envisage some great days ahead. They became inseparable friends.

On the weekends the trio would descend upon the restaurants and bars of the Latin Quarter. Their friendship grew and when not attending courses were often found together in the library or at a local café.

Claude had become well known amongst many of the students. He had become an active advocate for student democracy and a vocal representative for the students. The faculty gained respect for the good looking long haired skinny youth. He presented the students' ideas after careful thought and with elegance. While many of the ideas were radical he offended no one.

The intensity of their courses and hours of study steadily increased as weeks progressed. Finally, exhausted and looking for a release, they decided to throw a party at the pension. The news of the impending party swept through many of the student gatherings.

The academic year at the Sorbonne had commenced in early September. By the middle of October, the students were ready and looking forward to the party.

The weather was cool and crisp on the Friday evening of the party. Students in all forms of dress started arriving at the spacious de Passioné owned pension. As dusk gathered, well over a hundred students were either jammed inside the pension or standing in the stairway or on the street below talking.

Young men dressed in black high neck sweaters sporting scraggly beards or goatees and wearing traditional black berets engaged in nonsensical philosophy discussions. Some smoked cherry wood pipes and others drew on certain dubious cigarettes.

The sexual revolution was rampant amongst the students. Most of the girls were braless and wore sheer see-through blouses and were dressed in ultrashort miniskirts and go-go boots, while others wore retro clothing reminiscent of the 1920s.

Chapter 5

The party intensified. Inside the pension, the sounds of Thelonius Monk drifted above the loudly spoken conversations. Psychedelic lighting flashed different patterns and colors off the walls. On the table bottles of wine, whiskey and beer sat beside trays of various drugs and marijuana. The air was heady with the smell of pipe and cigarette smoke and the sweet smell of marijuana. Girls with their pupils dilated from drugs and alcohol giggled and attempted to flirt with certain of the younger members of the faculty who attended.

The pace of the party changed and modern rock music blared. The partygoers became less inhibited and the party spilled out onto the street. Bottles of wine were passed around and the festivity continued until a visit from the local gendarmes dampened the mood.

The gendarmes attempted to enter the pension but were pushed back by the crowd in the corridors and stairway. Whistles blew and they shouted at the crowd to quiet down. Their efforts were futile and soon they retreated, only to return thirty minutes later with reinforcements. As the gendarmes attempted to force their way inside, it triggered a massive brawl. Bottles flew through the air smashing and shattering on the ground. The shrieks of frightened girls pierced the air.

The street soon filled with neighbors who emerged from their homes to watch the melee unfolding in front of the otherwise quiet street.

A full-scale riot erupted. In desperation to get control, the commanding gendarme summoned for assistance and within minutes water cannons arrived and a high-pressure hose sprayed the students, knocking several to the ground. More gendarmes arrived in protective gear and swarmed the pension. Arrests were made. Claude was taken to the commander and handed notices of infraction.

The party was over.

Back in the house, Claude looked around at the debris and destruction. He turned off the flashing lights and turned up the main lighting and then fell back into a large overstuffed armchair. He fell into a deep drugged sleep.

It was ten in the morning when he awoke. Sunlight was streaming in through the leaded glass windows that looked out onto the street and adjacent park. Claude pulled himself from the chair and walked to the window. From the second floor, he looked down onto the street. The remnants of the party littered the small front lawn and sidewalk. There were wine bottles, cigarette butts, and other items scattered around. He was not happy to see this. He decided to shower and dress before going down to clean up the mess before the neighbors complained or lodged complaints.

He turned and headed to his bedroom. He opened the door and stood astonished. Somebody was asleep in his bed.

As he stood there the form in the bed threw back the covers to expose her face. As she sat up Claude realized she was a young eighteen or nineteen-year-old girl. She had pale white skin framed by the blackest hair Claude had ever seen. Her hair hung over her eyes in a fringe and dropped down the sides to her shoulders. He stared at her. Her eyes were of a violet color. She was beautiful. She smiled.

"Who are you? Why are you in my bed? Did I do something wrong last night? Oh, I am sorry. I didn't mean any harm. What did I do? "

"Claude. Good morning to you as well. Oh yes, you were a wild and passionate devil last night. I thought I would never be able to sleep," she replied, laughing.

Claude raised his hand over his mouth.

"I have no recollection. Why was I asleep in the chair out there?"

She threw back her head and continued to laugh mischievously. As she did so, she spun her legs out from beneath the bedding. She was fully clothed and wore long black leggings. Claude racked his brain trying to remember the events of the previous night that had lead to this.

"Claude, did you make me that coffee you promised?"

He was flustered.

"No, but we can go to the little café on the corner. I will order you the best coffee that can be found in Paris. First, you must tell me who you are and why you were in my bed."

"My name is Geneviève Martel. You were such a gentleman last night. You were so nice to me. I think you had a lot of wine, but you were not mean."

"I am sorry. I don't remember much of last night. Please tell me more."

"Yesterday I was called by Hopital Saint Anne. They had an emergency and needed blood. I have type O negative blood. It is not common and I went to donate. At the party last night I felt weak and fainted. You took control and carried me to this bed. You got me something warm to drink and made sure no one would enter the room. I thank you. Maybe I will repay you and buy the coffees and pastries."

She sprang off the bed and skipped over to Claude and kissed his cheek.

Claude reached for his old duffel coat and held her coat while she folded herself into it.

Together they descended the stairs and left the pension for the café.

At the bistro café, couples sat reading and enjoying the early morning. Claude held open the door and they selected a table near the window. The café was old. The tables were wrought iron and showed the years of service they had provided. A waiter wearing a floor-length apron attended their table and returned with fresh warm croissants and a French press of strong black coffee.

They chatted about University life, friends and family. Claude was taking more than a casual interest in Geneviève.

Two hours passed by before Claude and Geneviève left the café and slowly strolled back to the apartment.

Chapter 6

Upon their return to the apartment, Claude held open the heavy wooden door for Geneviève. She was barely inside when the voice of Marie-France boomed out from the kitchen area in the rear.

"Claude, what is this mess? There are beer bottles, wine bottles and dirty ashtrays everywhere. I did not bring you up to be a *cochon*. Get in here now. I want you to get this cleaned now."

Claude started toward the kitchen area. He surveyed the scene. Unfortunately, she was right. The partygoers had left a major mess.

As he walked past the front salon, he noticed a bra and some underwear thrown on the couch. He entered and quickly snatched them up before Marie-France would inevitably see them and start into a tirade.

He entered the kitchen. Marie-France stood with her hands firmly pushing into her hips. She was surrounded by empty bottles on the floor. Remnants of half eaten food littered the table and countertops. Coffee cups were knocked on their side with the contents spilled down the cupboard doors and pooled on the floor.

Geneviève followed behind Claude. As she entered the kitchen, Marie-France glared at her.

"Who is that little *putain* with you? Another of your great conquests I assume? You men of the de Passioné family certainly are concupiscent. You are no better than animals."

Claude's anger grew.

"I will have you know mother, that this young lady, who is called Geneviève, donated blood at the hospital yesterday. She collapsed here and we provided a place for her to sleep. She is a student and a friend. That is all. I would appreciate it if you could conduct yourself as a lady and my mother. Not some shrew."

Marie-France was shocked at his outburst. She was not going to let Claude take any control.

"This is all because of those Beaulieu brothers. Scum from the border town. They have the gutter values of the Spanish, not the elegance and fine breeding of we French. I want you to throw them out. I do not want them living here and distracting you."

Geneviève could not suppress her laughter. She found the ostentatious and domineering behavior of Marie-France hilarious.

"Claude, I will assist you to clean up. Then you can accompany me to visit with my family. This afternoon there is a function to recognize my brother's military award."

Marie-France's interest was piqued.

"What military award? For what was it awarded?"

"My brother was assigned duty in Nouméa as part of the New Caledonia Forces. One morning as he was driving to the base he noticed some young men in trouble with their boat. He stopped the car and went to their rescue. He brought one of the men ashore and performed life-saving procedures. The man he saved was the son of a diplomat. This afternoon the diplomat will attend to thank my brother Gerard."

Marie-France watched as Geneviève started to clean the tables and counter. Feeling shamed she decided to assist.

Sensing a social opportunity, Marie-France softened her harsh attack on them. She considered the possibility of expanding her contacts in high society.

"Tell me, dear. What is your family name? I wonder if I know any of your family. With our vast vineyard and winery holdings, we may have contact with them."

"No, I don't think so. My father had a military career and was assigned to a command in Algiers. After the fierce war for independence, my father returned to France and he too accepted a diplomatic post. He served as Military Attaché at the French Embassy in Ottawa, Canada until three years ago. Now he is retired. My mother, Monique prefers a simple life. She enjoys the arts and travel. Neither of my parents indulges in the social activities of la haute société. Our family name is LaForet."

Marie-France quickly realized she had been subtly censured.

Geneviève looked at Marie-France and studied her attire. For an older woman, she was not dressed as one would expect. Her black hair was swept up in a high beehive style. She wore a bright yellow leatherette mini skirt and matching vest. Her legs visibly blazed in bright red and black fishnet stockings that disappeared into orange go-go boots. Geneviève felt plain and austere beside her in her jeans and striped shirt. She watched as Marie-France withdrew a pink Sobranie cigarette and inserted it into a long ebony holder before lighting it ostentatiously with a gold lighter. Geneviève was not impressed by the heavy set woman.

Claude was perplexed in watching the interchange between them.

"When will you return to the Chateau mother?"

"I intend to spend the night here with you my boy. It is not often I see you now that you are here studying. I wish you would find a way to visit home more often."

Claude groaned. The prospect of Marie-France interfering in his social plans upset him.

"I have plans this evening. I have been invited to a dinner with members of the faculty. It is an exclusive affair and only certain students get selected."

"Well then, I will enjoy going as your companion."

Claude was shocked. There were no circumstances under which he wished for her to attend any function at the Sorbonne.

"I am sorry but that is not possible."
"How dare you refuse an old lady the companionship of her son and his obvious success?"

"It is not possible. In fact, I would be happier if you would return to the Chateau or stay at a hotel tonight. I don't know why you have come here other than to spy on me and create problems."

Marie-France stood in the middle of the kitchen with her mouth open. Suddenly she sobbed and crocodile tears ran from her eyes washing the mascara down her cheeks in dark streams.

"You are an ungrateful little bastard. You will regret this and I promise that you and that *catain* remember this morning."

"Yes, mother. I probably am a bastard given your promiscuity."

Marie-France was furious. She cruised across the room toward the front door. On the way, she whisked her sable coat off the wooden rack in the hallway.

As she draped herself in the coat, threw open the door and exited, Geneviève couldn't help thinking how much she looked like a giant bumble bee.

" Claude, how did you survive her all these years? She is not a nice person. Let us finish here. I can wait here while you dress and prepare for a nice afternoon with my family."

Chapter 7

The friendship between Geneviève, Claude, and the Beaulieu brothers grew deep. Geneviève visited and on occasion prepared meals. Often the four of them would sit at the old wooden table in the kitchen, with the empty Chianti bottles and candles as candlesticks, and hold long philosophical talks. During these sessions, Claude would softly play his favorite album of Jacques Lousier with the piano renditions of Bach. There were other times when Geneviève would beg Claude to play his xylophone which he had set up in the front salon. They were happy times.

The year dragged on and the workload steadily increased. Marie-France no longer visited, but Claude received intermittent visits from his father, Marquis Charles who seemed to be visiting Paris more frequently. Claude could guess the reason for those visits, although the Marquis protested they were all for business.

The academic year ended and Claude decided against returning to the Chateau to the ranting and disgusting behavior of Marie-France. He started looking for casual summer employment. His search did not go well. He was depressed. The Beaulieu brothers had gone to their home and Geneviève had left on an overseas trip with her family and a close friend she often referred to as her boyfriend. He had never met the boyfriend. Frustrated, he visited a local bar each morning and scanned the papers looking for job opportunities. As time progressed Claude was drinking heavily.

Claude was resigned to returning to the Chateau. He returned to the pension late one morning and found an envelope inserted in the edge of the frame of the door. He frowned and wondered why a letter was not in the mailbox instead of the door. He pulled the letter from the metal frame and examined the envelope. It was plain and bore no markings. Claude frowned and opened the door while still staring at the envelope. There was no stamp or return address. He found it very strange.

He walked to the kitchen and took a carafe of table wine from the counter and poured a glass. He then sat at the table and proceeded to tear open the envelope which contained a folded light blue note. He unfolded the note and read:

Dear Claude,

Please excuse my informal approach with this letter. I came to visit and found no one at home so I left this for you.
We met at the reception for Geneviève's brother. You may recall. My name is Lise. We talked about our family gallery on Boulevard Voltaire. I have been invited to spend the summer months at a cousin's home in America next year. I wish to go, but I work at Galleries des Images. I am wondering whether you would be interested in my position while I am away. Please come and visit us at the Gallerie

Lise Victor

Claude remembered the afternoon and the time he and Geneviève had spoken with Lise. She was a former student of the Sorbonne and they had spent hours discussing art and history. Claude had impressed her with his interpretations of art and its evolution through French history.

Claude found the telephone number for the Gallerie and called. The phone was answered by Lise.

"Claude. Thank you for calling me so soon. I guess you received my note."

"Yes. I am intrigued by it. When will you be leaving for America?"

"I have not yet decided. My cousin's family lives in Connecticut on the coast. As long as I am there by next spring as they are planning a Caribbean trip with friends who own a large private yacht that is kept in Miami. I have been invited to go with them. They will be sailing to Aruba, BonAire, and Curacao. I am so excited. When can you come for an interview? It will take months to train you in all aspects of my job."

Claude considered leaving that afternoon but quickly changed his mind. He was concerned about the smell of alcohol from his morning's heavy drinking.

"I can be there tomorrow morning."

"Good I will arrange for you to meet with me and my father at ten sharp. Please dress nicely. He is particular about that."

"I am looking forward to meeting your father, and of course, seeing you. Is there anything I should bring with me?"

"I remember you talking about a paper you had written on how art had evolved with French culture throughout the centuries. I suggest you bring a copy. I know my father will be intrigued by your dissertation."

"I will see you tomorrow at ten in the morning. Goodbye."

Chapter 8

Claude left the pension early and stopped at the corner café for a strong coffee and pastry. He scanned through the copy of his essay and reacquainted himself with the report he had written almost a year previously. Even after a year, the work impressed him. He left the café in high spirits and started the long walk to Boulevard Voltaire.

It took Claude twenty minutes to stroll the three kilometers from his apartment near the Sorbonne to Boulevard Voltaire. He casually walked along the main streets of Boulevard Saint-Germain and Boulevard Henri IV. Small delivery vans common to Paris and aggressive taxis sped by him with frequent horn blowing and the occasional shout from an open window. "Paris has its own unique drivers," he thought.

It took Claude another ten minutes to find the ***Galleries des Images.*** It was located in an unimposing building. The front façade of the building was a distinctive but boring old Normandy style. The Gallerie was at street level. The window appeared to be a heavy plate or armored glass as it possessed a slight greenish hue. The front door was contained in a polished chrome frame. An electronic entry system was located on another chrome panel attached directly to the building.

Claude approached the Gallerie and pressed the large beige knob. He waited and within minutes a smartly dressed young woman approached. She pressed the inside intercom and asked Claude's name and the reason for the visit.

Before Claude could answer Lise arrived at the door. There was the sound of hydraulics releasing and the door swung open. Claude found the level of security strange.

"Come on in Claude. You are right on time. Let me show you around."

Claude stepped into the Gallerie and looked around. The walls were a soft neutral pale white with the slightest hint of grey. Picture rails ran the length of each wall from which paintings of all sizes hung creating a kaleidoscope of color. Claude moved toward the wall of large paintings and slowly looked at each as he made his way along the display. He was shocked to identify several world-renowned artists' works on display. Lise stood back and allowed Claude to leisurely view the works. When he had circled the Gallerie he returned to Lise.

"You have an amazing collection on display. I am curious though. I do not see any works of new young artists including our famous street artists. I thought you would be supportive of them."

"We are Claude. Each year we sponsor a small festival. The works are not hung on the main floor but we have a special display area set up for new artists and their works. Follow me."

Claude walked alongside Lise until they reached a wide stairway built of what appeared to be blonde oak stairs. They descended the stairs into a huge cavernous area. Overhead lights shone on works displayed on easels positioned throughout and the walls were festooned with paintings. A table was at the entrance containing a number of brochures describing the individual artists and the works.

"This is impressive. Who comes to view this work? You seem to have heavy security here. I assume you don't just allow anyone from the public to visit these works."

"No. We have a select client list and host viewing evenings at which certain artists attend and present their work and describe the motivation to produce such a painting. Now let us go back upstairs and meet with my father."

They returned to the main floor of the Gallerie. Claude was confused by the configuration at the rear of the display area. A large plate glass window divided off a section of the room. On the right was an office with glass walls. Inside were the normal accouterments…a large mahogany desk, filing cabinets, boxes stacked neatly against the wall. He looked at the area to the left. It was totally empty. A strange piece of equipment was attached to the wall. It appeared to be a surveillance video camera. Claude frowned. He did not understand why it was mounted there.

"Lise, what is that?"

"My father is very security conscious. As you are aware, a number of galleries have been held up and robbed. He had an experience earlier in life that has made him cautious."

The door opened and a stately older man entered. Claude stood up from his chair and moved forward with his hand extended.

Antoine Victor recoiled.

"I am sorry young man I do not shake anyone's hands. That is a disgusting custom that results in the transmission of diseases and illnesses. I am Antoine Victor and I assume you are Claude de Passioné. I am pleased to meet you. My daughter has told me of the work you have done at the Sorbonne and that you are a special student there. She speaks very highly of you."

"I appreciate that sir."

"Now please tell me of your studies."

Antione leaned back in his chair and pressed his folded hands against his lips as he listened to Claude's achievements.

Claude spoke uninterrupted of his studies, exam results and achievements. When he was finished, Antoine spoke.

"I understand you have brought me a copy of your dissertation. I am looking forward to reading it. I will share my assessment with you. Now let us discuss our business. Lise has told you she is going to spend the summer with my brother and his family in the United States. She deserves the break and it is good for her to know the family. Her absence will leave a hole here in my operation. I need someone who is educated in art and trustworthy. I need to ask you some questions. Have you ever had problems with the law or been arrested?"

Claude choked. "Yes, sir. When I was first at the Sorbonne we held a student party that got out of control. I was handed notices of infraction. I was fined. That is the only interaction I have had with police or the authorities."

"I don't consider that too serious. I think everyone becomes over exuberant during the first year of study. If there is nothing else then we can continue.

While I am impressed by your academic qualities and that you were raised a de Passioné there is one problem. We have an image to uphold. I cannot hire you into a sales position with the scruffy appearance you have."

"I will have myself groomed and return them. I am sure you will be impressed. Tomorrow I will have that done. May I visit again in two days?"

"I like that spirit. Yes, come back at the same time please in two days."

Antoine waved his hand to signal their meeting was over.

Claude walked toward the front door with Lise. While walking he sniffed in the air. He had noticed a faint floral fragrance since his arrival. He couldn't place it. It did not seem harsh like cleaning material. Lise saw him sniffing the air.

"I see you have noticed. We inject a special agent into the ventilation system. It covers the chemical that is used to clean and filter the air. We condition the air to preserve the art. Some papers absorb humidity or other airborne contaminants. We treat against this. The scent you smell also assists in preventing that dry and musty smell which is common in museums and art galleries. The works here are very valuable and we are trusted by the artists and owners to protect the works. We maintain the temperature at twenty-four degrees and the humidity at forty percent. It creates a nice working climate."

Claude nodded but found the whole process and the Gallerie strange.

Chapter 9

As he walked away from the Gallerie, Claude reflected on the strange interview he had just experienced. He thought about the heavy security and the strange layout of the Gallerie. It was unlike any of the other ones he had visited in Paris. He had only met Lise a couple of times before the party at Geneviève's home. He was not feeling totally comfortable with her or Antoine, yet was fascinated at the prospect of working the summer at the Gallerie.

He recalled her comment about dress and appearance. He knew he had let his image slip into the poor student look. Antoine's comments stuck in his mind and he remembered the sharply tailored look of the older man. He guessed his age to be in the late seventies but looked younger in the lightweight grey linen suit and high necked pale blue shirt with a maroon tie. Claude decided to improve his image right at that moment. He would win the job he decided.

Claude walked to the bus stop to take the twenty-minute bus ride to Banque Palatine, 39 Boulevard Raspail. He waited patiently for the bus. As he did so he thought about the Banque and its history. He marveled that it was founded in 1780 and had survived the wars and yet still operated. The Banque had handled all of the de Passioné business affairs. He had witnessed executives visiting at the Chateau and the elaborate meals and entertainment that had been held with Banque executives as guests. He wondered what other relationships may exist between the family and the Banque.

After the bus stopped near the Banque, Claude crossed the busy street and entered the bank. He walked up to a desk and requested to see a manager. The clerk looked at Claude with his scruffy grooming and student attire.

"What is this about. Why do you need a manager? I think they are all in a meeting or busy. What can I help you with?"

Claude realized he was being stalled. He removed his passport and identity card and handed them to the clerk.

"I suggest you find a manager and show him this."
The clerk opened the passport to the identity page. He looked at the photo and then stared at Claude. There was some resemblance but Claude's beard and long hair made him unsure.

"Wait here. I will see if someone can assist you."

Claude sat across from the antique desk and waited. After what seemed eternity the clerk returned accompanied by an older man wearing a three-piece suit and heavy-rimmed glasses.

Claude stood to shake the man's hand and immediately recalled Antoine Victor's reaction. The manager had no such inhibition. He reached across the desk and shook Claude's hand vigorously.

"I am assistant manager of this branch. What can we assist you with?"

"My name is Claude de Passioné as you can see from my identity documents. I am here in Paris studying at the Sorbonne. Our family businesses, the de Passioné Vineyards and Wine Estates have been clients of the bank for many years. I need to withdraw some money from my trust account. Here is the amount I wish to withdraw.

He handed a handwritten paper to the manager who scanned it and then raised his eyebrows. He looked over at Claude.

"This is a large amount. I will need to check. I will need to phone our Head Office."

"Yes. Please do that. I am sure you will find everything is correct."

The manager excused himself and left. Upon his return, his whole demeanor toward Claude had changed. His politeness was disarming and in complete contradiction to the almost rude Parisian attitude, he had initially displayed.

Claude thought silently, "You arrogant little prick" but just smiled.

Please wait here Monsieur. There is no need for the heir to the vast de Passioné business to trouble himself with such mundane matters as dealing with a teller. I will have the funds brought here for you."

From the furtive glances Claude was seeing from the tellers and other worked it was obvious that his aristocratic background and vast family wealth had been disclosed.
The clerk returned with a long white envelope and handed it to Claude who opened it and counted the contents. He looked across to the manager.

"Thank you for your assistance today. I must leave as I have important business to complete before closing."

Claude pushed back from the antique desk with its gilt decorated edging and legs. He again shook the manager's hand and proceeded to walk across the vast marble floor. He was not unaware of the flirtatious smiles from many of the young women. Inwardly he smiled as he considered the days ahead.

After leaving the bank, he proceeded to the famous hair salon of Alexandre de Paris who had a reputation and famous and respected clientele. After arriving at the salon, Claude walked into the plush establishment where he was greeted with curious looks. A receptionist inquired about his needs and took his particulars. Again, it was not long before his identity caused a ripple of excitement. Alexandre himself appeared and introduced himself.

The straight edge razor gently removed the heavy beard. The attendant clipped and shaped until all that remained was a dark black goatee and mustache. Another female attendant took over to style and trim his hair. An hour later he emerged from the salon a changed man. With his light olive skin, black eyes, goatee, and jet black medium length hair, Claude looked better than many models. He was proud of his looks. He experienced many admiring smiles as he walked to Charvet, an exclusive tailor located on Place Vendóme. He recalled his father, the Marquis describing the famous establishment, and remembered the beautiful shirts and suits he had purchased and brought from Paris.

It was late in the afternoon when he located the store. He entered and introduced himself. The store staff recognized the de Passioné name and the business his father had given them over the years. He described his requirements to the staff.

"I will be working at a prestigious business, guiding wealthy clients with art collections. I will also be involved with some of the world's most prestigious art auction houses. I need suits and footwear."

The staff took measurements and set about selecting various suits and accessories. After a long session of looking at different styles and footwear, Claude made his selection. He ordered suits from Armani, Hugo Boss, and Saville Row. He selected a pearl grey lightweight fabric and the others in dark blue woolen serge. For shoes, he selected Black English brogues and two pairs of stylish slip-on shoes.

The tailor-made chalk marks for the adjustments and pinned the suits.

"They will be ready for you tomorrow afternoon."

Claude considered. "Is it possible to get one done for this evening? I have an important interview in the morning."

The tailor glanced at his large gold watch.

"If I start now it can be ready when we close at seven. I can only modify one suit. Which will it be?"

Claude selected the Saville Row and Black Brogue shoes.

"I will pick the suit up at seven. Please arrange to deliver the rest to my home." He wrote down his address and handed it to the salesman.

He was about to leave when a trench coat on display caught his eye. He stopped in front of it.

"Please include one of these coats with the delivery."

He left the tailors and headed across the street to a small bistro for an early dinner. He had firmly made up his mind to convince Antoine to hire him.

Chapter 10

In the morning Claude dressed in his new attire. He selected a medium blue Egyptian cotton shirt and a dark silver silk tie. He decided against wearing the suit vest as the temperatures had remained warm.

He admired his new appearance in the mirror and satisfied, set off to **Galleries des Images**. As he opened the door to leave the pension he looked up at the dark and threatening skies. Suddenly the sky lit up and exploded with bright green lightning. Nearby the sound of the loud crack and a tremor hit Claude. As he glanced skyward, heavy black clouds boomed as thunder shook the house. Huge raindrops started falling and the lightning continued flashing through the sky. Paris was experiencing a summer heat storm.

Claude pushed open the front door and retreated inside. The pension was in total darkness. There was no electricity. He looked at his watch and realized he would not arrive at the Gallerie on time for his interview. He fumbled in the darkness for the old wall phone. Upon placing the receiver to his ear he found it was dead.

Little did Claude know that a huge oak tree had been struck by the lightning and fallen across the electrical and phone lines. The Latin Quarter of Paris was without power or communications.

He cursed and wondered whether to attempt the trip. He finally decided to leave. He went to his room and foraged in the closet for his umbrella. It was an 1800's silver-handled Belle Époque parasol worth a small fortune. He was annoyed that his vanity had dictated and he had forgone the purchase of a raincoat. He hated them, as they reminded him of the Marquis who often wore a coat with his captain's hat, even though he did not own a boat. He wished he had brought the trench coat home with him that he had purchased the night previously.

The rain had eased when Claude opened the door to leave, though he could still hear the thunder rumbling in the distance. The streets were partially flooded and sirens wailed as police and ambulances raced through the narrow streets.

At the Gallerie, the young scatterbrained receptionist stared through the thick plate glass windows at him while he stood in the falling rain. Claude had briefly met her and considered she would be dangerous in the event she grew half a brain.

At the rear of the showroom, Lise saw him standing in the rain. She barked at the receptionist.

"Maudit Imbecile. Can't you see who it is? Go and let him in immediately."

The receptionist slid from behind the desk and teetered precariously on the new high heel shoes she had bought the day before. She almost made it to the door before falling on her chest and face. She laid spread-eagled on the floor.

Lise had seen the whole incident. She ran forward to help the receptionist to her feet. As she did so, the too tight chartreuse blouse burst open and two enormous breasts pounded out to freedom.

Claude stood in awe. Lise spun and went to open the door. He realized that this was not a good beginning for his art career.

The receptionist emitted a piercing wail and ran to the rear of the Gallerie in search of the women's washroom.

Lise could barely contain her temper.

"As soon as I can find a new one, she is gone. She is nothing but a slutty tramp. You men are all stupid when it comes to how they look. I didn't hire that. It was Antoine, my father. He likes those looks. Sometimes, in contradiction to his wealth, he is stupid. Now let us go and find him. I must say you look gorgeous dressed this way. I think you could be a movie star."

They walked up the small set of stairs and into Antoine's office, who stood when they entered.

"Claude. Is that you? I cannot believe the change. Yes, indeed. I can see you as an asset here at the gallery. Those wealthy women who think they know art will eat from your hand. Now please sit and we will discuss money and your duties."

Chapter 11

Working at the Gallerie was a satisfying and educational experience for Claude. He learned quickly. Within a couple of weeks, he had developed a routine for charming the female clientele. His popularity increased and soon he abandoned the more formal suits for casual artsy attire that accentuated his looks and personality. Antoine was thrilled as Claude had become a magnet to the well-heeled women. Many were finding excuses to visit with the flimsiest of excuses that ranged from asking Claude for advice on cleaning paintings to information on the artist. Several went as far as asking him to their homes to assist in determining the ideal location to hang their new purchases.

While Antoine was pleased with his new employee, Lise was disturbed. She had found herself with an unusual attraction to this younger man and was shocked to find herself fantasizing about him.

Claude was oblivious to her fascination with him until the Gallerie hosted an evening wine and cheese function for the wealthiest customers.

"Claude, can you assist me? I need to retrieve some promotional brochures from the storage room. I believe they are stored in a box high on the racking. I fear I am unable to reach them. We need to hand these out as they contain the schedule for our upcoming fall and winter auctions."

"That is fine. Let me take this wine to Madame Benoit. She is such a pain. It seems I can never be rid of her. I will join you in a few minutes."

Lise excused herself and left for the storage room. She entered and turned off the intense overhead fluorescent lights, but left the soft incandescent viewing lights on. She caught her reflection in the darkened glass window and fluffed up her hair.

The door to the storage room opened and Claude entered.

"Where is the box you wish me to take down?"

"It is on top of those shelves. It's the dark blue one. I think you will need the little ladder to reach there."

Claude pulled the step ladder from behind an old desk stored in the room. He set it up and started to climb toward the top of the shelving. As he did his foot slipped on one of the rungs. He dropped back while clinging to the side of the ladder. As he slid back he felt Lise' hands grab his buttocks. He steadied himself and remained still. As he hung on the ladder he became aware of her exploring fingers. She slipped her hand through his crotch and up to his manhood. Claude froze. She continued and started to massage him. He turned and looked back at her.

"Lise. What are you doing? This is wrong."

"Claude you fool. Is it not obvious to you that I am attracted to you? Why do you think I contacted you to work here? There are many young artists who would take this job willingly. Now come here to me."

As he crawled down the ladder he felt his huge erection rubbing against the belt of his trousers. He no sooner reached the floor when Lise spun around and grabbed his member. With one hand in his pants and the other around his back, she pulled herself to him and passionately kissed him.

He was startled. Lise pulled back from him and pulled open her blouse exposing milk-white skin and tiny breasts. She launched herself at him and within minutes the two of them were horizontal on the surface of the old stored desk. Her hands pushed against his chest and she mounted him like a jockey and rode him to the finish line.

Claude lay exhausted and watched as she tidied herself up. Her stockings were twisted at odd angles and her skirt was hoisted high to her stomach giving the appearance of a large beignet.

"Lise, I cannot work with you anymore. This was wrong."

"Claude I suggest you stop acting like a little boy who has just seen his first naked woman. Did you not see how I have felt and treated you over the past weeks? How can you be so stupid?"

He spun his legs out and off the desk and lowered himself to stand. His pants were around his ankles and as he bent to recover them, Lise laughed.

"That was the best cocktail ever."

Claude blushed. It was clear she was making fun of him and he resented it.

Chapter 12

For the next few weeks, life at the Gallerie became increasingly difficult for Claude. He became aware of the jealous stares and attitude of Lise as he attended to the various women, who came to seek his advice or make unnecessary purchases. The problem became exacerbated when certain of the women arrived with their daughters and unashamedly pushed them at Claude. He was seen as a catch. He came from the aristocracy, the family was wealthy beyond comprehension, and he had good looks and a charming personality. What more could a girl want?

The weather had started to cool as autumn approached. The leaves on the trees that lined the streets turned brown and fell to the ground where they were blown about with abandon. It was on one of these cool mornings when Madame Sophia Benoit arrived at the Gallerie with her eighteen-year-old twin daughters.

"Good morning, Claude. I am here to purchase some new works, but first let me introduce my daughters."

Claude looked at the girls and flashed them his disarming smile. They practically melted.

Madame Benoit took the hand of the taller twin with long curly golden hair. "This is my oldest twin, the firstborn. Meet Ginette."

"I am delighted Ginette. You are more beautiful than the paintings hanging on our walls here."

"This is the younger twin who gave me such a difficult time with her birth. Please meet Antoinette."

She placed her hand on the girls back and gently pushed the raven-haired beauty toward Claude.

"Again, such beauty. I am surprised they do not pave the sidewalks with gold for such a princess."

He took Antoinette's hand and raised it to his lips for a lingering kiss. She blushed a crimson red.

Madame Benoit had observed every movement. Her mind played a scene of a marriage to the famous aristocracy. She was delighted.

"Now girls I must leave you here while I go to the lower level to examine the works of some budding new artists. I am sure you are in good hands with Claude."

Claude recognized her deliberate move but played along. He glanced up toward Antoine's office and saw Lise standing and glowering at him. He smiled and turned away.

"It would be my pleasure to escort you both to that little café across the boulevard for coffee and pastries while Madam views the new works. I am sure she will be a while. We have just replaced all of the paintings with new works. It will take her some time to view them all."

The girls giggled as Claude reached for his trench coat which he threw on with a great flourish. He could not believe his luck to be taking a break away from the Gallerie and Lise with two beautiful girls. He intended it to be a coffee to remember.

He escorted the girls across the street with one on each arm. He smugly observed the looks of other men passing him by.

Upon entering the café, Oscar, the Romanian owner immediately recognized Claude, who stopped in the café frequently.

"Good morning. Please come and sit at our best table. It is nice and warm in here. Better to be in here than out in that blustery wind."

Oscar seated them in a circular booth that was quiet and comfortable. The girls were demure and smiled at Claude as he ordered pastries and coffees.

They sat talking for thirty minutes. The conversation drifted from music to life at the university to Claude's life at the Chateau. He was fully taken by their gracious manners.

An hour passed and Claude suggested they return to the Gallerie. The girls pouted.

Ginette stood to leave and turned to Claude.

"We have had fun with you and you are nice. It would be nice to meet you again."

Claude considered this and an idea entered his head.

"Girls. I play with a small group at a nightclub on Saturday evenings. Would you like to come and hear the band and maybe have some drinks and a few dances?"

The Benoit sisters looked at each other.

It was Antoinette who spoke.

"Yes, we would love that. Where is the club? What instrument do you play or do you sing?"

"It is **LE LAPIN CHAUD** and is located in the 4th arrondissement of Paris. I play the xylophone. We play a lot of jazz. I would love you to come as my guest. I will arrange for a table and passes at the door."

"What time should we go to the club?"

"I will meet you there at nine this Saturday night."

They returned to the Gallerie and found Madame Benoit in an intense and animated discussion with Antoine and Lise. As they entered the conversation died. Claude noticed that the door concealed in the wall at the rear of Antoine's office was slightly ajar. He had often wondered about that door and the security system that secured it. He was determined to find out what secrets it held.

Claude thought about Madame Benoit and her fortune. She had married André Benoit in the Gaspé region of Quebec, Canada. André was an entrepreneur and had invested heavily in a mining company. The company prospered and André made millions which he then invested into a chain of slaughterhouses across Canada and the United States. He had made a fortune. As a result of his untimely and suspicious death, Madame Benoit had inherited the fortune. She proved to be a shrewd businesswoman and parlayed the businesses into an enormous fortune. The circumstances surrounding Andre's death were suspicious and many, including the police, considered that she had arranged his death.

"My business here is complete. We shall now leave and take lunch at Chez Voltaire. Maybe Claude would like to join us?"

Lise spoke rapidly and somewhat harshly.

"Claude has a task to perform here with our inventory. Besides he has been out with your delightful daughters for the past hour. Thank you but he has work here to do."

Madame Benoit was startled at the severe response.

"Well I am sure there will be another time. I suggest you and Antoine remember what we have just discussed. I will return later in the week. I expect all will then be in order."

The trio turned and left the Gallerie. Claude stood with Lise at his side. He was confused. As he turned he saw Antoine in his office on the phone. Again he was gesticulating wildly as he spoke. The door was closed and the thick glass walls prevented him from hearing the conversation. He turned to Lise.

"You didn't say anything about performing an inventory today. This is a surprise."

"It is not the case. It is better that you stay away from that Benoit family. No good will happen to you if you get involved. Besides, we will need to get things in order before I leave in the spring to spend summer in America. You will have the winter months to learn the intricacies of operating a gallery and the auction process. I am assuming you will make the time since you will still be studying at the Sorbonne."

"I look forward to that. You can be assured I will perform well and both you and your father will be pleased."

Lise looked down and twisted her hands.

"Claude…what happened. I am sorry. I have such strong feelings for you. Can we start as more than just friends?"

"Lise, that is not possible. You are the boss, and you are older than me."

Lise bristled at the mention of her age and being older.

"There is no bigger age difference between you and me as there is between you and those twin Benoit trollops."
She slammed down the books she was holding and quickly walked off.

Chapter 13

The next week at the Gallerie was awkward. While it was virtually impossible, Claude avoided as much contact as possible with Lise. He knew that his employment at the Gallerie would probably be ending very soon. He was a little despondent at the prospect of losing his job due to her female jealousy and infatuation.

Claude was working with a new artist in the downstairs display area when Antoine summoned him. He feared that would happen, but climbed up the stairs and made his way to the office. He noticed the concealed door had been closed and a bookcase pulled in front of it. Claude's curiosity was peaked.

"Claude, I have called you in to discuss a situation with Lise."

Claude assumed the worst.

"The time has come for you to take a larger role here. Lise is going to be traveling to Marseille, London, Munich and New York beginning next week. The next 3 days will be busy. Can you stay and work longer hours? Lise will need the help to prepare some works for auction before she leaves."

Claude was relieved.

"Yes, of course, I will stay longer. My studies at the Sorbonne will not start for a few weeks yet."

Each day Claude worked into the evening. It was during these later hours that he watched older men arrive and be ushered into Antoine's office. The meetings seemed friendly with smiles, laughter, and smoking of cigars. Claude had seen the concealed door opened on several occasions and the visiting men escorted in. It seemed they stayed for between fifteen and thirty minutes. Claude was puzzled.

It was later in the week when he and Lise were alone one evening when Claude decided to ask her about the concealed door.

"I have noticed that there have been visitors who get taken into that room. What is in there?"

"I am not at liberty to say. We call it 'The Inner Sanctum' I will tell you though there are valuable pieces of art that we store in there for certain clients. There is not a work in there valued at less than ten million dollars. Only owners of the art are allowed in and even then they can only view the art they own. The room is climatically controlled. Some of the art is extremely old and fragile."

The explanation satisfied his immediate curiosity but fired up other questions in his mind. He wondered what works were in there. His vivid imagination thought to the spate of art thefts where famous pieces had been stolen from museums and private collections. His mind wandered and he thought of the plundering and theft of art by the Nazi

Germans during WWII. He chuckled to himself as he imagined all sorts of wild possibilities.

"Will I ever be allowed to enter and see the pieces stored there?"

"No. The only people permitted to enter are the owners, Antoine, I and a couple of museum curators. Please do not ask again."

Throughout the rest of the week, Claude worked with Lise to prepare catalogs for the auctions she was arranging in the different cities. The closer it got to the date of her departure she softened her stance with Claude. It was almost as if nothing had taken place.

The weekend was approaching fast and Claude was looking forward to his evening with the Benoit twins. On Thursday evening he returned to his pension and found an envelope stuffed in the door. He went through to the kitchen and poured some wine before ripping open the letter. It was a note from Geneviève. She had returned to Paris and had visited earlier that afternoon. Claude was excited and searched for her telephone number. Her phone rang unanswered. Claude decided he would prepare a meal and call her in an hour. As he was preparing the food, his ancient doorbell rang. He went to the door and was met by a very tanned and happy Geneviève. He wrapped his arms around her and hugged her for a long while.

"I am so happy you are here. I was just preparing food. Have you eaten this evening?"

"No. I was hoping to surprise you and take you for dinner."

"I can stop now. Yes, let's go out. I want to hear about your trip. Why are you home early? I thought you were staying until the end of summer."

Claude had no sooner spoken the words when he saw the sad expression on Geneviève's face.

"I will tell you over dinner and drinks."

Chapter 14

In the bistro, Geneviève poured out her heart to Claude. He sat silently until she had finished.

"Geneviève you have never spoken of your friend to me. I never knew you were in a serious romantic relationship. This is all a surprise. Why did you keep something like this so quiet?"

"I wasn't sure that he and I would become more than friends. It was only over the past year that we became lovers."

"You say that he is gone. Are you sure that he will never return to you?"

At that comment, Geneviève wailed. Other restaurant patrons turned toward their table and stared at Claude with looks of disgust and anger. Claude arose from his chair and went around the table. He hugged her and attempted to calm the situation. A waiter quickly approached. Claude asked him to bring a glass of water.

After a few minutes, Geneviève regained her composure.

"I am so sorry Claude. I didn't mean to create this scene. I should explain more to you.
My boyfriend had arranged a three-day weekend trip to the Bahamas. We had decided we both needed time away from family. It was to be just the two of us. I had no idea he had carefully planned the weekend to contain major surprises.

We arrived at the hotel on the beach and were checked into The President's Suite. I was so impressed. From the bedroom, there was a magnificent panoramic view of Cable Beach and the Caribbean Sea. We were only in the room for less than five minutes when room service arrived with a huge bouquet of flowers and a trolley with an ice bucket containing a bottle of Verve Cliquot and two champagne flutes. There was an assortment of cheeses, smoked salmon and caviar as well.

My boyfriend, Ramon suddenly dropped to his knees and presented a ring and asked me to marry him. I was shocked. I had actually fallen deeply in love with him over the year. I accepted and we were both so happy.

That night we dined early and went for a walk on the beach before it was dark.

We awoke the next morning and Ramon slid open the huge glass doors to go out onto the balcony. It was windy but warm. I was going to join him when the wind gusted and Ramon was blown across the deck. He grasped the railing but it broke. Ramon sailed down the six stories and crashed onto the table of the family that was having breakfast on the patio below. He landed in their Eggs Benedict. The yellow yolks sprayed and splattered everywhere. He died with Canadian back bacon all over his face. Claude, I will never eat Eggs Benedict again."

The patrons of the restaurant had listened intently to Geneviève's story. It was totally quiet. Claude was speechless.

She started sobbing again and conversation amongst the patrons resumed. Claude noticed that every so often people would glance over and look at them.

"I am truly sorry. Would you like to leave? We can go back to my place. Maybe you will be more relaxed there."

"No Claude. I need to deal with this and continue with my life. You are a true friend and I could tell you. I don't want to discuss this with others. I hope to forget this when classes at the Sorbonne resume and my mind is focused on my studies."

"Has the rest of your family returned yet?"

"No, they are due to arrive on Tuesday. My father met with some prominent lawyers and politicians while we were vacationing. I called them from the Bahamas and told them I was returning to Paris. Ramon's body has been flown to his family in Puerto Rico. I will not go to the service. It is too painful."

They sat in silence for the longest time.

The waiter returned to the table. Claude had been considering the Eggs Florentine but quickly changed his mind.

"Geneviève have you chosen?"

"Yes. I am ordering the porterhouse steak on a sautéed bed of mushrooms and onions drenched in a burgundy reduction."

Claude looked at her in amazement. He had never known her to eat such large or heavy meals. He wondered whether this was her way of dealing with grief.

"I would like the crepes bourguignon. Please send the wine steward."

Claude perused the wine menu and smiled when he saw that one of the Passion Fields estate finest Cabernet wines were listed. He ordered a bottle for them to share.

They leisurely ate the meals and when finished, Claude walked Geneviève to her home before turning back to visit at a little wine bar prior to returning to the pension.

He was looking forward to Saturday and the evening at LE LAPIN CHAUD club with the Benoit girls.

Chapter 15

Saturday mornings in Paris were Claude's favorite time. He was not due to work at the ***Gallerie des Images*** until it opened in the afternoon. He strolled through the streets stopping at food stands and looking at items in the stalls set up by the street sellers. Claude's particular attention was drawn by the musicians who played accordions, guitars and harmonicas. On passing, he would throw some coins into the hats and other receptacle left by the musicians for contributions. His favorite visit was to the local artists who had set up easels and were completing works while surrounded by displays of their work. He was impressed at the quality of some and felt they exceeded those on display in the new artist's area of the gallery.

Hours passed as he immersed himself in the noise and smells of the market. Grilled food aromas drifted through the assembled vendors. Sounds of music and lilting voices filled the air. Peals of children's laughter rose and fell. It was a happy place and Claude slipped into a mood of contentment. Not only was he happy at the market, but also the anticipation of the evening ahead with the Benoit sisters. Life was good for him in Paris.

Armed with baguettes and fresh flowers Claude returned to his pension. As he approached he noticed a man standing across the promenade. He seemed to be looking at Claude's home. Claude wasn't sure but felt he had seen this man before. He shrugged. There were, after all, a lot of people in Paris and it was easy to mistake someone. He looked across the street and the man had turned away and was walking at a brisk pace away from him. Again, Claude thought he had seen him before. Then he realized this man had come into the gallery several days earlier. Claude considered it coincidence and nothing to worry about. He had nothing to hide.

Inside, he decided to shower and dress in more casual attire for his Saturday afternoon of entertaining the ladies who would be visiting to hold idle chats with him. Instead of wearing his tailored suit, he dressed in tight black trousers and a puffy white renaissance shirt. He inserted a maroon cravat and stood back to admire the effect in the bedroom mirror. He was satisfied.

He threw on his trench coat and left the pension. As he did so, he noticed the man again. This time he was lighting a cigarette and standing in a store entrance near the corner. Claude was tempted to cross over and confront him, but decided caution would be wise.

His trio to the *Gallerie des Images* was uneventful. People scurried around looking after activities only performed on weekends. Claude was focused on the evening ahead.

He was surprised to arrive at the Gallerie and find a number of people already inside. The new receptionist was circulating and offering glasses of wine from a tray. He observed Lise deep in conversation with two professorial-looking men. He looked up to the office and Antoine had a group of men seated in front of his desk. He did not look happy.

Claude went to the small room at the back that was exclusively for staff usage. He removed his coat and threw it across the back of a chair. He looked in the mirror and combed back his hair then went out onto the gallery display floor.

Sophia Benoit cornered him immediately.

"I am happy you are taking my twins to a club tonight. They are really nice girls. I am sure you will all have a nice time. How I envy all of you young people?"

"They will be looked after. I will see that they are the most important guests of the club. It will be a special night."

"They are so lucky to be going with such a handsome man. I wish I had one like you at that age. Instead, I only had nonsense from rural men. My André was an exception. A brilliant kind man and I am not ashamed to say that he was a lover like no one else. He could give me all I needed."

"It is nice to see you. Now I must go to Lise. She is waving to me to join her and her clients."

As Claude turned to walk across the floor, he looked out the front window. Standing and looking into the gallery was the man he had seen outside his home. He was accompanied by two somber looking men in drab clothes.

Claude reached Lise and her little group.

"Please excuse me. I need to speak privately with Lise."

"What are you doing? Those are very important clients. We sell millions of dollars of art to their hotels and businesses."

Claude leaned forward to her and quietly explained his apprehension and observations. As he did so, Lise turned away and stared up into her father's office.

"Thank you, Claude. You are most observant. I will go and speak with Antoine and we will tell our security people about this."

She spun and almost ran to Antoine's office. He watched as she entered. The men inside stood as she entered. She stood and spoke. The men looked from one to another. One of the older men was talking. The others were facing and listening to him. They all turned and looked at Antoine who then reached down to his desk and removed an object. The men shuffled into a ragged line and followed Antoine as he opened the concealed door to the Inner Sanctum.

Chapter 16

At the gallery, the crowd of clients slowly thinned as the afternoon grew late. Claude had entertained several society members and made some significant sales. When the gallery was empty, Lise approached him.

"You will need to find more time. I have urgent business in London and will be leaving on Monday morning. Can you arrange to be here? Will it be possible with your courses at Sorbonne?"

"My classes have only just started. I will arrange a schedule so I can be here and still have enough study time."

It was too early for Claude to go to the club and yet it made no sense for him to return to the pension. He decided to phone Geneviève and ask her to join him for an early dinner. She eagerly accepted.

Geneviève met Claude at the gallery. Together they walked to a bistro that was well known for its Provincial cuisine.

"Claude, I have been wondering. This year you will graduate. Will you return to the Chateau and the de Passioné wine business or will you stay in Paris?"

"I do not yet know. I will have my degrees in both business and art. I must admit that even when I arrived at the Sorbonne, the thought of studying business did not appeal in the least. Now I find I have enjoyed it. It is possible I will go back. It is Marie-France that I have my problems

with. She has controlled me and hurt me. When I was a very young boy, I made some mistakes. I remember that I wet in my pants. I could not help it. She took off my clothes and tied a string around my part. It hurt. She left me like this for a day. I remember crying and asking her to take it off and give me my clothes. It was cold. There was snow outside. She just laughed at me.
I hate her."

"I did not know she was cruel to you. Now I understand things you have said before. I thought you were just saying those things."

"I don't want to discuss this anymore. Let us talk about you. What are you going to do now you are back?"

"I have applied to the School of Medicine. I am hoping to be accepted. I wish to be a pediatrician. I have never told you this. I kept it secret until I was sure I could graduate the Sorbonne."

"I am so proud of you and hope this dream comes true. I will help in any way I can."

"What will you do after you graduate?"

"I will need time away from France and family. I have decided to take a little money from my trust and travel for a year or two. I hope that by being away I will be able to make the correct decisions."

Silence fell between them. They were never lovers yet the bond was tight.

They sipped on their wine and ordered typical bistro meals. Claude ordered the steak entrecote and Geneviève ordered the specialty duck.

Throughout the meal, they chatted about events at the Sorbonne and her vacation trip. Claude was careful to stay away from any reference to Ramon. When dinner was over, Claude looked at his watch and realized he needed to leave for the club. He was about to leave Geneviève and head to the club alone but changed his mind.

Geneiéve, I am playing at **le lapin chaud** tonight. Why don't you come with me? I am escorting the daughters of a client from the gallery. It will be fun. It is not a crowded club. We play jazz and the customers dance and drink wine. Please come."

They took a taxi to the club. Claude was recognized and welcomed inside. He spoke to the manager for the night and they were taken to a table between the stage and the dance floor where there were huge overstuffed chairs, a black onyx topped table, and a long couch. Claude made sure Geneviève was settled and then left to change into the costume that the band members wore.

The group started playing. It was soft jazz. Geneviève listened and recognized the tune. It was from the Jacques Lousier Play Bach album which was one of Claude's favorites. The band went upbeat and the club was rapidly filling.

After an hour, Claude returned to Geneviève as the group took a break. He glanced at his watch. It was nine.

"I must go and welcome the daughters of one of the gallery's best clients. I will return shortly with them."

The Benoit sisters were waiting when he exited the club door. He beckoned to them. Some in the line started booing and calling insults as the girls were escorted passed the waiting patrons. He took them down to the front of the club where Geneviève sat sipping a spritzer.

"I would like to introduce the Benoit sisters. This is Ginette and Antoinette."

The sisters icily stared at her. Instantly feeling the hostility, she decided to leave.

"Claude, I must now leave. There is a function tonight and I promised to be there. It was nice to meet you, girls."

She turned hastily and quickly made her way to the exit. Claude did not see the sniggers on the Benoit twin's faces.

One of the members of the musical group called to him to rejoin them as they were ready to play again. For another two hours, they continued to play until a new group was ready to replace them. Claude was pleased their session was over and went to join the girls. He sat himself down on the couch and ordered a brandy. The girls moved from their chairs and positioned themselves on either side of him. He could feel their warm bodies pressed against him and their breath brushing past his neck.

The group started to play 'The Girl from Ipanema' and Claude used it as his chance to break the situation.

"Which of you girls would care to join me for this dance?"

Antoinette stood and extended her hand. They moved out onto the dance floor and swayed to the music. Antoinette kept leading Claude and had his back turned away from the seated patrons. She watched as Ginette removed a glass vial from her purse and proceeded to pour its contents into Claude's drink.

As they slow danced, she nestled her chin into Claude's neck and shoulder. He was in heaven.

Chapter 17

Claude experienced a strange feeling of euphoria and calmness. He tried to keep his thoughts focused on the girls and yet he seemed to drift away. He started to feel tired but did not wish to leave the club.

By the time the club closed he was extremely mellow. It was late. The Benoit sisters asked to return with him to his home for more drinks. He agreed. After the brief taxi ride, they arrived at his home and stumbled into the kitchen. Claude found a bottle of Brandy and they sat talking until late.

Antoinette decided it was time to leave, but Ginette decided otherwise.

"It will be morning in a few hours. Can we stay here and leave early?"

"Yes, that will be fine. My roommates are not here so you can use their room. Excuse me while I go to the toilet."

Claude left and wove his way to the bathroom. While he was gone, Antoinette and Ginette conspired.

"I don't understand. I used a normal amount. He is not acting like the others. I am going to use another."

She reached into her purse and removed another vial and proceeded to pour its contents into the glass of brandy he had left on the table. He returned to find them sweet and smiling.

"I am going to finish my drink and go upstairs to bed. I will wait for you to finish your drinks and take you up to the bedroom."

Fifteen minutes passed by and the effects of the drug hit Claude. He felt strange and decided that maybe he had drunk too much that evening. He told the Benoit twins to go with him and he would open the room for them.

The trio climbed the stairs to the second floor where the bedrooms were located. Claude took the girls to his roommate's bedroom and left. He stripped naked and crashed back onto his bed. It was late yet he was not tired. He felt happy and floating. He pulled himself under the covers and thought of the evening he had experienced. Things were different in Paris.

Claude was dozing when he heard their laughter. His bedroom door inched open and the Benoit sisters entered totally naked. Each jumped into Claude's bed on either side of him. They both started kissing and fondling him. Ginette raised herself and straddled him.

She laughed. "Now we will enjoy a ménage à trois."

Claude found himself unable to resist as the drugs controlled his system and for almost an hour the sisters sexually feasted on his body. Exhausted they all fell asleep. Claude was sandwiched between the sisters.

At six in the morning, a loud thumping and the sound of splintering wood awoke Claude. He attempted to sit up in the bed to go and investigate. Before he could get out of the bed, heavily armed police crashed into his bedroom shouting to stay where he was. Claude froze. He was confused and the drugs in his system were making it even more complicated.

A short man in uniform walked up to the bed. "I am Inspector Cloutier. You are under arrest."

As he spoke the girls threw back the covers and ran naked from the room to the roommate's bedroom where they locked themselves in.

"Mon Dieu. A ménage à trois!! What sort of animal are you?"

Claude struggled to reply. Two large gendarmes stepped forward and pulled him from the bed. They laughed when they saw he was naked, but stopped when the eyes fell to his lower extremities.

"Sacrebleu. Let's get him dressed."

Before handing Claude the pile of clothes he had stripped off only hours ago, they thoroughly searched them. He dressed in the same avant-garde clothing he had worn to the gallery the previous afternoon.

As he dressed, Claude wondered what was happening.

"Why am I being arrested? I have done nothing. This is some mistake."

"Be quiet. You are under arrest by the prosecutor's order. It will all be explained at the police station. Now don't resist. Come with us."

One of the gendarmes stepped forward and grabbed Claude's wrists. He locked heavy metal handcuffs around them and started to pull Claude from the room.

Claude was marched down the stairs and passed the broken front door they had smashed to gain entry. They pulled him onto the street where three Renault 8 police cars were haphazardly parked with their blue lights flashing.

He was roughly pushed into the rear seat of the closest car and a burly cop crawled in beside him. With the unique siren of a French police car blaring they pulled away and left a number of neighbors standing on front steps and the sidewalk who had come out at the early hour to see what was happening.

After the short but harrowing drive through the early morning traffic, they arrived at 4 rue de la Montagne Sainte-Geneviève, the home of the 5th Arrondissement police station, a grey and ominous looking building

The door of the car was opened by another officer who had run to the car. There were no handles in the rear of the police car. The burly cop exited and then pulled Claude from the car. He was joined by two other officers and Claude was half dragged up the stairs into the station.

Inside the police station, they turned right and through heavy wooden double doors and down a corridor. There were a number of doors off the corridor and they proceeded to the end door. The burly cop stepped forward and unlocked it. They shoved Claude into the room. It was painted in a faded sickly light green with bright white-blue overhead fluorescent lights. In the center of the room, a grey metal desk was placed with six cheap chairs around it. Attached to the cement block wall was a metal bench.

The cop motioned to Claude to sit on the bench and then left the room. Claude sat for what seemed hours. Finally, the door clicked open and several men entered. Claude looked at the man leading them. It was the same man he had seen watching his home and later staring through the windows of the gallery. None of the men were smiling.

One of the gendarmes who had entered with them walked to the bench and lifted Claude and took him to a chair at the table. The other men took up positions at the table. No one had spoken yet. Other than a hum from the overhead lights that room was totally silent.

The man Claude identified spoke.

"I am Detective Gérard. I have checked your id. I cannot believe we have one of the famous de Passioné family members sitting here. Your presence makes us concerned that your family may also be involved in these matters. You have been arrested and face several charges. You are being held in extended custody which has been authorized by the Judge of Liberties due to the serious and complex offenses you are charged with. Those charges include conspiracy to commit a crime, participating in organized crime, theft, accessory to murder and smuggling. You will be held in custody for a period of up to six days while further investigations are made. Your detention is also to prevent you from communicating with the others involved. You are allowed to have assistance from a lawyer at this time and a physician should you need one."

Claude sat in total bewilderment. He knew he was in serious trouble but had no idea of what or why.

"Do you want us to provide the duty lawyer here or do you wish to contact your own?'

"Can I call and arrange for my own?"

"Yes. The officers will escort you to a phone you can use and then you will be placed in a holding cell with the general population. You will be held there until your lawyer arrives here."

Claude was trying hard to suppress hid panic. He felt sick. The drugs from the previous night and morning were creating havoc in his empty stomach. He knew this was some horrible mistake and decided to stay quiet until he spoke with a lawyer. He did not have a lawyer in Paris. It was impossible to contact a de Passioné lawyer to attend. An idea hit him.

The officers took him to a wall phone. As his hands were handcuffed they asked him the number to dial and then held the phone to his ear. He listened as it rang and rang at the other end.

Chapter 18

He was about to hang up the phone when it was answered by a groggy sounding Geneviève.

"Geneviève, I am in trouble. I have been arrested. I don't know why. I am at the police station at the 5th Arrondissement in custody. I desperately need a lawyer. Can your father help?'

"Let me run and ask him."

Claude listened and heard the deep voice of her father responding to her questions.

"He will be there around noon. I will come with him. He advises you to say nothing until he is present. What did you do last night?"

"No. Please don't come. You might get implicated in whatever this strange situation is. They will not let you in to see me."

Before Claude could answer the officer took the phone. "You only get a few minutes. This is not a social club."

Claude was taken through another corridor. He heard the shouting from the prisoners and them banging on the bars. As they approached the cell, he smelled stale urine and excrement in the air. They stopped in front of the huge metal cage. The prisoners inside went quiet as they watched the new addition pushed into the cell.

"Place your hands through those bars. We will remove those handcuffs now that you are secured behind those bars."

He pushed his wrists out through the bars and after the cuffs were removed rubbed his wrists. The other prisoners were looking at him in the strange clothing he was wearing.

A huge prisoner with a shaven head, tattooed arms and heavy jowls headed toward him.

"Give me the cigarettes pretty boy. Give em now."

The prisoner fronted up to Claude and pushed his huge chest against him.

"I don't have any. I don't smoke and they have taken all my possessions before they put me in here."

Claude felt the heavy blow in his chest that was followed by yet another to his side. He fell to the filthy floor. Blood and vomit spewed from his mouth. He lost consciousness. The other prisoners crowded around shouting and tried to incite a fight. The huge man kicked Claude in the ribs. There was more shouting. Guards came running to investigate. Recognizing the situation as dangerous they spayed a pepper spray into the cell. With mask s attached they entered the cell and bent over Claude. The extent of his injuries was evident.

"Go quickly. Get the doctor. I think we will need to move him immediately."

Five minutes went by until the doctor arrived. He examined the injuries.

"This man is seriously injured. I cannot treat him here. Call an ambulance. He needs to be treated at a hospital."

The prison guards ran to the administration office to call the ambulance and arrange for police to accompany Claude to Emergency.

At the hospital, his injuries were quickly assessed. He was taken to be X-Rayed.

"Please get me the results without delay. I fear this man has severe internal damage."

The doctor walked to get a coffee from the hospital café before returning to the radiology department where he waited. The radiologist returned with the x-rays. He requested the doctor to join him in an office equipped with a backlit lightbox. He attached the x-rays to the box.

"Here you will see that these ribs are broken. In particular, look at this one here. It has been snapped into two pieces and is close to the lung which could be punctured by the jagged edge around the break. I suggest surgery to remove or repair this damage."

The doctor stood looking at the x-rays while trying to decide whether surgery would help.

"I will need time to consult with my associates. Please have him admitted. Ask the admitting staff to administer morphine. Send a copy of these x-rays with him. I am going to discuss this with the other surgeons."

Chapter 19

The lawyer parked in the allocated parking at the side of the police station. He acknowledged a few of the officers he knew as he climbed the stairs to the front entrance. Inside he immediately went to the main desk and presented his credentials and requested a meeting with his client.

The desk officer looked at the log and frowned.

"There is a note here that I am to call Detective Gérard upon your arrival. Please take a seat over there while I find him."

The lawyer looked at the chairs with disgust. They were made with cheap curved plywood backs and seats attached to tubular metal frames. He stood waiting and watched as the desk officer went about trying to locate the detective. He looked up and beckoned the lawyer to the desk.

"Detective Gérard is at the hospital and is returning. He will be here in thirty minutes. You may wish to go and enjoy a coffee at the café across the street while you wait. Anything would be more comfortable than those chairs," he laughed.

Hugo Martel was less than impressed at having to wait for the detective.

" I will expect him here in thirty minutes. I suggest you contact him and tell him that. If he is not here then, I will be speaking with his superiors. I am sure you know who I am and the power I wield politically and otherwise."

The desk officer smiled at Hugo but silently thought to himself how he, like many Parisians, disliked the bombastic politician with the overinflated ego.

"Yes. I will get a message to him now."

Hugo, politician, and lawyer left the police station and headed toward the café.

He returned exactly thirty minutes later and found Detective Gérard waiting for him at the reception desk. They exchanged pleasantries and headed off to an office.

"I would like to see my client now. I want him present in these conversations to hear and understand the charges you have brought against him."

Detective pointed to a comfortable chair at the side of the office. Hugo sat and wondered why they were in this office. He did not have to wait long.

"There is a problem. Your client, Claude de Passioné has been injured as a result of an altercation in the holding cell. He is presently in the Saint Agnes Hospital awaiting surgery. We will need to contact the immediate family to authorize this surgery. His situation is serious. Do you have contact with the de Passioné family or their legal representatives? I am told by the doctors that the surgery needs to be done immediately."

"Before I contact anyone, please tell me the details. Was this an assault by the police or another prisoner?"

Detective Gérard bristled at the inference of police brutality. He was well aware of the reputation of the Parisian police and the many incidents that had occurred during recent riots.

"He was attacked by another prisoner. The doctors advise me that he has multiple broken ribs, one of which is snapped and threatening to puncture his lung. They wish to operate to prevent that. In addition, it seems there may be other injuries. We are still investigating the incident and I do not have more information to share with you."

"This is a deplorable situation. You have my client under arrest and have allowed him to be injured by placing him in a harmful situation. I assume you have him guarded at the hospital as well? You have stripped him of his freedom based on an allegation or do you have proof to show me?"

The detective shifted uncomfortably in his chair.

"The information we have, plus your client's involvement is solid. We do not arrest people in such a manner unless we are sure of the information. Your client is implicated in a huge crime."

"Normally I would wait for you to provide all the details when my client is with me and present. Under these circumstances, I suggest you explain fully."

Hugo Martel removed a tallow pad from his briefcase and placed it on the table.
"Now, tell me all you have including evidence and the sources of your information."

Detective Gérard folded his hands on the table. He looked distressed."

"I will tell you what I can at this moment. Your client, Claude de Passioné, has been arrested for his role in an international art smuggling operation. We have had him under observation for weeks. He attended at Gallerie de Arts almost daily and has been seen in the company of Lise Victor and her father Antoine. There is only so much I can tell you now because as we speak, Interpol detectives and art experts are at the gallery. We have arrested Antoine at his home. We have yet to locate his daughter. They were the key figures in the operation. We had undercover agents gather evidence. There are many stolen pieces of art at the gallery in storage in a private area with highly restricted access. These were stolen from museums, universities and private collections. In addition to these were a number of valuable paintings that had been stolen from Jewish and other wealthy families by the Nazis during the war. Many are priceless pieces. It seems your client was involved in handling sales of this art.

The art was smuggled abroad. Many of the ancient French masterpieces are protected by French export law. The trafficking in illicit antiques is a huge international problem. There are many dangerous figures associated with this business. The Victors were a key part of a French network. There have been murders, bombings, hijackings, fraudulent money transactions and other crimes that have been committed with this network. Your client has been involved and will face justice here and abroad where art crimes have been committed.

The case against the Victors and your client has been presented by us to the prosecutor. Given the severity of the crime, he has issued authority for us to hold all the suspects until trial. There are arrests being made in Italy, Holland, Spain, and England as we speak. This is a huge investigation. The statutes regarding detainment under French law will not apply."

Hugo actively scribbled down the key information.

"I would like to visit my client in the hospital. Please make the arrangements now."

Chapter 20

Hugo was taken to the third floor of the hospital by the armed gendarme. Another gendarme sat outside the door of the hospital room. Hugo waited while the door was unlocked and he was allowed to enter.

"I wish to see my client in private."

"We are under orders that he not be left alone with anyone."

"Where do you think he will go? Look at him."

Claude lay on the cream colored metal bed. A saline drip was attached to his right arm. His left arm was handcuffed to the railing of the bed and a wide brown leather strap across his lower stomach restrained him to the bed.

Hugo was furious.

"Release that restraining belt now. This man has severe injuries in that area of the chest and I am sure that is aggravating the situation."

"We will need to get permission from our superiors. We have very strict orders regarding this man's custody."

"Then I suggest you do it now before I make it very unpleasant for all of you."

The gendarme was aware of Hugo's massive influence as a politician and a lawyer. He left to contact his commanding officer. He returned ten minutes later with a nurse and the belt was removed. Claude had remained unconscious throughout. Hugo stopped the nurse.

"Since I arrived he has been asleep. When will I be able to speak with him?"

The nurse took a clipboard with notes and a chart from the end of the bed. She thumbed through the papers.

"He has been given heavy sedation and a large amount of morphine. He will sleep for hours."

Hugo left the room and spoke to the gendarme waiting outside.

"Please contact Detective Gérard. I wish to meet with him immediately."

At the police station, Hugo was ushered into a sparsely furnished meeting room. The detective arrived within minutes.

"I would like you to share with me the information you have that incriminates my client. I would also like the contact for the others investigating this matter and specifically Interpol."

"I will need to get special clearance for this. I will need to speak to my superiors and probably make a request to the prosecutor. It will take some time."

"I am not prepared to wait too long. I will commence with legal proceedings regarding his injury, false arrest, damages and more. If you delay I can promise you that your future career will be shoveling dog shit from the sidewalks of Paris."

Hugo left the police station in a mood. He hated dealing with the low-level bureaucrats who were too scared to take any initiative for fear of reprimand. He considered them spineless and unworthy.

He went to his car and drove home ignoring all the traffic signs and at a speed well in excess of the posted limits. At his home he stormed through the front door, his mood still foul.

"Geneviève. Where are you? Come and see me now please."

She ran down the stairs from her room. It was obvious from his voice that all wasn't well and she did not wish to aggravate him further.

"Please sit down. We need to discuss what you have got me into."

Hugo told her of the charges against Claude and the happenings at the police station and hospital.

"Is he alright? Can I go and see him. He is one of my best friends."

"No Geneviève. He is heavily sedated, plus they have him guarded. They will not admit you. He has been isolated away from anyone who may have knowledge of the situation. Now tell me everything you know about Claude de Passioné.

"I met him at a student party at his house. He lives with two other students. They are brothers from near the Spanish French border. They are both studying to become doctors. Claude did not go out too much. We stayed at the pension a lot. We cooked and drank wine and listened to music. All four of us had fun. We had huge debates but no one got offended. We were the best of friends."

"Did he discuss his home life or things he was involved with outside of the Sorbonne?"

"Not really. It was just after I met Claude that I had the unfortunate experience of meeting his mother. She is crazy and a mean one. She was the reason Claude stayed in Paris and took that job at the gallery. He did not want to return to the Chateau and her. Claude did not need the money. The de Passioné family is so wealthy, as I'm sure you know. Claude wanted to stay in Paris and needed to find a job that would interest him. I had met Lise Victor at the Sorbonne. She was older than me and several years ahead in her studies. I saw her at a party and she told me of a trip she had planned and was looking for someone to work in the gallery. I suggested Claude. That is all I know."

"Did Claude ever speak of his job or what happened at the gallery?"

"No. Our life was about friends, the Sorbonne, music and the future. We never spoke about the gallery or his job."

"Do you think he was involved with these people?"
"No. There was no reason. For him, it was interesting to meet people who purchased and collected art. He liked the social aspect. He did not need money, so why would he take such a risk?"

"That's what I have been wondering."

Chapter 21

The phone in Hugo's study rang steadily. It was early morning. He made his way from the kitchen where he was preparing a breakfast for the study. He gruffly answered.

"Good morning, Hugo. It is Detective Gérard and I am calling you as a courtesy. The patient has regained consciousness and is talking. I am going to the hospital with an investigator from Interpol. I am wondering if you wish to be present. I will be driving past your home and stop and drive you. It will be easier at this time of day to go with an official police car. We will not have issues with traffic."

Hugo thought of the snarled traffic at that time of the morning and made a quick decision.

"Thank you, detective. Yes, I would indeed appreciate that, besides I will meet the representative from Interpol."

Thirty minutes later, the white Renault 8 with a blue flashing light screeched to a halt outside his luxury home on Saint-Germain-des-Prés. Hugo bounded out to the car and silently laughed when he observed his neighbors looking on in curiosity. He squeezed himself into the small car.

Detective Gérard introduced Hugo to Inspector Rudy van der Horne from Interpol.

"I am most eager to interview your client. Detective Gérard has told me of this Claude de Passioné. It makes no sense that the wealthy heir apparent would participate in such criminal activities and place himself in such jeopardy. I wonder whether he did it for the thrill and excitement."

"I can assure you that from what I know of the young man, he certainly did not. I will be arguing for him to be released from the arrest that has erroneously been made."

They sped on in silence toward the hospital with the unique French police siren wailing, as they moved through the early morning traffic. At the hospital, they pulled into an area reserved for official vehicles.

The hospital was busy even at that early hour. They passed by the Emergency area and observed the people waiting for attention. There was the normal collection of those with cuts and some drunks sporting the damage of earlier brawls and fights. It was a particularly unpleasant scene.

Detective Gérard walked at a brisk pace until they reached the elevators. The hospital had a disinfectant and ether-like smell. They rode to the third floor and headed to Claude's room. Upon entering they were greeted by a young doctor.

Detective Gérard showed the doctor his badge and spoke.

"We are here to visit Claude de Passioné. We have several questions for him. Is he in a state to answer them?"

The doctor looked over at Claude who was semi-conscious.

"He has been given some sedatives and will be very groggy. I ask that you do not stress him. We are preparing him for surgery this morning. We are just waiting for a family member to arrive, and then we will be giving an anesthetic. The surgery is scheduled to take place in an hour. We are hoping the family member will arrive shortly."

Hugo introduced himself.

"What is the surgery to treat?"

"The patient has suffered some serious internal injuries. There is a broken rib and part of it is protruding outwards. The other part is pushed in and could easily penetrate his lung. Several others are broken. We will be removing the badly broken rib. We have him on a high dosage of painkiller at present. We have also detected that his kidneys are bruised. After this surgery, he will need to be immobile for at least six weeks, possibly longer.

He will be strapped to prevent the cracked and broken ribs from moving. He will be given medicine to assist him with urinating due to the kidney bruising. Your friend here has a couple of difficult months ahead of him. Now I must leave as I need to visit other patients. The nurses will be by to start the preparation soon."

As the doctor left the room, Hugo went to the side of the bed. He was appalled to see Claude's wrist still handcuffed to a lower rail on the bed.

"Detective I hardly believe this is necessary. Please have it removed. This man is not going anywhere."

A gendarme was summoned from the corridor outside to remove the handcuff.
Hugo continued. "Claude can you hear and understand me. I am Hugo Martel, a lawyer. I am also Geneviève's father. I am here to assist you. Do you understand what has happened to you?"

Claude's eyes flickered. He attempted to speak but was prevented by a heavy yellow crusting on his lips. It was from the heavy medication that had been administered through the night. Hugo went to the small basin and wet a cloth. He wiped away the crust.

Again he asked Claude if he was aware of the situation. Claude babbled an unintelligent response. The sedatives had rendered him senseless.

Detective Gérard spoke.

"Well, gentlemen it seems there is no point in remaining here."

They were about to leave when the door to the room opened and Marquis de Passioné entered, escorted by a doctor and the gendarme who had been on guard outside.

Chapter 22

Marquis de Passioné strode into the hospital room with an air of superiority. He was attired in a long navy serge wool coat. On his head, he wore his usual matching navy sailors cap.

"What has happened to my son? Who are you, people? It seems like a crowd in here. Explain your presence here."

"I am Detective Gérard and this is Inspector van der Horne from Interpol. I am sure you know Hugo Martel. He is acting as counsel for your boy. It is fortuitous that we should meet here. We will leave you with the doctor and the patient but will want to speak with you before you leave."

The trio left the room and waited for the Marquis and doctor to emerge from the room. Another doctor wearing green surgical scrubs and wheeling a trolley with bottles and stainless trays entered the room. He was accompanied by two nurses. Shortly thereafter the Marquis emerged looking grim.

"You wish to speak to me."

"Yes. Are you driving, or should we drive you to the police station? We need a statement from you regarding the charges against Claude."

"I have my own transportation. I have a chauffeur waiting to take me to the Ritz. Have the gendarme provide him the address and we will accompany you there. Please excuse us, but I wish to speak privately with Mr. Martel."

The detective and inspector move down the corridor to a small waiting area near the nurses' station.

"Please tell me what this is about. Why was Claude arrested? Do you have details?"

Hugo Martel replied with the information he had been provided.

"That is preposterous. Under no circumstances would Claude get involved with something like this. For one thing, he is too stupid."

Hugo was surprised at the Marquis' harsh reaction. He decided to attend the meeting with the Detective and the Marquis.

"You can come with me. I will have us driven directly to the police station. The chauffeur can wait. Will you require to be driven after the meeting?"

"No afterward I will go to my office. There are a number of people I will need to contact about this matter."

Traffic had thinned and they drove behind the Renault with its distinctive siren. Some cars pulled over but many ignored the wail of the siren and the importance of the police.

The Marquis and Hugo climbed the stairs to the reception area and were quickly taken to an interview room. They were seated at the same table Claude had sat at hours earlier.

The detective started the interview.

"I am sure that Mr. Martel has advised you of the details regarding the apprehension of your son. We do not understand why the son of a wealthy family would be involved with an international trafficking and smuggling operation. Can you explain?"

The Marquis sighed. "I am sure you have made a huge mistake. There is no reason."

"You realize that we now suspect the de Passioné family of involvement. I have requested the prosecutor to issue the necessary paperwork for us to have your Chateau searched for stolen art and antique items."

The Marquis exploded. He stood and slammed his fist down on the table and burst forth with a long drawn out series of profanities and curses.

A gendarme ran into the investigation room and seized him from behind.

"Let him go. I think he is going to be spending a long time with us. I am arresting him for further questioning. We will not put him in the general holding area. Take him to an isolation cell. He can think about the situation there."

The Marquis turned to Hugo.

"Stop this nonsense now. They cannot arrest me. I am an innocent man who came to assist with my son."

"I cannot represent both you and Claude. I will recommend someone to you. Please go quietly with them. I am leaving now to make those phone calls I told you of."

The Marquis was taken by each arm and struggled as he was pulled from the room.

Hugo stood and asked the detective to advise him of any developments.

Chapter 23

Surgery was successfully performed on Claude and after six hours he was taken to a recovery room. The nurses checked saline drips and took readings of his pulse and other vital signs. Claude was heavily sedated and was not expected to regain consciousness for many hours.

At Hugo's office, he was busy phoning his government contacts. He had many questions that needed answers. He asked about past interceptions of smuggled art and likely markets. He obtained names of convicted criminals who had been caught and incarcerated. The scope of international art and antique trafficking was huge as was the money aspect. Hugo had heard of discoveries of lost or stolen art but never realized the magnitude of the problem.

He called several art dealers he had met at social functions and explained why he was calling. He asked for their thoughts on who was involved in the Gallerie des Images case. He drew a blank. Either the contacts did not know or wished to remain quiet.

As he sat considering how to obtain the information, his door opened and Geneviève walked into his office. She had a serious expression on her face.

"Father, how is Claude? Do you know?"

"I do not. I will phone the hospital."

The phone rang many times before it was answered. Hugo explained his situation and after a lengthy delay was connected to the surgeon who had performed the operation. They spoke for several minutes before Hugo hung up.

"The doctor advises the surgery went well but Claude will have a long and difficult recovery. It seems we can visit."

Geneviève's face lit up. While she and Claude were not lovers, their friendship was deep.

"When can we leave? I am anxious. I wish to see him."

"You must have a really special friendship with him. Are you sure that is all it is?"

"He is kind. He helped me and has continued to listen and give me advice. We truly are just friends."

Hugo arose from his desk and reached for his coat. His office was warm and the air stale. The overhead lights glared down on his desk. As he was taking his coat from the rack, the phone on his desk rang. For a minute he wondered whether he should answer. He finally walked back to his desk and snatched the receiver from its cradle.

He stood in silence while the voice of Detective Gérard announced the news.

"We have arrested Antoine Victor. He has been questioned for the past few hours. He has decided to cooperate with us. He is squealing like a pig. We are getting names of many involved in the trafficking ring. He has signed a legal document here that exonerates Claude de Passioné. It seems he was just an employee. We have not been able to locate Lise Victor. We believe she has fled the country. It is possible she may have told Claude where she was going. We will need to speak to him again."

"As his lawyer, I tell you that you will not speak to him further at this time. I will determine what he knows of her whereabouts. You and the other investigators will now make any requests through me."

"Hugo you are mistaken. We have the authority and will use it."

"I suggest you think carefully about that. Remember that he is my client and I can take actions you may well regret."

Hugo slammed the phone down and turned to Genévieve.

"Let us leave now and visit Claude."

"Why are you so angry? Who was that on the phone? What is wrong?"

"That detective. He is arrogant. I intend to make his life difficult. He has a confession from Antoine Vector that states that Claude is not involved with the crimes. Now he wants to investigate whether Claude knows what has happened to the daughter, Lise. If he wants to pursue things he will need to speak with me."

"You must calm down. It is not good to see you like this. I am pleased you feel so strongly about Claude. I knew he was not involved. He is a good person."

"We will go to the hospital. I suspect Claude will be drugged and may not be very coherent. His surgery was lengthy and he is on painkillers. It will be a short visit."

They left the office and Hugo decided to take a taxi instead of driving.

As they drove through Paris, Geneviève looked at the buildings and the pedestrians dressed in early winter clothing. Paris seemed drab and grey. She was growing to dislike the city.

At the hospital, Hugo encountered one of the reporters from The Paris International.

"Mr. Martel. Mr. Martel. Mr. Martel. We understand that one of the accused in the stolen art trafficking ring was injured while in police custody and is in the hospital. Are you representing him? What is his name? Is he the only one?"

Hugo cursed. Obviously, someone in the police had leaked the information.

"I have no comment. I am accompanying my daughter to see a friend. Now let me through."

He pushed the reporter to the side and entered the hospital where they took the elevator up to the third floor. The gendarme guarding the door was no longer stationed there.

They opened the door and found Claude lying on the bed with an array of tubes connected to his body looking like a giant octopus. A raven-haired young nurse was standing by the bed holding a bedpan. Even though he was drugged, Claude was appreciating the minute. A faint smile curled at the edge of his lips. Beneath the white sheets and with his head nestled in the pillow, Claude looked handsome with his black hair, olive skin, and mustache. Geneviève quickly realized that the nurse was infatuated with Claude. She moved to dismiss the nurse.

"Please give us some privacy. This man with me is his lawyer. We need to talk confidential matters."

Hugo looked at his daughter in amazement. "Just friends," he thought.

Chapter 24

Later in the afternoon, Hugo received a visit from Detective Gérard at his office.

"I have come to ask your assistance. We have been unable to locate Lise Victor. We believe that your client, Claude de Passioné may know her whereabouts. It is an offense to keep such information from us. Will you speak with him? I would like to be present with you. Are you in agreement with this?"

Hugo thought for several minutes before answering.

"I have some concerns. I understand your request and the penalty for not cooperating with the police, but I am worried about his safety, should he provide the information if he has any. That trafficking ring is large and operates in several countries. It is likely they will resort to violence as punishment if they feel he has betrayed her."

"I would not ask this if it wasn't important. It isn't just to arrest her for a minor role, we have interrogated another and have a confession she was a major player in the operation. There are millions of dollars hidden in a Cayman Island Bank. She is involved in other criminal activities with drugs, guns and the killing of other gang members who were in competition with her."

"You have just confirmed my fears. I will speak to Claude, though I doubt he knows much of her activities."

"It is important we try to get this information quickly. She may still be in France and that will make it easier to apprehend her."

"I will be visiting the hospital tomorrow morning with my daughter. You are welcome to join us but I caution you to proceed very carefully. He has had major surgery and is drugged. It is possible he may not understand your questions. His answers may not be accurate."

"I will meet you and your daughter in the morning at your house. Again we will take a police car to the hospital."

The detective turned and exited the office.

Hugo tidied up some papers on his desk and sat quietly thinking of what he had just been told. The police were uncovering more than he believed possible. He picked up the phone and called his contact.

An hour passed before he left his office and headed for the rendezvous. He stopped and looked in various shop windows and glanced around for any signs of being followed. After he was convinced that he was not being tailed, he hailed a taxi and took it to the **Gare de l'Est for the long trip from France.** Before purchasing the ticket he called Geneviève to tell her that he had an urgent business matter and would not be home that evening. He
Advised her to go with the detective in the morning and visit Claude. At the station, he met his contact

In the morning, Detective Gérard arrived to drive Hugo and Geneviève to the hospital. He frowned when he found that Hugo had left on business. Not deterred by the fact he drove to the hospital.

Claude was awake and propped up with an assortment of pillows supporting him. Many of the intravenous tubes had been removed and he looked particularly alert. Again, the raven-haired nurse was fussing over him and holding an empty bedpan. It was obvious to Geneviève he was enjoying the attention. She felt a pang of jealousy arise. The nurse turned to leave and she noticed the top buttons of her blouse were undone and the blouse hung open. Her jealousy increased.

She glanced down the bed and saw the sheets were raised like a circus tent below Claude's stomach, held aloft by his erect member. She realized then that the nurse had indeed given Claude some special attention.

Geneviève spun on her heel and marched from the room. Claude's tent-like structure collapsed. He tried to call to her but could only muster up a croaking sound. The detective had watched the whole performance with amusement. He walked to Claude and rested his hand on his shoulder.

"I need to ask you a couple of questions regarding the gallery. Are you able to answer?"

Claude nodded as the detective waited patiently. Alone in the room with Claude, he started the questioning.

"We have been unable to locate Lise Victor. Do you know where she is?"

He attempted to answer and Detective Gérard leaned his head down toward Claude to understand the whispered response. Claude told him of her planned travel to the art auctions. The detective scribbled the information into a small black notebook.

"Did you ever see Hugo Martel at the gallery?"

"Never."

"Did you recognize any of the visitors who were admitted to the rear storage room?"

"I only met people who came into the gallery to view the art in the main area. On occasion, there were wine and cheese evenings with artists in attendance. I never really got to know many of them well."

Detective Gérard soon concluded that the discussion was pointless. He bid farewell to Claude and left to find Geneviève. She was nowhere to be found. He left the hospital and drove back to the police station with thoughts of the crime running through his head. He planned to speak with the inspectors from Interpol. Something was disturbing him.

Chapter 25

Claude's recovery from the operation was fast. Weeks passed by with visits from the Marquis and one from Marie-France. His roommates visited on weekends and kept him informed of happenings at the university. He wondered why Geneviève never visited again. He was puzzled.

The day of his discharge arrived. Still, with the bandages bound around his ribs, two nurses gently lowered him into a wheelchair. An orderly pushed the wheelchair from the room and along the corridor. Nurses lined the edges of the corridor to wish Claude farewell. He was the heartthrob of the ward. At the end of the line, the raven-haired nurse stood sobbing gently. Claude asked the orderly to stop and motioned the nurse toward him. He reached up to her to give a hug but soon they were in a passionate kiss. Claude tasted the salty tears that ran down her face and curled onto her lips. The other nurses looked on in astonishment.

Outside the hospital, Claude was assisted onto a pair of crutches in order to reach the waiting car and the Marquis. The orderly and the chauffeur helped him into the front seat.

Ascending the front steps at the pension was a long and painful process. The roommates, Jean and Henri Beaulieu came out to assist and finally were able to get Claude into the house. They took him into the front salon, where he sat exhausted. The Marquis paced the room.

"I think we need to celebrate now Claude is home. Do you have any of our fine wines here?"

"We have a selection in our little cellar. Let me fetch one for us. Do you prefer a red or white?"

"It is early. I think we should sample a chilled white. Preferably an Alsace."

The Beaulieu brothers exchanged looks and Henri left for the wine. He returned minutes later with the wine and four chilled glasses. The Marquis was pleased.

While they sat, Claude discussed his predicament and wondered how he would graduate at the Sorbonne after missing weeks of tuition. The Marquis responded.

"I will arrange for you to receive private lessons for you to catch up. I have connections at the Sorbonne. It will be fine."

Claude turned to the Beaulieus. "Have you seen Geneviève Martel. She did not come to the hospital to visit."

"No. We have not seen or heard from her. We tried to phone her but the number no longer works. We tried to contact her father but his office is deserted. It is strange. Could she be involved in that art smuggling scheme?"

They sat for a few minutes in silence, pondering the question.

Claude spoke. "I have known her for years now. She has never acted strange or disappeared before. I do not believe she was involved. But what has happened to Hugo Martel? It is strange that such a prominent politician and lawyer would just abandon his career. It is very strange. I don't like it."

Henri went to get another bottle of the Alsace. He was walking by the phone when it rang. After answering the call, he called Claude.

"It is Detective Gérard for you."

The Marquis responded.

"Claude is in pain and it is difficult for him. I will speak to the detective. Anything he has to say to Claude he can say to me."

The Marquis marched to the phone and announced himself and stated why he was taking the call. Within minutes he went totally quiet and his face expressed concern. He hung up and returned to sit with Claude and the Beaulieu brothers. He was now in a somber mood.

Claude was curious. Finally, he could not contain his curiosity.

"I gather from your reactions that it was not a good call from the detective."

"No. It was not good news. The detective is on his way here now. He says it is important and involves life and death. He seemed panicked."

Henri walked around the group and refilled their wine glasses. They sat talking and wondering why the detective needed to visit them and what could be so important.
Almost an hour passed before there was a pounding on the door. Jacques went to admit the detective. He took his coat and escorted him into the salon. He then went to the kitchen and returned with a chair for himself and another wine glass which he handed to Detective Gérard. The detective politely declined.

"I wish to update you on the art smuggling investigation. We followed up at the auction houses that Claude had provided us where Lise was meant to visit. Our foreign counterparts and Interpol were able to investigate and further stolen art has been recovered. Some are masterpieces that disappeared years ago. This trafficking ring is proving to be much larger than we first believed. It seems that Lise Victor was the brains behind the elaborate scheme.

I want Claude to take extra caution as we are worried that his life may be in danger.

The bodies of Hugo and Geneiève Martel were found off the coast of Sicily last night. A local fisherman thought he had caught a whale. It turned out to be that fat Hugo.

Claude gasped. Suddenly the pieces were falling into place.

Chapter 26

Claude recovered within weeks and returned to the Sorbonne to continue his studies. He was deeply saddened at the demise of Geneième. His personality had changed. He was an angry young man.

Claude threw himself into his studies; however, in need of distraction, he immersed himself with a plethora of girls. The frequency of visits to the pension became a source of annoyance to the Beaulieu brothers.

Late spring arrived in Paris and the moods of Claude and the Beaulieus changed. There was activity on the streets, including music, art, and buskers who performed into the night. An abundance of flowers sprang up in planters carefully arranged by storekeepers and restaurant owners. The city took on a new life….and so did Claude.

The upcoming academic year was to be his final year. Claude's life was full of contradiction and confusion. Unable to finally decide on a career or returning to the de Passioné business he made a decision. He called Marie-France to announce he was returning home for a week to discuss his future. She was ecstatic; convinced he had decided to step into the family's wine business.

Friday arrived and Claude took the train to the closest station to the Chateau. He was met by the family chauffeur. It was mid-afternoon when they arrived at the large sprawling home.

Marie-France bounced down the front steps. Claude immediately realized the type of week he would endure.

Marie-France was dressed as a hippie. She wore a tie-dyed with bright orange bell bottom jeans and open-toed Jesus sandals. Her hair hung over her shoulder in a long braid.

Claude looked at her and thought, "Shit. She's sixty years old but trying to be twenty-five."

She held his arm as they entered the Chateau. They had no sooner walked into the huge marble-floored foyer when they were confronted with the yelping and barking of a dog. Claude was confused. The family had never owned a dog. Suddenly a large apricot poodle ran to them. Claude bent to pat the dog's orange head but quickly recoiled from the stench of the dog's breath from the rotting teeth and diseased gums.

"Isn't she beautiful? I won her in a contest at the local butchers. Her name is Fifi La Rue."

Claude looked at the smelly beast with disgust. The dog circled him and then relieved itself at his feet. He was not amused.

"I can't believe you have a smelly animal like this in the house. It is a horrible dog."

"Don't speak about Fifi like that. She is better than many people including you and your insolence."

Marie-France stormed off with the dog leaving Claude standing on the foyer.

Claude returned to the entrance and took the cases the chauffeur had unloaded from the car and proceeded to his room. The reception was what he had expected and the reason for the plans he had made.

After he placed his effects in his room he decided to take a stroll in the vineyards. He needed the solitude to compose in his mind the way in which to announce his plans to the Marquis and Marie-France.

A late summer breeze rustled through the densely leafed vines. Claude looked at the abundance of the grapes. It had been a good year as the weather had been ideal for the growing season.

As he walked, the silence was sporadically interrupted by the loud report of shotguns fired by the workers to scare off the birds from the ripening grapes.

Claude continued to walk for several hours, pausing once in a while and sitting on old tree stumps that had been left after the fields had been cleared of shrub and forest. He felt sad. He loved the Chateau and the land but hated the prospect of living under the same roof with Marie-France for a week. He was not as worried about the Marquis as he knew he would seldom be there as he was too busy with his frequent dalliances.

The sun had set when Claude returned to the Chateau. In the early dusk, he observed a luxury Jaguar car parked in the courtyard. He did not know the car. His curiosity arose.

As he entered, Marie-France ran to him.

"I am sorry that we argued earlier. I am tired. I have not been feeling well recently. Please dress for dinner. We have special guests this evening. They are of special importance."

"Who are these important guests and why should I want to meet them?"

"They are the owners of Banque Crédit du Vin. The Marquis had made an offer to purchase two vineyards that the bank previously financed. The owners are in financial trouble and they have offered us an excellent arrangement. One day when you operate the vineyards and wineries you will need these contacts. Please hurry and dress. We will dine after drinks in the salon. Please hurry. The chefs have prepared a special dinner for this evening. I want it to be a night that they will enjoy and remember."

Claude digested her words. He barely accepted how she changed personalities when there was something to gain, whether social or financial. She was a hypocrite in his mind.

Thirty minutes passed before he joined the group in the salon. The guests politely stared at him as he entered wearing black matador pants festooned with black buttons on the side and a white satin high neck regency shirt with a large neckcloth. On his feet, he wore black pointed boots.

Marie-France thought to herself how handsome he looked and how he looked like a fancy pirate. She gushed forth as she rushed to proudly introduce him.
"This is my son, Claude. He is studying arts and business at the Sorbonne. The Marquis and I are so proud of our boy."

Claude was surprised at the mix of the three guests. In particular, the impeccably groomed young woman he guessed to be in her mid-forties. He bowed slightly and introduced himself. She was flanked on either side by two handsome older men in their sixties. They had silver grey hair neatly trimmed. Their faces glowed with the tan and relaxed look of the wealthy who enjoyed the finer items in life.

Marie-France fussed around them like a mother hen ensuring that the drinks and hor d'oeuvres were served frequently and with grace.

"Let me introduce myself. I am Chantal Marchand. I am the manager responsible for the bank's business in the district of Bordeaux. These two gentlemen are the owners and senior executives of the bank, Charles Gagne and Yves Chartrand." The two men shook Claude's hand in greeting. Charles could not resist a comment.

"You dress very differently to the young people today."

"I take pride in my appearance."

As they engaged in polite conversation, the head chef announced from the doorway that the dinner was ready for serving. Marie-France motioned the group toward the dining room. The Marquis took Chantal's arm and walked slowly beside her. In the dining room, he pulled back a large antique chair from the table for her and assisted her to the table. Marie-France watched and glowered.

Chapter 27

The dinner was served and the conversation and wine flowed freely.

Dinner consisted of an entrée of Garbure, the thick French soup of ham, cabbage vegetables, with cheese and bread. The plat principal was fresh poached salmon with a lemon sauce and freshly harvested vegetables. This was followed by a salad and then a cheese plate with many different varieties. A demitasse of strong coffee was served to each of them and a tray of individual desserts was placed on the table.

The guests were astonished at the pleasurable meal.

Charles Gagne finally put down his wine glass and spoke.

"I think we should now discuss the business, which is the reason we have come here. You are aware that we invested in wineries owned by the Berger family. Recent poor health and the poor harvest of the past three years have resulted in the inability of the family to continue running the wineries. The bank is not prepared to continue to support them. We have commenced legal proceedings to assume the title of the operations. We will naturally work with the family during a change of ownership. It is our plan to recover the money we have invested and to sell the properties at a small profit for the family."

Silence descended around the table. Claude looked at Marie-Franc and then focused on the Marquis. He was deep in thought.
"What is it that you are proposing to us? We are busy here with our own wines. It has not been in our minds to expand. Why should we consider this?"

Claude recognized the maneuvering process that the Marquis had commenced. He had seen it before.

It was Yves who answered.

"Our proposal is actually a very simple one. We wish to be repaid in full for the investment. We will sell for a twenty-five percent premium in order to reimburse the Berger family."

The Marquis was deep in thought. He did not speak for a long while.

"Gentlemen, let us retire to the salon where we can discuss this in detail. Claude and Marie-France will join us."

As they were seated in the salon, a waiter arrived and politely offered after dinner drinks. The Marquis requested a bottle of his finest Courvoisier. With drinks in hand, they settled into a lengthy conversation about wine production in the region and the possible yields the Berger properties should produce. The Marquis sent for paper and pens. When he received them he started making notes. He determined the amount the bank was requesting and the premium. He offset the amount by the possible yield of the vineyards and wineries. When he was finished he lay the notes down.

"I am prepared to share my quick analysis of the situation with you. The debt you request and the cost to transfer the properties and the operating cost of taking over the operations are impossible. I cannot consider your proposal."

"We were hoping for a friendly transaction and avoid the spectacle of a public sale and the eviction of the family."

Claude had been listening quietly. Now he spoke.

"I have some questions. I have studied such business arrangements at the Sorbonne. There are a number of other options that could satisfy everyone."

All eyes turned to him.

"I will speak with my father privately. If he agrees, then we will need to meet again."

Both The Marquis and Marie-France were astonished by Claude's outspoken comments.

"Yes, that is acceptable to us. Now let us speak of other things. I am a football fan and Chantal is a ballet and opera aficionado. The business can wait until you and your father have spoken. Now, we shall speak of other things.

The conversation continued for hours. Shortly after midnight, the bankers left. The Marquis promised to contact them with the next couple of days.

When they were alone, The Marquis and Marie-France decided it was time to speak with Claude.

"We were surprised by your participation in that meeting. Can we assume that you are now coming to your senses and will accept your position at the business as a family member? I think the Sorbonne has helped you and also that accident of yours."

Claude knew the moment had arrived for him to deliver the news. He had not planned on this so early in his weeklong stay.

"I came here this week as I have made plans for when I complete my studies this year at the Sorbonne. During my time at the hospital, I thought about my life. I had never experienced the danger I had been placed in. I realized that I needed more experience in life. I have decided to travel the world for the next two years. I need the exposure and I wish to learn about different cultures."

Marie-France gasped and fainted, falling off the chaise lounge onto her beloved Fifi La Rue. The dog yelped and sprinted from the room, leaving a trail of liquid behind it.

The Marquis ran over to lift Marie-France from her slumped heap on the floor. As he lifted her back onto the chaise he was surprised at her weight. It seemed to him that she had lost a lot of weight. He looked at her in detail. He had not noticed the deepening of the wrinkles on her face and neck or the sagging of her figure. Now it was obvious.

Claude watched them and thought to himself what a sorry, rich and privileged pair they were and how they had wasted their lives and opportunities.

Chapter 28

The following morning Claude worked with the Marquis to examine the dossier of financials and reports the bankers had left with them. Claude was surprised that he enjoyed the task. It was clear that the Berger vineyards and wineries were in serious trouble.

"I have some ideas. At the Sorbonne, we studied methods of saving troubled businesses. I have some thoughts on how we could apply them and save the business. First, there are other matters we must understand. Can you have our vintners and estate manager here this afternoon to meet us? I will explain later what my idea is, but first I need to speak with them."

"If you are sure that we could make this a success, then I will have them here. You do realize the risk we are taking in doing this. The risk is financial and once others know our plans they may try to interfere."

They stopped and joined Marie-France for lunch. At the lunch, she barely ate. The Marquis observed her carefully. He noticed a tremor in her hands and how she would occasionally drift into a trance. He vowed to have her examined by their doctor.

As they sat talking after lunch, a servant entered and announced that the staff had arrived for the meeting. Claude and the Marquis excused themselves and left to greet them.

In the salon, Claude addressed them.

"I must stress that what we are about to discuss must be held in confidence. If you cannot make that commitment we need to know now."

There was agreement amongst the staff. The Marquis then spoke.

"We have been approached with the possibility of purchasing the Berger vineyards and wineries. As I am sure you know, the businesses have not been performing well and the Berger family have suffered some personal misfortunes. We are examining the situation. My son, Claude, has ideas but wishes to speak with you first."

"I have spent time with my father reviewing the financial affairs of the business. I believe it is possible to return the operations to profit, but need your assistance. I have here the information regarding the size of the vineyards, the number, and type of vines and the last two years grape yield. I need you to look at this information and determine whether the yields can be improved. The wineries can be supplemented by purchasing grapes from other vineyards. While this is not ideal, we have that as an option."

For the balance of the afternoon, the staff reviewed the documents. It was late when they finished. The head vintner spoke.

"We cannot make any decisions just based on those papers. I suggest we need to visit and see what equipment they have, examine the vines for any disease, and investigate the number and quality of the workers. Until we do that I cannot establish the probability of making the business work."

The Marquis leaned back in his chair and considered the comment.

"I will contact the bank in the morning and arrange for us to visit. I will tell them that we need a complete disclosure of all aspects of the business. If we do not get this then we will not proceed further."

With the work finished, the Marquis sent for a servant to bring some of the best wines to relax and socialize with his staff.

Claude excused himself. He had noticed that Marie-France had been absent from the Chateau. He checked the rooms downstairs and then proceeded upstairs, calling her name. There was no response.

In the distance, he heard a dog barking. He believed it was Fifi La Rue. The barking seemed to be coming from the vineyard in front of the Chateau. Claude decided to investigate. He pulled on some work boots and started to walk through the vineyard in the direction of the barking.

The barking became louder as he approached the entranceway to the Chateau. He saw Fifi La Rue pacing in and out of the vines. Claude ran forward. Marie-France lay on the ground in an unconscious state and dropped to his knees beside her. He felt her weak pulse and decided to carry her back to the Chateau over his shoulder. He was amazed at how little she weighed. He thought back and remembered her as a strong and somewhat sturdy woman.

Back at the Chateau they placed her on a bed and called for a doctor. She was pale and gasping for air and mumbling incoherently. Claude sat on the edge of the bed and held her hands. Even though she had berated him for most of his life, he still had some affection for her.

An hour passed before the doctor arrived at the Chateau. He examined Marie-France but found no immediate cause for her situation and recommended she be taken to the hospital.

Claude and the Marquis followed the ambulance to **L'hôpital Saint-André** hospital. The doctors performed a quick diagnosis and scheduled a series of tests after which they decided to admit her for observation.

Back at the Chateau, Claude sat alone thinking of the options to take over the failing Berger business. It was early morning before he retired for some sleep.

Chapter 29

The Marquis was anxious to return to the hospital and visit Marie-France. As he was preparing to leave the Chateau the phone rang. He considered not answering, but on second thought turned and snatched the receiver from its cradle.

"This is Charles de Passioné."

He listened intently as Chantal from the bank spoke.

"We have prepared an offer to sell our interest in the Berger operation. We would like to visit and present the offer to you. Can we make an appointment?"

"It is too soon. I have to visit Marie-France who was taken to hospital this morning and until we visit the Bergers and inspect the vineyards and wineries there is no point in the meeting. I trust you will facilitate setting up the meeting. I will be here at the Chateau this afternoon. If you are able to arrange the visit for tomorrow please call me then."

Chantal agreed and the Marquis left for the drive to the hospital. He was ten minutes away from the Chateau when he decided to take a detour and drive to the Berger vineyards.

As he drove through the undulating hills, his thoughts were focused on the meeting with the bank owners. He still wondered why they wished to dispose of their investment so quickly. It was troubling him.

Soon the characteristics of the land changed and the road climbed up an incline. The land sloped down to the Garonne River. Large plantings of vines ran in neat rows down toward the river.

He arrived at the Berger vineyards and pulled off the road. He parked and left the car to walk and visually inspect the estate. The buildings appeared in need of maintenance. He crossed over the road to get a closer look at the vines. Many seemed distressed with reddish leaves. The Marquis examined the soil at the base of several vines. It was dry and the vines were suffering from a lack of irrigation.

The condition of the buildings and vines further troubled him. He wondered what the bankers had not told him and were attempting to hide.

He was aware of the serious incidents that had befallen the Bergers. Three years previously, their vineyards had been severely damaged by raging hail storms due to their location. The Bergers attempted replanting new vines but had unable to produce enough to have a successful harvest. In desperation, they purchased grapes from neighboring growers. The costs had spiraled and the family had suffered losses.

The Marquis had seen enough. He turned back toward the city and drove to L'hôpital Saint-André. He parked and walked to the entrance. The old hospital had been modernized inside and was busting with activity. He requested information and asked to meet with the doctor assigned to Marie-France.

A young doctor soon arrived in the reception area and took him into an office. The office was dark with pale sickly green walls and a flickering overhead fluorescent light. They sat and the doctor spoke.

"We have examined Marie-France. It appears she suffered a vasovagal syncope. During the examination, we uncovered some other issues that will need treatment. She has vascular dementia. It is in the early stages."

The doctor sat silently while the Marquis tried to digest the information.

"I do not know what vasovagal syncope is. Can you please explain?"

"An incident is generally brought on by a sudden moment of extreme emotional distress. The heart and blood pressure drop and the flow to the brain are momentarily diminished. By itself, it is generally not serious, but in her case, we believe that it has happened before and that has resulted in damage to the vessels that supply the brain with blood. Her condition will worsen. We can treat it but the chances of reversing the condition are not good. You should prepare for her to worsen. She will experience periods of forgetfulness and extreme mood swings. I do not know her past. Was she a placid woman?"

The Marquis could not suppress his laugh.

"No. She is far from placid."

"Can you recall what may have caused her such emotional anxiety?"

The Marquis thought back to the discussion they had been having. He recalled Claude's announcement of his planned travels away from France and the home.

"Yes, I do. Our son announced he was leaving for several years to travel the world. She dominated his life and could never bear the thought of him having female companions or, God forbid, marriage."

"I can see how that could trigger the vasovagal syncope. I suggest you find a quiet and relaxed time to discuss with her the dementia situation. I warn you that most patients immediately reject the diagnosis. It will be a difficult conversation. I suggest I be with you to advise her of the treatments and outlook for her future."

They left the office and proceeded to the room where Marie-France lay in the huge cream colored bed. She looked at them as they entered and a frown creased her forehead. She pointed at the doctor.

"Who is he? Why is he here?"

"He is your doctor. You experienced a bad fall after you fainted. You are at L'hôpital Saint-André. The doctor has a diagnosis to discuss with you."

"Where is my Claude? Why isn't he here? Is he sick?"

"No, he is at the Chateau. He is working on some plans for the business and his trip."

The mention of Claude's upcoming trip triggered an uncontrolled outburst.
"My boy. My boy. You're sending him away," she wailed in a loud and piercing voice.

Several nurses rushed into the room. Marie-France attempted to reach out to hit the doctor. The nurses grabbed her arms and held her down while the doctor injected a sedative into her arm. He turned to the Marquis.

"You can expect this condition to worsen. I suspect the incident she experienced last night has done more damage than we first thought. I am sorry. I don't believe that this is the time to tell her of her condition."

The doctor turned and left the room. The nurses continued to hold Marie-France until she drifted into a sleep.

The Marquis thanked them and returned to his car to drive back to the Chateau.

Chapter 30

At the Chateau, Claude was carefully reading through the financial reports and the assessors report on the Berger vineyards and wineries. There were errors and it seemed some of the information was missing. He put the reports aside and pondered the situation.

It troubled him the way the bank had approached selling out their investment. Claude thought back to the business courses at the Sorbonne and especially those that dealt with purchasing troubled companies. The problem was that those courses did not deal with farms and vineyards, but rather companies with buildings, assets and hard products. The vineyards had none of these, other than the few old buildings and residence. In addition, the vineyards ability to produce was at the whim of the weather.

He sat for some time considering this. It would be a huge risk for the de Passioné family. If it failed they would lose one month's profit. That was hardly a pittance.

Claude was surprised at his level of interest in the family business and that he wanted to be involved in the possible takeover of the Berger states. The Sorbonne had changed a part of him, yet a wild streak still existed.

He was interrupted by the arrival of the Marquis who strode into the salon still wearing his sailor's cap and had his coat collard turned up. There was a cool wind blowing in from the west and directly off the Pacific Ocean.

"What happened at the hospital? Did they diagnose the problem?"

"Yes. It appears Marie-France suffered what they described as a vasovagal syncope. I did not know what this was. It seems that when it occurred the supply of blood to her brain was affected. There is permanent damage and they diagnosed dementia. I believe she has been demented for many years."

The Marquis removed his coat and threw it onto a chaise lounge. He walked to a large glass fronted wine cabinet and selected a bottle.

"Claude please come and sit with me. I would like to speak with you. I have things to discuss."

"Let me put away these papers. I have been going through them in detail. Some things worry me based on what I read in those reports."

Together they sat and sipped the wine. Claude was anxious. He was unsure what the Marquis wished to discuss.

"Claude, things are changing fast for the de Passioné family. I have been thinking about your plan to travel for a while. I support your decision. Things here are not going to be the same now with Marie-France being ill. It is best you leave soon as I am hoping you will return and take control of the business. I know we have talked about this in the past and your reluctance to do so. I have seen changes in you since the Sorbonne and I believe you will excel at running the business."

"I must admit that this challenge of evaluating the Berger Estate with a view to buying it has created great curiosity in me. When do you think I should leave for the trip?"

"You will need to finish up at the Sorbonne. I would plan on staying for a month or two and then leave. By that time we will know what Marie-France's condition is and whether the Berger deal will be complete."

The phone jangled alive. Claude arose and quickly answered it. He listened to Chantal from the bank confirm an appointment with the Bergers for the following morning. When the arrangements were complete, Claude returned to advise the Marquis and continue the discussion.

"Before we continue, I must contact my best vintner and vineyard manager that they will need to join us at the Berger Estate."

Plans were made for the next morning.

"I have performed a detailed analysis of those reports. There is something hidden in them. I cannot fully understand the position of the bank. Those vineyards and wineries produced record crops and amounts of fine wine just a few years ago. Why are they so eager to sell out their investment?"

"I was thinking the same and while driving back from the hospital I continued and drove to the Berger Estates. I performed a brief visual inspection. There is a lot of work to be done and the vines are in poor shape. There will need to be a replanting of many. We will need to determine the length of time that the wineries will be unproductive. I am sure we will have a surplus from our vineyards that could be used and we could buy in from other vineyards."

They sat together talking and Claude explained his analysis to the Marquis, who was impressed by the business knowledge he had gained at the Sorbonne.

It was late at night when they retired.

Chapter 31

Along with the head vintner and vineyard men, they drove to the Berger estates. The owners of the bank were anxiously awaiting them. Berger Senior was looking nervous and glanced from face to face of the newly arrived party. He had met with the Marquis on several occasions and yet had never developed much of a relationship with him.

It was Yves from the bank who took control after the introductions were completed.

"Gentlemen, where shall we start? I believe everyone is aware of why we are here this morning. It is the bank's position that we are selling out our interest in this business and the Marquis is the ideal businessman to assume control and make the purchase."

Claude was amazed at the man's arrogance. He knew that this was no more than an exploratory visit. They were a long way from making any decision. He looked over to his father who was stone-faced. He showed no reaction. Instead, he turned to Berger.

"Please explain why the bank wishes to dispose of this business."

Berger looked down at the ground and stayed quiet for some time.

"We have not had good business these past few years. The vines were weakened by French Blight and were only recovering along with the newly painted ones when we experienced those hail storms. Our grape yields have been poor. We were not the only vineyard to experience this and the other vineyards did not have a surplus to sell us. Consequently, our production of wine has dropped by over thirty percent. We have attempted to negotiate new financial arrangements but have been unsuccessful.

The bank is not prepared to help us further. We have tried to improve our situation but it seems hopeless. I do not know where we will live or what work I will have if our business is sold at a low price. The bank will take all the money to repay their investment. We will be broken people. This is the only business I know. I don't know what will happen to my family."

The bankers looked on with disinterest.

The Marquis spoke.

"Please give us some privacy. I would like our vintner and vineyard manager to meet with their equivalents here. It is important for them to ascertain the situation."

Berger left the group and went to summon his men. The Marquis, Claude and bank owners stood in silence while they waited. This further endorsed Claude's belief that something was wrong with the whole situation.

It was fifteen minutes later before Berger returned accompanied by two rugged looking men dressed in stained coveralls. They had the appearance of hard-working men. Their faces were lined and wrinkled from exposure to the elements.

The Marquis introduced his men and then turned to the bankers.

"I will go with the men and start an inspection. I wish to do this privately, along with my son. You can either wait for our return or leave and return to your bank. There will be no decision today."

A look of annoyance passed across the bankers' faces.

"We will leave now. Please do not wait too long to contact us. As I explained we are ready to commence proceedings to seize the business."

"I will contact you when I have had the opportunity to review everything. Until then, there will be no communication from me."

It was the first time Claude had seen his father be forceful in business. He was surprised.

The vintner spoke first after the bank owners had left.

"I would like to visit and withdraw some samples of the current wines that are fermenting. What I find will assist us to know what is happening with the soil and the vines."

Berger nodded his agreement and led the group across an open field to the barns containing the winemaking equipment and barrels. On the way, he started to relax and chatted to Claude who listened attentively to the story of the difficulties the Bergers had endured. He felt sorry for them.

"Monsieur Berger, I am confused. Why is the bank in a hurry to sell out the business?"

"There is a rumor that the owner Yves Chartrand has family who has wanted our property for some time now. They have already forced some others off their land. The bank acts to finance and invest in farms that have had problems and then create a situation where the owners are forced to sell, often at prices that are low. They could have assisted us and protested their investment. By the time I found out about their plan it was too late. We could have survived and planted new vines. They have placed many demands on us. We were unable to repay the demands. These vineyards can produce again. We need money to refresh the vines. The bank refused the payment for our sprays and fertilizers. They are forcing us to fail."

Claude considered this. He moved back to speak to the Marquis and briefed him on the discussion.

"Let us wait until our men look at the winery and the vines."

They walked to a huge building containing the winemaking equipment. Inside the building, the Marquis head vintner laid his case down on a nearby worktable. He snapped open the case and removed a wine thief. He proceeded to the nearest barrel.

"Is this the youngest wine? Is this wine that has been fermented in the last few months? Is it the latest wine from the recent harvest?"

Berger nodded to his men to answer and assist.

The wine thief was lowered into the huge cask and a sample was drawn off and released into a glass flask. The vintners talked about the acidity, the sugar level, the clarity of the wine. The Marquis men seemed satisfied. They continued onto the newer wines ready for bottling. Again the vintner withdrew samples. This time more wine was extracted for tasting by the Marquis and Claude. The heavy red wine was bitter. They spat the wine into a makeshift spittoon

"This wine is undrinkable. There is no allowable technique here in Bordeaux that will save this acid."

The Marquis's men conferred and decided to inspect the vines. The Marquis agreed and turned to Berger.

"I think we should go and speak. Your operation here is a disaster."

They walked back to the Berger home while the vintners and vineyard managers left for the fields.

In the home, they were offered fresh coffee and pastries. Berger sat with them in the salon.

"I cannot fight them. I believe they have gone to you to have you refuse to participate in the purchase. They have created a situation that is bad and that was their intent. They will repossess the vineyards and winery at a greatly reduced price. I will be left owing money and with no home, work or way to pay them."

He dropped his head into his weathered and calloused hands and started weeping.

The Marquis looked across the room at Claude.

"I think we need to investigate the financial records you have. My son will be able to assist with this. We would like to take your records with us."

Berger agreed and left to fetch his business records.

Chapter 32

Back at the Chateau Claude and the Marquis examined the records that Berger had provided to them. A deep frown creased Claude's forehead. He set the Berger papers down and proceeded to the desk to retrieve the records that Chantal from the bank had delivered.

"There is something wrong here. The information is not the same. Look, the wine production report from the bank shows a much larger volume than Bergers."

He continued and compared the asset listings. Again the bank's records were inflated. The values had been factored into the sale price of the winery and vineyards resulting in a much higher valuation than was realistic given the condition of the estate.

The Marquis was furious.

"For years our family has given that bank our business and personal banking. Do they think I am stupid? I will end this now."

The Marquis stormed from the room and strode to his office. He grabbed up the phone. Claude heard the shouted conversation which lasted minutes until the phone was slammed down. The Marquis returned to the salon and faced Claude.

"I may be getting older but not senile yet." He suddenly grabbed at his chest and rubbed his heart area. His face reddened.

"This is not good for you. Sit here and calm down. There is too much pressure with Marie-France and this attempt by the bank to deceive us. Let me deal with this matter. I have an idea and will prepare a proposal for the bank. I will discuss it with you when you feel a little better."

Claude heard the phone ringing in the Marquis' office. He ran to the office and snatched the receiver from the cradle. It was Chantal from the bank.

"I understand your father called and is angry. I am sure there has been some mistake made. Yves is embarrassed and has asked me to visit and handle whatever the error is. Can I come now?"

"No, it is not a good time. The Marquis is upset and it has affected him. He is resting. I don't believe that a simple error has been made by you and your colleagues. Do not mistake the Marquis or me as fools. What you have attempted is dishonest and fraudulent. I don't believe the Marquis wishes to proceed any further with the deal. I will discuss it with him and call you if we are still interested. Until then we really have nothing to talk about."

He hung up the phone and upon returning to the salon found his father in a deep sleep.

He poured himself a glass of Burgundy and went "

to sit at the small desk near the window which looked out over the fields. He carefully compared the reports and noted the differences. Several hours slipped by until he was finished.

He looked over at the Marquis who was still in a deep sleep. He decided to wake him.

"Are you feeling better? You looked very pale."

"I feel tired but I am fine.

Claude told him of the phone call from Chantal. The Marquis scowled.

"I do not want to discuss this any further. I am going into the hospital to visit Marie-France."

He stood and positioned his sailor's cap on his head and draped a light jacket over his shoulder and moved toward the door.

"I am not going to allow you to drive. Either I will drive with you or have one of our servants take you. Which do you prefer?"

"I would rather you come with me."

"Please wait. I will need to change into better clothes for the visit."

Ten minutes later Claude joined the Marquis. He had changed into a clean white high necked regency shirt and tight black trousers and black buckled shoes. The Marquis looked at him and considered him dressed for the theater rather than a hospital visit.

They decided to have a chauffeur drive them to the hospital. During the drive, they sat and discussed the discrepancies between the bank's valuation and the information provided by Berger.

The Marquis was still disturbed by the situation. After a period of silence, he turned to Claude.

"We really don't need to buy that estate. I don't see it will benefit us. In fact, it will require more work to fix the vineyards. We will advise the bank of this decision."

"I estimate that the valuation prepared by the bank is in excess of the real information provided by Berger is about thirty percent too high. I suggest we don't respond to the bank until we speak with our head vintner and vineyard manager. Let us get their opinion before we respond."

"There must be some rationale why the bank is acting this way. I cannot decide why they are doing this."

They arrived at the hospital and exited the car. Inside the hospital, they proceeded to the ward where Marie-France was being treated.

Upon entering her room they were surprised to see her out of bed and sitting in a cream-colored metal chair. She was dressed in a blue-green hospital robe. Claude gasped. One side of her head was totally shaved.

Marie-France stared at them with a dazed look and glassy eyes. The room smelled of anesthetic and was hot. Claude momentarily experienced a bout of dizziness.

Marie-France had not spoken to them. The Marquis spoke to her.

"Are you able to hear us? Do you know what is happening?"

She continued to look at them with a blank expression.

The door opened and a young dark haired doctor entered.

Chapter 33

The following morning Claude and the Marquis met with the vintner and vineyard manager to review the wisdom of acquiring the Berger estate.

The vineyard manager spoke in detail.

"The vines are in poor shape. Those that are producing cannot yield enough grapes to sustain the winery. I have looked at the size of the vineyard and it could produce adequate volume but there will need to be significant replanting of about a quarter of the vines. It will be at least a year or more before those new vines produce. If the winery is to continue during that period it will be necessary to purchase grapes from others."

He produced some handwritten calculations detailing the costs of bringing the vineyards up to full production capacity. Claude and the Marquis scoured the papers. When they were finished the head vintner addressed them.

"The inspection of the equipment in the winery satisfied me. The equipment is in excellent condition with many new components. I do not see the requirement to spend on any changes and this time. I spoke with the workers and they do seem to be qualified and knowledgeable. In my opinion, we could produce some fine wines in that winery."

The Marquis and Claude listened intently as the conversation continued and they advised their workers of the gross exaggeration of the valuation.

The head vintner finally spoke.

"I have an idea of their game. You may not know but that Yves Chartrand has a private investment in another vineyard. I think it is his strategy to create a situation where the price the bank sets is of no interest to other potential purchasers, including us. He will force a low bid on the property and have his vineyard interests buy the Berger estate at an extremely low price. The Berger family will be evicted and own nothing. Before I came here to work with you I had experience with one of Yves Chartrand's vineyards. He is a crook."

The conversation continued for hours. It was decided that Claude and the Marquis would make a visit to the Berger's to discuss the latest developments.

At the Berger's they were greeted and invited into the house. They were seated in the large salon at the front of the house. Coffee was offered and they started with small talk and finally, the situation with the bank was introduced. The Marquis spoke.

"We will not be proceeding with the bank. I will be advising them of this later today. Claude had designed a proposal that we will try to conclude with them. We do not trust them anymore. Here is our proposal in brief.

We will set a price. That price will be lower than what they are requesting. We will divide the deal into three components. We will structure an ownership of three parties….you, the bank and us. We will pay the bank two thirds which will cover your part of the purchase. You will, of course, execute the appropriate legal documentation. The bank will hold a one-third interest which we will purchase over time. You will continue to live here and work the operation. We will supplement the supply of grapes and labor to assist in restoring the vineyards."

Berger sat in disbelief.

"Why would you want the bank as a partner when they have acted dishonestly?"

"We will control them and prevent their ability to take any action against you. Over time we will buy them out completely. It is not any fault of yours that the vines were infected with French Blight and then subjected to those damaging hail storms. If you are in agreement with our proposal we will advise the bank and start the process."

The conversation intensified and an agreement was reached to present the proposal to the bank. After several hours Claude and the Marquis returned to the Chateau.

In the Chateau they went to the cellar and selected a bottle of vintage Bordeaux before retreating to the huge kitchen area to sit and discuss the structure of the proposal over the glass of wine. Hours past and the daylight started to fade. The Marquis decided to return to the hospital. Claude deferred and advised he would stay and prepare the offer to the bank.

Sitting in the dimly lit kitchen, Claude laid out the papers and started to draft the offer. He was interrupted by one of the servants announcing a visitor wished to see Claude.

He went to the front entrance and found Chantal Marchand waiting for him.

"Good evening. What are you doing here? I didn't expect any visitors. The Marquis is not here. He is visiting my mother in the hospital."

While he wasn't positive he thought he saw a faint smile at the corner of Chantal's lips.

"Can I come in? I have come to discuss the Berger situation."

Claude ushered her into the salon and left to bring her a glass of the Bordeaux. He returned and sat across from her.

She raised her glass in a toast.

"Here is to the successful completion of a deal for the Berger Estate."

Claude looked at her and changed the subject of their conversation. It did not take long before she switched the conversation back.

"I understand that your father was in contact with Yves Chartrand this afternoon and it was an unpleasant telephone call. There is no need for that to happen. I am sure we can work things out."

Chantal slid forward in her chair and laid some papers on the table and smiled seductively at Claude.

"What I have to propose may be very interesting. The bank has another partner who will work with us to purchase the Berger property and evict them. We can then sell the property to you at a lower price."

Claude was offended.

Chantal slid further forward on the chair causing her skirt to ride up and expose her fleshy thighs. She then leaned forward allowing her low cut blouse to sag open exposing her ample breasts to Claude.

She reached across and started to massage Claude's leg. He decided to play along and reached down to adjust his trouser crotch.

She took this as a sign her guiles were working.

Claude was uncomfortable but decided to enjoy the show, though he thought to himself he had seen melons at the outdoor market in the Latin Quarter that looked better. He smiled at her and stood. In doing so, he loudly broke wind and then turned to walk to the guest bathroom. As he walked a series of retorts followed him. He turned to Chantal and spoke.

"Excuse me. It must be the tripe and beans I had for lunch."

Chantal was annoyed. Her plan had fallen apart. She had expected to seduce him in the ideal conditions with the mother in the hospital and the father visiting.

She rose and quickly gathered her papers and ran to the door.

Claude returned to the salon laughing.

The Marquis did not return to the Chateau that evening.

Chapter 34

In the morning Claude sat alone in the salon. The Marquis had not returned and there had not been any phone call to the staff to leave a message as to his whereabouts. Claude was becoming frustrated. He felt trapped again into the family and the business. He had only planned to stay a few days before returning to the Sorbonne to complete his studies and plan for his globetrotting trip.

It was mid-afternoon and still, there was no sign of the Marquis. Claude was angry and decided on a plan. He spent the balance of the afternoon writing a proposal for the Marquis to present to the bank and Berger. He decided it was time to leave. He wondered whether Marie-France was really that ill or just faking her state of illness, which she was a master at doing.

He hastily scribbled a note to the Marquis and placed it with the dossier containing the proposal. He then left to pack his meager clothing for the return to Paris. When he had completed the task, Claude summoned one of the servants to drive him back to his pension. He had no further interest in the business or the takeover of the Berger Estates. He felt betrayed and used by both Marie-France and the Marquis. Claude was anxious to finish his studies and start his trip. That way he could be away from their attempted control of him.

A young staff member, Jacques offered to drive Claude into Paris. He entered the salon to assist Claude with his luggage. He turned and spoke to Claude.

"Sir, would it be permitted for me to spend the night in Paris? I have a fiancé there and would like to visit and take her for dinner."

Claude liked this young man and often felt sorry for him as both the Marquis and Marie-France ordered him around like a dog.

"Of course that is fine. In fact, spend the morning there."

As it was a six hundred kilometer drive to Paris, it would be late when they arrived. Claude had assumed that Jacques would stay in Paris overnight instead of attempting to drive back to the Chateau.

It was four in the afternoon when they departed for Paris. Jacques had chosen the Citroen car for the trip. It was older but drove smoothly and was quiet inside. Claude decided he would sit up front with Jacques. He liked the man and together they would enjoy a great conversation.

They drove northward toward Paris. The late afternoon sun sank in the west and the countryside was bathed in the light of dusk. After almost three hours they arrived at the old town of Chateauroux.

"I suggest we stop and have dinner here. I know a bistro near the Inde River. It will be busy at this time but the weather is good and we can sit on the outside patio."

Jacques nodded his agreement but was silently worried that the restaurant prices would be expensive. He was ashamed to mention this to Claude.

"Monsieur de Passioné, I am not all that hungry, but I can join you."
Claude was not convinced.

"Is it because of money? This will be my way to thank you for taking the time to drive me. You will be my guest."

Jacques started to object.

"No. It is final and my decision. We will eat well before continuing to Paris. It will be late when we arrive there."

They wound through narrow streets and finally found a location to park not far from the bistro. Claude slipped off the seat and stood beside the car stretching. Soon they entered the small and intimate restaurant. It was full and the conversation was loud.

A tall maître d greeted them.

"Good evening gentlemen. Do you have reservations?"

"No, we are just driving through on our way to Paris and decided to stop here for a splendid dinner. I have been here several times in the past with my father. I remember how delicious the food was."

The man looked at Claude closely then frowned.

"May I ask who your father is? I cannot seem to remember you."

"He is Marquis de Passioné"

The man gasped. "Of course we can accommodate a de Passioné. Do you have a preference for where you would like to sit?"

"I think a sheltered table on the patio. It is still warm this evening."

"Yes, sir and I will have the chef visit and explain our fine selection for this evening."

Jacques sat in awe. He had never experienced service such as this. He now realized the power of money and title.

The maître d escorted them to a table next to a low wall that allowed for a magnificent view of the river and old town.

In crossing to the table, Claude noticed a woman seated alone. She had long black hair. He stared at her and felt he knew her. Then it dawned on him. It was the raven-haired nurse who had given him special treatment in hospital. He smiled when he recalled the erotic event.

Claude occasionally looked across at her. He noticed she was alone. Every once in a while she would raise her wrist and glance at her watch. Claude assumed she was waiting for someone to join her. She had not eaten. A glass of white wine sat on the table in front of her half drunk.

The sommelier arrived at their table and presented his recommended wines for the evening. Claude selected a Château Lafite Rothschild.

Jacques and Claude sat sipping the wine and relaxing. Fifteen minutes had passed and nobody had joined her. Claude decided to speak to her and arose and walked across to her table.

She looked up at and recognized him immediately.
"Claude. What are you doing here?"

"I am on my way back to Paris after visiting at my parents Chateau. More importantly, what are you doing here all alone?"

"I am taking time away from the hospital. I was invited by friends of our family to visit and stay. I spent time cycling and visiting many of the famous buildings here. I love this part of France."

"I am here with one of our staff who is driving me back to Paris. Would you like to join us or are you expecting company?"

"No, I am alone. I was checking the time as I am taking a bus back to Paris this evening. I did not want to miss it."

"Then that is perfect. Come and be my guest and we will drive you there tonight. It will be more comfortable than the bus."

She blushed and as she went to stand Claude, pulled back her chair and helped her to his table where he introduced her to Jacques as the nurse who had helped him in hospital.

The conversation was light and all three laughed and joked. Finally, the maître d and chef joined them to present the dinner menu for the evening.

The chef addressed them.

"Good evening. It will be my pleasure to prepare a special meal for the esteemed de Passioné guests. Here are my recommendations for this evening.

Terrine de campagne maison au foie gras et sa confiture d'oignon

Hampe de boeuf grillée aux échalotes confites

Fromage blanc et son coulis de fruits rouges

Soupe de poires à l'orange et zestes confits"

He continued.

"All are freshly made with fresh produce and delicious."

After some discussion, the group decided to order everything the chef had recommended.

The chef smiled and bowed and left to prepare their feast.

"Let us relax and enjoy. Jacques, you will stay in Paris tonight with your friend. Take your time there. Leave tomorrow late in the morning to return to the Chateau. I will advise them."

It was then that Claude realized he did not know her full name. He asked.

"My name is Fleur Des Champs."

Throughout the meal, they joked and laughed. Jacques refrained from drinking since he was driving, but both Claude and Fleur enjoyed several bottles between them.

It was ten at night when they finally left the restaurant to continue the drive.

Chapter 35

It was close to one in the morning when Jacques pulled up at Claude's pension. Claude turned to Fleur.

"I will get Jacques to drive you to where you wish to stay tonight."

"I am where I wish to stay tonight. Here with you."

Claude and Fleur stumbled from the car and climbed the stairs of the pension. Claude's roommates were away in Spain so the house was empty and private.

They fumbled their way through the front doorway laughing and speaking loudly. Several lights came on in the buildings across the street and a shout to quiet down was shouted from one of the upper windows.

After clumsily making their way upstairs to the bedrooms, Claude showed Fleur the room she could use and sleep in. She pushed him back and laughed.

"Claude you are being silly. Tonight we will finish what we could not at the hospital. I will be in your bed so do not snore."

She took Claude by the hand and led him to the bed. Sitting on the edge of the bed she unbuttoned his shirt and ran her hands across his muscular hairy chest. Her ring caught in some of the hairs and ripped a clump of hair away from the nipple area. Claude let out a small yelp. She reached down and unfastened his belt and slid her hand into the front of his tight black trousers. Claude reached down and embraced her. She rolled back and stripped her blouse away and released her bra exposing milk-white breasts. Claude dropped his head onto them. She writhed and removed what little clothing remained and then turned her attention to Claude. Within minutes they were both naked and caressing each other. She slipped her hand down his torso and found him as hard as a rock. She thought, "This is what I remember from our tryst in the hospital."

They exchanged passionate kisses until she slid her leg across him and pushed him into her. She gyrated and thrust until she heard him moan and felt the warm silky smooth sensation in her. She continued to vigorously partake until she called out in ecstasy and her body trembled with pleasure. As she withdrew from him, Claude ejaculated again. The warm juice of his love flowed across her stomach.

Exhausted they fell into a deep sleep.

Claude awoke late in the morning and found Fleur sitting at the end of his bed in his flowing Japanese bathrobe. He went to speak but she reached up and placed a finger on his lips.

"You have awoken a love in me that I thought was gone forever. I was badly hurt by a man. I swore it would never happen again, but you have started something in me."

Claude sat up. His mouth tasted foul. He imagined it tasted like the bottom of a birdcage had been emptied in it. He swung his legs out of the bed and stood. He was totally naked and noticed that Fleur's eyes were riveted on his member. He grabbed an old pair of jeans and hastily pulled them on before reaching for her and hugging her.

"Let's go and get some coffee and breakfast. I know a place."

She readily agreed.

After they dressed they walked out into the Latin Quarter and strolled at a leisurely pace to the small bistro Claude often frequented.

"Today I must return to the Sorbonne. I am about to complete my studies. There are a number of matters I must attend to. What will you do today?"

"I wish to visit my family. I do not see them very often. I work strange hours at the hospital."

"I would like to invite you to have dinner with me tonight. There is a special restaurant I would like to visit with you. It is a little more formal than where we ate last evening. Do you wish to join me?"

"Of course I will. I look forward to that. Where should we meet at and at what time?"

"Come to my home. We will leave from there at seven tonight. Now I must leave."

He bent over the table to kiss her and quickly left the bistro after leaving money on the counter. She remained for another ten minutes and then gathered herself and left. She was feeling great and looking forward to the evening ahead.

Claude finished his business at the Sorbonne and returned to his home. He called the Chateau and spoke with the head of the staff. The Marquis had not returned and nobody had heard from him. Claude was mildly concerned.
He sat and pondered his situation. He did not want to immediately return to the Chateau and had dreamed of his plans to travel and the adventures he might experience.

It was late in the afternoon when he made the awkward decision to visit Marie-France in the hospital. He hailed a taxi at the curb for the long drive to the hospital.

At the hospital, he first stopped at the nurse's station to inquire about Marie-France and her condition. A somewhat matronly nurse advised him of recent developments.

"I must tell you that she has been recovering nicely. She is funny. She has been ordering all of us around and playing the role of a queen. We understand she has had a mental condition but she has been behaving and helping us when we ask her. The doctors are predicting that she will regain her mental state with the new medication she is taking. It is important she takes that medicine every day or she will slip back into a bad state."

In Marie-France's room, the shades had been drawn for protection from the sun and to create a calm environment for her to sleep. Claude stood at the foot of her bed and looked at her for the longest time. He could see the beauty that had once been there and drawn the Marquis to her. She was in a deep sleep.

Claude turned and was about to leave when a nurse entered the room.

"Do not leave. It is time to wake her for more tests and medication. You can stay for another ten minutes and then we must move her."

The nurse placed her hand on Marie France's shoulder and gently shook her awake, She awoke in a startled manner but immediately calmed when she saw Claude standing at the end of the bed. A huge smile spread on her face. She raised her hand toward Claude who moved forward and took it in his.

"Nurse you see how beautiful my boy is and he's not married."

The nurse blushed and smiled.

"Yes, indeed he is handsome."

Claude spoke.

"I am sorry for her behavior. I don't wish to embarrass you."

"No that is all right. We expect all sorts of things to happen when dealing with older patients who are suffering from some mental illness. I am not offended and I do think you are both charming and attractive."

Claude smiled his most disarming smile. It seemed he had a thing or two to offer these nurses.

"I will return to visit at another time. I do not wish to delay my mother's treatment."

He turned and left the room. The nurse stood with her mouth partially open.

Chapter 36

He arrived back in Paris in time to meet Fleur at his pension. Together they walked to his favorite restaurant, **Le Pied du Cochon.** He noticed that Fleur was quiet and hardly spoke. He wondered what could be occupying her mind. He cast his thoughts back to the evening and the passion they had shared.

At the restaurant, they were taken to a table toward the rear. Once they were seated, Claude ordered a bottle of wine.

"Fleur that was special last night. Will you stay with me tonight?"

Claude was excited at the prospect of spending another night filled with passion.

Fleur looked across the table and gave him a faint smile but did not answer.

"Is there something wrong? You have hardly spoken."

She picked up the menu and pretended to be reading it. After a minute she stood and excused herself.

"I need to go to the ladies room."

She hurried away and forcibly pushed the door open. She grasped the edge of the counter and the tears streamed down her face. She stayed there for several minutes until she heard the door opening behind her and an elderly woman entered. Fleur dabbed at her eyes and went through the motions of fixing her makeup. She returned to the table to find Claude looking at her with a quizzical look on his face.

"Are you alright? I am concerned. You are like a different person today."

"Claude, I cannot stay with you or be late tonight. My husband is returning tonight from a business trip to Germany."

His jaw dropped open.

"I didn't know you were married. I would never have taken advantage of a married woman."

"Don't feel bad. I had fun too. Besides I've been married several times now. It never lasts."

Claude was shocked and as he watched her, she again burst into tears.

"There is something wrong. This is not normal. Why are you so upset? Shall I leave? Is it me? Have I caused you all this grief?"

"No Claude. It is not you. My husband is a brute. He beats me and kicks me like a dog. I fear that one day he will lose control and kill me."

Claude did not know how to respond. He thought that the night was a disaster and could not get any worse. He was wrong.

Finally, he spoke to her in a calming manner.

"Why don't you leave him? You are young and have a job as a nurse. Surely you could start a new life."

"He has taken everything from me. I have no money. He controls every move I make. If he finds out about last night he will hunt you down."

"I do not scare that easily. Besides, I have certain resources I know. I can look after myself, but it is you that we need to save. If you need money I can assist. I am the son of Marquis Charles de Passioné. I am sure you are aware of the family and our wealth. It would be my pleasure to help you."

More tears flowed. Other diners were watching and Claude felt embarrassed. He reached across the table and took her hand.

"It will be alright. We will make a plan for you to leave without having to fear for your safety."

He smiled and sensed a sigh of relief on Fleur's face. He signaled the waiter to come to their table. As he was asking about the different selection of the evening's menu, the front door of the restaurant opened a cold wind blew in as a couple arrived. Claude was shocked.

Entering the restaurant was a man wearing a navy sailor's cap. He was accompanied by a tall elegant lady. They were escorted to a private booth. It was the Marquis.

He stopped mid-sentence and stared at the pair. The waiter turned to look at what had distracted Claude. He smiled

"Oh, that is the famous Marquis de Passioné. He visits here often when he is in Paris. That lady with him is also famous. She is the Countess Francesca Cortelli from Italy. She is wealthy and owns large Chianti wineries.

On hearing this, Claude assumed they were here on business until she leaned toward the Marquis who bent forward and they locked in a passionate kiss.

The waiter smiled.

"It is nice. They come here together almost every month. I understand the wife of the Marquis has gone crazy and he is alone. I am told his wife went crazy years ago."

Claude scowled at the waiter. Pointing in the direction of the booth he shouted.

"That is my father and it is my mother you are talking about. You bloody imbecile. You know nothing. I saw my mother this afternoon. She suffered a blackout and has had treatment. She is eccentric but fine. And now we will leave this establishment never to return."

He threw some loose coins onto the table and abruptly stood to leave.

"Fleur, come with me. We will go somewhere private and enjoy what remains of this evening."

He took Fleur by the arm and assisted her with her coat. They were walking to leave when Claude turned and went to the booth. He said nothing but just stared at the Marquis who attempted a blubbered greeting. Before he could finish, Claude turned away and left.

Huddled together against the cool wind, Claude started to explain how he would help her. After a few minutes, she stopped.

"Claude I really must go now. I am sorry tonight did not work out."

She waved for a taxi to stop and then sped away, leaving Claude on the sidewalk. He was confused. Dejected he returned to his pension.

Chapter 37

The next morning there was an impatient knocking at the door. Claude bounded down the stairs to find the Marquis standing at the front door.

"We need to discuss last night. The woman you saw me having dinner with is the Countess Cortelli."

Claude interrupted. "I know who she is and it didn't look like a casual dinner to me."

"Don't be so fast to judge. The Countess has decided to be a partner in the purchase of the Berger Estate. She is prepared to buy out the interest of the bank. It is great news. I want you to come back with me and work on the purchase."

"I prepared a dossier for you. It is on the desk in the salon. I have no interest in returning or being any part of that deal. I am sure you will manage. Now I must leave as today is my final day at the Sorbonne."

Claude attempted to close the door but the Marquis jammed his foot in the doorway preventing it from closing.

"You must come back. It will be an invaluable experience for you and prepare you for when you take over the business."

"I told you that I am preparing to travel for a while. I will return on the weekend to visit mother. Now I need to leave. Go back and look after your wife, Marie-France."

"You cannot do this. I forbid you. I will stop the bank from allowing you access to your trust account. You will be penniless in a week."

"Who are you to forbid me anything? For years I have watched as you carried on with countless women. You are a hypocrite, a liar, and a cheat. Now please leave or I will not visit this weekend and neither you nor Marie-France will see me before I depart. The choice is yours."

The Marquis shrugged and turned away. Claude gathered his papers and headed for his final day at the Sorbonne.

For the balance of the week, he made travel plans and prepared for his trip. He had not heard from Fleur. This disturbed him.

His patience was gone and he decided to visit the hospital where she worked. On checking with the head nurse he was advised she had not been to work all that week. Claude was truly worried. He asked the nurse if she was aware of the problems in Fleur's marriage. She denied any knowledge.

Claude left the hospital. He never saw or heard from Fleur again.

Chapter 38

The weekend arrived and Claude, true to his word, traveled back to the Chateau. Marie-France had been discharged from the hospital and was back in full force ordering around the servants and acting strangely.

Claude had taken the train to Bordeaux and arranged for Jacques to drive him from the station to the Chateau. He and Jacques had become friends. During the drive, Claude asked about recent developments with the family at the Chateau.

"I do not wish to speak badly, but you are going to have some big surprises. Since her return, Marie-France has been different. The Marquis has not been at the Chateau very often. He has been traveling a lot."

As they drove down the long driveway to the front of the Chateau, Claude was surprised at the long line of motorbikes parked there.

"What is this? Who owns those bikes? What is going on?"

"I warned you to expect some big surprises and this is one of them."

They had barely pulled up when Marie-France appeared at the top of the stairs. Claude stared at her in disbelief. Gone were the expensive but tacky brightly colored hippie clothes. Marie-France was dressed head to toe in black motorcycle leathers. A silver chain hung from epaulets on the jacket and attached to a wide leather belt with a huge pewter buckle. She was wearing knee-high riding boots with a thick heel.

Claude eased himself out of the car and moved toward her.

"What are you wearing? Who owns all these motorbikes?"

"Claude I am so excited. I have found a new interest. I have joined a motorcycle club. Those bikes belong to my new friends. Come in and meet them. We are having a little social meeting."

Unsure of the situation, Claude followed her up the stairs and in through the foyer and into the salon. Seated in the salon were almost thirty scruffy older men and several haggard women. The air was blue with cigarette and marijuana smoke. The visitors fell silent when Claude walked in. He looked around at the assembled group. Most were wearing leather biker gear and looked extremely rough.

Marie-France bubbled to the center of the room and proudly introduced her son. Claude stared at them and his instant hostility was visible. One of the burly men, with a fat stomach hanging over his belt and falling to his crotch spoke.

"I think we need to go and leave our friend Marie-France with Prince Charming here."

The group stood and shuffled to the door. There was a thunderous roar as the bikes were kicked into action and as they thundered off down the long driveway toward the main gates, exhaust fumes, dust, and oily smoke spewed into the air.

When they were alone, Claude turned to Marie-France.

"Have you gone mad? Do you know that most of those people are criminals and involved in drugs and guns? I cannot believe what I have returned to find. How did you link up with them?

"I met one of those nice men in the mental ward of the hospital when I was there. He introduced me to his friends and they asked me to join their club. I am so excited. Of course to join there was a fee to pay to be a member."

Claude groaned. This was worse than he thought.

"How much of a fee did you pay?"

Marie-France hesitated as she tried to remember. Finally, she spat out the amount. Claude was in shock. It was in excess of an executive's annual salary. It occurred to him at that moment that her mental faculties were compromised. He didn't understand why the Marquis had not intervened.

He decided to remain calm and gently persuade Marie-France to change clothing and join him for an early meal at a nearby restaurant. Initially, she was reluctant, but after some mild persuasion, she agreed.

As they were leaving the Chateau, the Marquis arrive home. He was in good humor. When he saw Claude he smiled and went to him. He grabbed Claude's hand and shook it vigorously.

"I am so happy. Your suggestions and work helped us to complete the purchase of the Berger Estate. The negotiations were very difficult and your analysis assisted us. We were able to convince the bank to sell us their share. The woman, Chantal was very bitter. I don't think she likes you, Claude."
Claude smiled and thought "If you only knew."

"I am pleased it has ended positively for you. Who else are owners?"

"The Bergers will stay. I loaned them money to secure their position and of course, the Cortellis from Italy."

At the mention of the Cortelli name, Claude recalled the scene he had witnessed at the restaurant between the Countess and the Marquis.

"It is a good arrangement. The Cortellis have invited me to visit in Italy. They are looking for a new investor and partner. I am hoping that Marie-France will join me and we can have a vacation on the Amalfi Coast."

At the mention of a trip, Marie-France became ecstatic. She bubbled with enthusiasm. Claude felt storm clouds gathering. He did not trust the Countess Cortelli.

Chapter 39

At the restaurant, Claude described the trip he had planned. The Marquis and Marie-France sat in silence as he told them of his plans. He thought he sensed a jealousy in Marie-France.

"I will be starting in the United States. I have booked a flight on Air France from Paris to Los Angeles. I will spend some time exploring California. I will stay about 3 months there. Because it will be winter in the northern hemisphere, I intend to spend time exploring the islands of the South Pacific. I will fly to Tahiti then visit Fiji, The Cook Islands, Noumea, and back to Hawaii. After I will fly to New Zealand where I will stay and work for a year. Finally, I will spend some time in Australia before returning to Europe. I expect to be gone for between two to three years. I will contact you often."

The Marquis sat quietly. He said nothing. He didn't have to as Marie-France started her uncontrollable wailing. The restaurant patrons stared at the performance.

"Please stop that. Your tantrums are not going to dissuade me from making this trip. I will return to Paris and pack this coming week. I leave on Friday."

His announcement provoked Marie-France into yet another louder outburst. Embarrassed, Claude stood and left them. He decided to leave in the morning.

Back at the Chateau he found Jacques and planned the return trip to Paris before retiring for the night.

He was tired of the games that both the Marquis and Marie-France were playing.

In the morning he spent little time saying farewell to the Marquis, Marie-France and the staff. Jacques loaded his bags into the car and they left for Paris.

During the drive, Jacques and Claude became engaged in a lengthy conversation. They were no longer in an employee and employer relationship.

"Claude, I hope that one day soon I will be asked to work in managing the vineyard and assisting with the winery. I do not wish to stay as a house servant. I want to progress and learn a valuable trade."

"I am sure that the opportunity will present itself. I will mention this to my father, though he is busy with the matters related to the purchase of the Berger Estate. There may be an opportunity now. He is going to need more staff."

It was early afternoon when they arrived in Paris. Claude left to pack the last of his items for his trip and Jacques left to spend time with his girlfriend.

Part 2

World Travels

Chapter 40

Claude boarded the Air France flight bound for Los Angeles. He has decided that for the long twelve-hour flight he would treat himself so had purchased a first class ticket. As the flight left at ten in the morning, Claude had not eaten breakfast. He had awoken late and panicked.

At the airport, he had rushed to check his baggage. Being a first-class passenger he was greeted and assisted pleasantly. On the plane, he was served Champagne the moment he was seated but requested a strong French coffee instead. The flight attendant was young and attractive. She offered Claude a croissant with his coffee. He was hungry and gladly accepted.

The trip was off to a good start.

Claude relaxed back into his seat and closed his eyes. There was no one in the seats either side of him. He listened to the huge jet engines of the Boeing 747 whine into life. They revved and then slowed. He felt the bump as the tractor commenced pushing the plane back from the gate. Finally, he would be free from Marie-France, the Marquis, and the family business. He felt a veil of relaxation come over him.

The engines roared and the plane lurched forward. Claude smiled to himself. Now his adventure could begin.

The engines whined as the plane climbed in altitude. There was some mild turbulence and then he heard the engines slow and the plane leveled off. At this point, the flight attendants sprung from their seats and circulated throughout the aircraft.

Claude had heard derogatory things about Air France but was surprised at the courtesy and service.

After thirty minutes the cabin crew returned with printed menus and handed them to the passengers along with hot towels. Claude scanned the menu and selected an espresso coffee with pastries, fruit, yogurt and a Croque-Monsieur followed by lemon cream crepes and fresh berries. He was hungry.

The young flight attendant who had brought him his coffee earlier took his selection. She flashed him a charming smile. He was sure she was flirting with him.

After the breakfast, Claude settled back in his seat to sleep. The attendant returned with a pillow and blanket for him that she lay on his lap, along with a toiletry kit.

"It is a long flight. If there is anything at all you need from me to make you more comfortable, please tell me."

She slightly puckered her lips and with a mischievous smile returned to the others at the front of the cabin, where Claude could hear them laughing.

He drifted off into a deep sleep. Several hours passed by until he felt a hand on his shoulder gently shaking him awake.

"You have been sleeping for three hours. Soon we will serve a light luncheon. Would you care for a drink beforehand?"

"I would, but first I must use the toilet."

He released his seatbelt and stretched as he stood in the spacious aisle. He made his way to the washroom and was surprised at the small size of it. It got him wondering about all the stories he had heard of amorous escapades on flights.

Claude returned to his seat and selected Chablis for his drink. For lunch, he selected Vodka cured Finnish smoked salmon with capers and a cream cheese.

After lunch, the passengers were settled in for the lengthy balance of the flight. Two of the flight attendants came and sat either side of Claude and started a conversation.

"Are you going to Los Angeles for business?"

"No, I am taking some time and traveling around the world. I have been studying at the Sorbonne and need time to make some important decisions. I want to do this before settling into a career."

"Have you been to California before? It is a busy place."

For the next hour, Claude sat and chatted with the girls. They regaled Claude with stories of their adventures and escapades in California. They were a lively and fun group.

The remainder of the flight progressed without any particular incident. The cabin crew circulated and spoke with various passengers; drinks were frequently offered and some slept or read.

It was just after the noon hour when the captain announced the initial descent into LAX.

Claude listened to the grinding noises as the wheels of the jumbo were lowered. The pitch of the engines slowed and sped up as the aircraft was directed to LAX by air traffic control.

Claude was fascinated by flight and how it had evolved. He pondered the intricacies of the systems that kept the plane on course and assisted with the landing. He decided that one day he would take lessons and learn to fly.

Chapter 41

The heavy plane gently touched down and taxied to the arrival gates. When the engines died, the cabin attendants assisted the first class passengers with personal items and small baggage.

Claude gathered up his reading materials and reached for a light jacket he had placed in the overhead bin. Before he could reach it, the young flight attendant retrieved it for him. She turned to him with a charming smile. As she handed him the jacket, she slid a card into his hand.

"This is where I will be staying tonight. I hope to see you."

"I will call you at this hotel. Goodbye for now."

He exited through the forward door and started the long walk to the Customs and Immigration area. After a slight delay, while his papers were checked, he entered the baggage hall.

Outside of the airport building, loudspeakers blared out informing travelers' not to leave parked cars and to not leave unaccompanied baggage.

With his bags gathered he hailed a courtesy van to transport him to the rental car offices, where he joined a long queue of customers waiting to rent.

Finally, Claude was served and taken to the Chrysler he had rented for the month. He looked at it in horror. It was pale mustard yellow with a hideous black fake leather roof and a putrid white interior. American design and culture amazed him with its bad taste.

He drove from the rental car parking lot out onto the Freeway and headed slightly south of the airport. He had decided to rest soon after arrival and start his adventures the next morning.

As he drove he noticed the famous arches of a McDonalds ahead and decided he would stop and try a real American hamburger. He parked in the large sealed lot and headed in through the greasy glass door. The tan tiled floor was coated in a fine layer of grease. Years of use and cleaning had created a hard surface of grime. At the counter, he ordered his food. He sat at a booth with a chipped white Formica table. He unwrapped the hamburger and sunk his teeth into it expecting flavors to burst into his mouth. Instead, he bit off a nondescript piece of grey meat that was coated in a strange tasting mayonnaise. It had a dry cardboard taste. Claude threw it down on the tray and sprinted for the door. Outside he spat the contents of his mouth into a sorry looking garden bed planted with cacti.

He drove another mile and pulled into the entrance of The Marriott Hotel where a clumsily dressed bellhop in a white jacket with red epaulets and towering hat like a tropical hunter's hat bounded forward to open his door.

"Are you staying with us, Sir?'

"Yes, I will be staying overnight, but will need my car as I will be going out later."

"Very good, Sir. I will have the Valet park your car and I will assist you with your luggage."

Claude was escorted to the front desk and went through the formalities of registering. When complete a bellboy with a brass cart arrived to take him and his bags to the room. The bellboy looked at the key for the suite number.

"That is a beautiful suite. It is on the top floor. It is used by many dignitaries we have visiting America."

Claude was enjoying his arrival in America, though he found it rushed and busy. The tranquility he had known in France was absent. Even Paris seemed more relaxed in his mind.

The bellboy opened the door and placed the bags on a fold out rack near the bathroom door. He then went over to check on the air conditioning and over to the bar fridge. Claude realized he was killing time while waiting for a tip. Claude withdrew a ten dollar note and pushed it into the bellboy's hand. He was thrilled.
"If there is anything you need to make your stay more comfortable, call the front desk and ask for me. My name is Anthony."

"Thank you, Anthony. I am going to freshen up and rest after that long trip."

When he was alone Claude stripped naked and stood in the scalding hot shower. He felt the tiredness hit him hard. He dried off and dressed before calling the front desk to request a wakeup call in two hours and then fell onto the bed.

It was just before five when the bedside phone buzzed. Groggily Claude answered. He thanked the operator and decided to take another shorter shower.

He emerged from the shower relaxed and refreshed. He dried off and put on the plush white bathrobe provided by the hotel and proceeded to the mini fridge and selected a California white wine. He poured a glass and sat thinking. He was surprised at the quality of the wine.

After thirty minutes he took the card the flight attendant had given him and dialed the number.

The phone was answered on the first ring and Claude asked for the attendant by name. There was a slight hold and she picked up the phone.

"Hello. It is Claude. We met today on the flight from Paris."

"I remember you, Claude. Where are you staying?"

"I am at the Marriott here. Where are you?"

"I am at the Hilton. The airline has a special arrangement. Can I see you tonight or are you busy?"

"I will be at your hotel in thirty minutes."

Claude dressed in one of his high necked Regency shirts and the same tight black trousers. He pulled on his buckled loafers and left his room.

He rode the elevator down to the lobby. Guests who were checking in or waiting for others looked at him with smirks and curiosity.

Chapter 42

At the Hilton, he found her waiting at the front entrance. He jumped from his car and escorted her. He opened the door and assisted her in.

"This may seem rude, but I have forgotten your name. I think I was tired from my travels."

She laughed. "My name is Julia."

He enjoyed her cheery disposition and a soft laugh. She reminded him of someone. He fell silent while he considered who she reminded him of. Then it struck. Genevieve. He felt a pang of immediate sorrow but pushed it from his mind. They drove on in silence.

"Claude, you are very quiet. Is something wrong? Did I do or say something incorrect?"

"Not at all. I had a friend in Paris and you reminded me of her for a minute. That was a long time ago."

"Can I ask you what happened?"

"I was young. I suffered an accident and was in the hospital and that is when I lost contact with her. It was years ago now."

Julia looked at him for a while and then turned away.

"Claude, are you married or have a fiancée or long-term girlfriend. I don't want to create a problem."

"No. I am alone. I was studying at the Sorbonne until recently. I decided I needed to leave France and my family to experience the world and other cultures. There is no time for lengthy relationships at present."

"I understand. I too have recently lost a friend. I needed a change and that is why I joined Air France so I could travel and meet new people and see new places. It was hard. We were together for three years. He left me for an older wealthy woman."

Claude immediately thought of Marie-France. It now occurred to him that she probably didn't realize the damage she did to others relationships.

"Where did this woman live in France? Do you know her name?"

"Why?"

"I am just curious."

Julia sat quietly chewing at her bottom lip.

"Claude, it is still painful to discuss. Can we stop and talk about something else?"

"I am sorry. I didn't mean to probe."

Claude continued to drive until they reached Redondo beach with a collection of seaside restaurants and bars. He had heard about the "Purple Orange." It was renowned for its strong 151 Proof Rum drinks and raucous live music.

He drove the car into the adjacent parking area and together they entered the club. It was packed. Loud music drowned out any chance of conversation. Claude leaned into Julia and asked what she wished to drink. She shrugged. Claude went off to the bar and soon returned with a couple of large glasses containing a slightly amber-colored drink.

"What are these?" Julia shouted over the music.

"They are 151 Proof Mai Tais. Enjoy."

For the next half hour, they sipped the drinks and danced. Julia reached out and took Claude's arm.

"Let's go somewhere quiet. I am hungry."

They left the bar and found a cozy seafood restaurant. The interior was decorated with fishing nets and floats. Black and white pictures of old fishing boats hung haphazardly on the walls. Claude loved the atmosphere of the place.

Julia perused the menu and ordered lobster bisque with sourdough rolls to start. For her main course, she chose a lobster thermidor. Claude chose a small salad followed by a lobster Newburgh.

For the wine, he selected California Chablis from a vineyard he had heard the Marquis speak of. It was located in Northern California in the Napa Valley. It was then that the idea hit him. He would visit that winery.

"Julia, how long will you be here in California? Do you fly back to France tomorrow?"

"No. I had requested to spend time here on vacation. I will be here for a week."

"What have you planned for your week?"

"I will do some touristy things. Go to Disney, visit Universal Studios, go and tour the homes of Hollywood actors. What will you be doing?"

"Tomorrow I will drive to Orange County and Dana Point. I will join a fishing trip. It is the time of the year when the Bonita is in season. They are like a smaller tuna and catching one is exciting. They really fight and you need to work hard to get it to the boat."

"That sounds like fun. Unfortunately, I don't have anyone to do things like that with. I would love to do that."

"I can take you. It will be early. I am leaving for Dana Point at five in the morning."

"Are you sure? I can be ready for five."

They ate their dinners and made small talk until it was time to leave. Claude drove back to the Hilton and left the car to open the door for Julia. She slowly stepped out and hugged Claude and kissed him passionately.

"Claude, I would ask you to come to my room for a drink, but I have a roommate from the airline sharing the room. I would really like to spend more time with you."

Claude thought for a minute.

"Julia. It is late. In five hours I need to be here to pick you up. That will be soon. Go and get a good nights sleep, or what is left of the night."

She hugged Claude tight and kissed him again. He felt an old familiar arousal. He looked at her and she smiled back mischievously. He bent and opened the door to the rental car. She slid herself in and they drove to the Marriott.

In Claude's room, he dimmed the lights and they opened a bottle of champagne. It was only a short time until they were locked together on the king-sized bed.

Disappointment soon arrived. Whether it was his tiredness from the flight or another reason. He recalled Geneviève and was unable to rise to the occasion.

They talked a while and fell into a deep sleep until the phone buzzed with their wakeup call.

Claude was surprised to find that at that hour of the morning his arousal was inextinguishable. The day started with a bang.

They showered together and quickly dressed to go and start the drive to Dana Point. Already the California highways were busy. Almost an hour later they pulled into the marina. Claude spotted the sign for the fishing charter he had booked.

"There is the boat over there under that sign. See, its called **Dad and Donny's Charters.** I'll go over and get us checked in. Why don't you wait in the café there."

He pointed to a small building set at the end of the pier.

After completing the check-in arrangements he joined Julia for a light breakfast.

Chapter 43

The day went by quickly on the water. The fish were plentiful and both Claude and Julia enjoyed fighting them onto the boat. It was in the early evening when they returned to shore, tired but excited.

"Julia, there is little that I want to see in Los Angeles now. I am going to drive up the Pacific Coast Highway to San Francisco. I would love your company if you are interested."

She stood staring at him, unsure how to answer.

"Claude, I would love that. Are you sure you want me to come with you?"

"Yes. Why not? You have the time. We will have some fun. No work for you and a new adventure for me."

"I will need to go to the Hilton to get clothing and to tell my friends of my plans."

"I will drive you there now. I will come for you in the morning around seven. Will you be ready?"

Julia was giddy with excitement. She couldn't believe she was going to see California with a handsome escort.

On the drive to the Hilton, she chattered away. Her happiness created an aurora of contentment for Claude.

He left her at the hotel and drove himself back to the Marriott, where he packed his possessions and made arrangements for a hotel in San Francisco.
At seven in the morning, Claude arrived at the Hilton to meet Julia and start the drive north up the Pacific Coast Highway to San Francisco.

She was happy to see him and bubbled with enthusiasm. In the car, she settled in for the drive. The Los Angeles traffic was heavy and slow going even at that early hour. They made their way north of the city on Highway 101 and continued north through Ventura arriving in Santa Barbara shortly before ten in the morning.

Claude parked and they strolled the beach for a while before returning to the Stearns Wharf pier for a breakfast in the little restaurant. Julia was happy and childlike as she pointed out different boats and the surfers riding the waves in the early morning sun. She could barely contain herself when a huge seal surfaced near the edge of the pier.

After they ate, they continued to stroll the beach before traveling into the town center to visit some stores.

It was just before noon when they continued the drive. The road followed the coast and climbed and fell over the many hills. The scenery was breathtaking. The mountains plunged deeply into the sea and Highway 1 cut a majestic trail through them.

Claude jumped and almost drove off the road when Julia screamed. She had seen a pod of migrating whales with their plumes of water spouting from the surface of the ocean. He was amused by all her excited reactions to nature and the new experience.

They continued until they reached Carmel some 5 hours later. Claude found the entrance to their hotel and drove up the steep driveway. As he stopped a smartly dressed young man sprinted to the car and opened Julia's door. She was taken aback at the grandeur of the grounds and the hotel itself. The hotel was older and had magnificent views out over the sea from its elevated height.

Claude checked them in and was delighted when he was informed they had been given a 3 room luxury suite.

Upon entering the suite, Julia gasped.

"Claude, I never expected anything like this."

She ran into the bedroom with the oversize bed. There was floor to ceiling windows providing a panoramic view of the Pacific Ocean. An ensuite bathroom off the bedroom contained a giant Jacuzzi and subdued ceiling lighting. An expansive mirror spanned the width of the bathroom over a marble countertop. All the fittings were gold.

Claude tipped the bellboy well. He collapsed onto the bed and watched with joy as Julia flitted around the rooms. He was enjoying this life and had relaxed into a state he had never known while in France.

Tired from the day's drive, Claude fell into a light sleep. When he awoke, Julia was sitting reading a book the hotel provided with a history of the area. As he stirred she turned and smiled.

"Claude, you were talking in your sleep. Who is Geneviève?"

His jaw fell open.

"Did I say her name? She was a friend in Paris during my university years. It was Geneviève who came to visit me in hospital. I am ashamed as I betrayed her."

Claude sat on the chair next to Julia and told her of the escapade he had with the raven-haired nurse in the hospital. Instead of being shocked it seemed to excite her. She reached over and squeezed his hand. He looked at her and into her eyes. They seemed enlarged and eager.

"Julia, its time for us to dine. I understand that the restaurant here is rated as a five star one. Let's go a little early and secure a nice table with an ocean view."

She looked disappointed but agreed.

The dining room was a building in itself. They walked up a cedar planked ramp and through tall shaded glass doors. Inside they were met by a distinguished looking man holding thick leather-bound menus to his chest.

"Good evening. Are you here to dine with us or will it just be cocktails?"

"We are here to dine. Hopefully, you can seat us at a table with a view."

"Of course. Follow me please."

They crossed over a polished blonde oak hardwood floor and were offered a booth with high backed seating and a view.

Claude beamed.

"This is magnificent. Thank you."
For a few minutes, they sat quietly taking in the surrounds of the dining room and the view.

Within a few minutes, the Sommelier arrived. He wore a silver tastevin that hung from a silver chain around his neck. Claude felt he was back in France for a moment. He had chosen the hotel perfectly.

The Sommelier produced a wine list that Claude considered thicker than an old phone book. He thought that this was so typical in America. Things were always bigger.

Claude ordered a bottle of Freemark Abbey Cabernet Bosché. He had heard about the winery from the Marquis and was eager to try the wine from the one-hundred-year-old plus establishment.

Before dinner, they ordered Dry Martinis which they sipped in leisure. They were finished when the waiter arrived to take their orders.

Julia ordered first.

"Thank you. I will have The Oysters on the Half Shell for the appetizer, and a mixed green salad. For the main dinner, I would like the Filet Mignon and Lobster. I would also like the fresh hot Blackberry tart with French Vanilla Icecream."

Claude followed.

"For me, I would Jumbo Prawns, a Vintage Clam Chowder and I will also have the Filet Mignon and Lobster. Please ask for the Filet to be medium rare."

The waiter left with their orders.

They dined at a leisurely pace before returning to their suite.

Claude decided to soak in the giant Jacuzzi before retiring for the night. He poured himself a cognac while it filled with warm water. He found a sachet of a bubble bath and emptied the contents into the water. A huge foam of bubbles soon covered the water and tumbled over the sides. He stripped and jumped naked into the water. He lay soaking with his back to the door. Hw was almost dozing off when Julia walked in. She called him. Claude turned to see her drop the plush bathrobe. She stood naked in front of him. She looked like a white sculpted statue. She let out a loud giggle and jumped in beside him. They played like kids in the water for almost an hour before the temptation was too much and the fierce lovemaking began. Exhausted they made their way to bed. They crawled into bed and embraced with exhaustion. Sleep came fast.

Chapter 44

Sun streamed through the windows into their room. Julia arose and looked out to the east at the pink and orange sky. The sun had barely risen and cast a long shining beam across the ocean. She turned to see that Claude was still in a deep sleep. She was unsure whether to wake him or let him sleep. She took some clothing and silently went to take a shower. When she laws finished, she emerged from the bathroom to find Claude had made coffee using the appliances in the room. She walked to him and hugged him.

"I am so happy. You make me smile. This trip is great. What will we be doing today?"

"We will be driving up to San Francisco. It is not that far, only a few hours. Today we can relax a little."

"Ever since I was a little girl I wanted to see San Francisco. It looks beautiful in pictures."

"Well, we will be there this afternoon. Then you can experience it for real."

Claude showered and dressed in more casual clothing that was better suited to California. He still looked stunning, even without his typical classic style clothes.

They returned to the dining room for breakfast. She chose fresh berries, sprinkled with sugar and drenched in heavy cream. Claude was hungry and on a whim ordered a plate of kippers and eggs. Julia scrunched up her nose when his meal was brought to the table.

"How can you eat those disgusting things?"
Claude laughed. "Easily."

When they had finished their breakfasts, they checked out of the hotel and drove into Carmel by the sea and visited some of the touristy stores. Claude bought Julia a hand carved seal on a rock. She loved it.

That afternoon they cruised slowly toward San Francisco, stopping at various locations including the Hearst Castle. Claude looked at it and shook his head. It was not European and seemed incongruously out of place, perched next to the ocean coastline.

It was late afternoon when they arrived in the city. Claude drove them down to a hotel situated by Fishermans Wharf. He had not booked ahead. He parked and entered the hotel. The lobby was overflowing with Japanese tourists. The noise was deafening. At the front desk, he inquired about the availability if a room in a quiet part of the hotel. The clerk advised him the hotel was fully booked with the exception of the penthouse suite and that it was quiet. Claude decided to take the suite.

Once they were settled into the room, they decided to walk along the Fishermans Wharf promenade. The breeze off the harbor waters was cool and both Julia and Claude wore jackets. On the promenade, there were buskers juggling and fire-eaters, musicians and clowns. Julia felt like she was visiting a carnival. Claude would stop to listen to some of the performers and if impressed threw some change into the hats or other containers put out to collect money.

Hours slipped by and dusk was creeping in.

"Julia let's stop at Aliotos for dinner tonight. I have heard about it from many people who visited here."
They dined on a selection of fresh crab and lobster accompanied by some fine white California wines.

Claude was becoming more impressed with the local wines. He was looking forward to their continued trip up the coast and through the Napa Valley.

In the morning, Claude realized he had not been in contact with Marie-France or the Marquis. He looked at his gold watch. It was eight in the morning. He calculated that it was, therefore, five in the afternoon in Bordeaux. He picked up the room phone and gave the operator the details to call France. It took minutes but finally, he was connected. He could hear the phone ringing at the other end at the Chateau and waited. It rang for a long while before it was answered.

When it was answered, it was Claude's new friend Jacques. Claude told him where he was and of his adventure so far, then asked to speak to either the Marquis or Marie-France.

"I am sorry, but neither are here. Your mother has gone out with her motorbike and friends and your father has gone to Italy."

Claude thanked him and hung up. Nothing had changed. He felt a little depressed. Julia had watched as he had called. She sensed his mood.

"Come on, Claude. Let's start that trip north. I know you are eager to see the Napa Valley. You can call them tonight. There is a nine-hour time difference so if you call late you should be able to connect in the morning."

Claude recognized she was attempting to cheer him up and reacted accordingly.

The valet arranged for his car to be brought up from the underground parking and soon they were weaving their way through the chaotic San Francisco early morning traffic to the Golden Gate Bridge. Julia's eyes were wide with excitement as they crossed the bridge. Claude signaled and took the exit to Sausalito.

He drove along the narrow street near the wharf and found somewhere to park. They exited the car and walked around the few stores and looked back across the bay to the City of San Francisco. The city glowed in the early sun.

Back in the car, they continued the drive up Highway 1 until they reached the road that leads into Bodega Bay. They dropped down a gentle incline on to the small road that ran along the beachfront.

Claude started to excitedly tell Julia about Bodega Bay and some of the history. He told her of how it had been the location of Alfred Hitchcock's The Birds film. Julia had not heard of the film but nonetheless was fascinated.

Claude loved the ruggedness of the area. He watched the swirling mists coming in off the ocean and the surf crashing on the shore. Their grey haziness floated up over the dark sands and created an eerie feeling. The atmosphere felt isolated, even though it was populated with houses and stores. Fishing boats bobbed in the water, moored at the wharf. Claude loved Bodega Bay.

He drove back along the bay and found the sign to their hotel, The Inn at the Tides. They checked in and took their luggage to the room. Claude decided he wanted to spend some time beach walking and left alone to explore while Julia rested.

Chapter 45

Claude walked and explored the area. He found there were horses for rent to ride the beach and reserved for the following morning. He stopped into the Tides restaurant. It was exactly how he had seen it in the film, The Birds. He ordered a beer and sat at the long wooden bar and glanced out at the boats moored alongside. The whole area had a certain seductive effect on him.

When he returned he found Julia dressed and eager to leave for dinner. He had planned a surprise evening. He changed into slightly more formal clothing and joined her.

"Tonight we will take a drive to a special place. It is the Mark West Lodge in Santa Rosa. It will be a nice drive at this time of day."

They drove through sparsely populated land and some small vineyards. It was different from the French wine districts that Claude was familiar with.

They arrived at the Lodge and were seated in the bar while waiting for their table to be prepared. As they sat chatting, Claude became intrigued by a younger man he heard speaking in a strange English accent. He listened carefully but could not place it. His curiosity could not be checked. He went over to the man.

"Excuse me for this interruption. I have heard you speaking and I am confused. You speak English but not the way I was taught. I am from France and cannot decide where your accent is from."

The man looked at Claude and grinned a somewhat crooked smile.

"No worries, Mate. I'm from Australia. Up here to teach these Yanks how to make wine. I guess you must like wine then since you're from bloody France."

"Yes, I do like wine. I have been drinking it since I was a baby."

"Well, Mate. I feel sorry for you. Pity, it wasn't our good Aussie wine instead of that French shit."

Claude was astounded. It was the first time in his life that anyone had insulted France or French wines to his face. He was at a temporary loss for words. Julia looked on unsure what would happen next. Claude went to speak but the large Australian put up his hand and burst into laughter.

"Struth, you shoulda seen yourself. Thought you were about to shit yourself for a minute. Here let me buy you a good wine. No offense, Mate."

Claude started to understand the man's strange sense of humor.

The Australian thrust his hand forward to shake Claudes.

"Me names Barry, Barry Jones. I'm up here helping one of the wineries try to make wine as we have at home. Bloody hopeless bunch they are. These Yanks have no idea yet. You can't just buy everything and think it will result in a good product. I guess I'm probably boring you though. So tell me sport, what do you do in France. You look a bit of a dandy to me."

Claude choked on his wine. For all his gruffness, Claude was taking a liking to Barry.

"I am doing some traveling at present. I do know a little about wine. Maybe you don't know much about French wineries and vineyards, but I certainly do."

"Go on, Mate. You're too bloody young to know much at all. Probably think that thing between your legs is too piss with. Well, one day you'll find out different."

Julia had been listening and watching. The last comment was too much for her and she broke into hysterics. Barry looked at her.

"Ok Claude, boy. Whose the Sheila with you?"

"She is a friend and traveling companion. Now let me teach you something. My name is Claude de Passioné. Maybe you might have heard of our wines."

Barry almost dropped his glass.

"Why the hell didn't ya tell me that cobber. No harm meant. Just a bit of fun with you being a frog."

Claude shook his head. It was obvious that their cultures were far apart.

"I am not offended. In fact, I find you a bit funny and also a bit brash."

A waiter interrupted them to advise Claude their table was ready. Claude shook Barry's hand.

"Maybe we will meet up some day. I am interested in the wine business here."

"Tell you what. After you eat, come and see me. I'll arrange for you to visit the winery. I'm the head vintner there so I don't need to go ask anyone. Now go and enjoy some tucker. We'll chat after."

Julia had watched the whole interchange.

"I think his manner is charming in a strange way. I liked him. He sounds rough but I think he's a nice person. All talk. Beneath that rugged exterior I believe, is a good man."

When dinner was over, Claude and Julia found Barry at the bar making jokes. He saw them approaching and left to join them.

"I will get us a quiet table so we can chat."

It was obvious that Barry was well known. He had no trouble having a private booth made available.

"Sorry if I offended you. I was just having a joke. People here are a bit too serious. I do know the vineyards and wines of de Passioné. It is one of the brands we fear coming onto the market in Australia. I am flattered to meet a de Passioné in person."

Julia was aghast. She had no idea she had been traveling with the wealthy son of a Marquis of some fame.

"Where are you and the young lady staying?"

"We are at Bodega Bay."

"If you have time tomorrow, please come and visit. The winery is in the Russian River area. The name is Devil's Lair. The wine they are producing certainly does that name justice. I'm not sure I can save that winery. Lots of issues. Still, I'll be trying hard. Hate failure."

Julia and Claude took the information and then returned to Inn at the Tides. They were exhausted.

Chapter 46

They awoke to a glorious sunny California morning. Claude decided to order a breakfast that they could take and eat on the beach.

As they rode the rented horses along the beach, high surf crashed onto the black sandy shore with a roar, and as the water receded, a loud hiss sounded as shells and small pebbles rolled back with the water.

After riding the horses, they returned and sat on the sand to eat the breakfast. When they had finished eating, Claude removed his shoes and rolled up his trouser legs and walked the length of the beach at the water's edge. He was wondering what he had started with Julia. She didn't fit into his traveling plans. He would need to find a way to tell her that he just wishes to be a friend and not a lover.

After he returned he found Julia sitting and reading a book.

"I have been thinking. Let's go and visit Barry Jones at the Devil's Lair winery. It's still early and we will be there by noon."

Julia enthusiastically leaped to her feet, eager for another adventure.

They drove for almost two hours before arriving at a sign announcing the winery. Claude was amazed at the size of the neighboring vineyards. They extended down an incline and into a ravine. He estimated the width of the plantings to be in excess of a mile and the depth stretched as far as he could see. It made the de Passioné estate in France seem small by comparison. He slowly drove to what appeared to be an office at the front of the winery. He had no sooner stopped when Barry came bursting out through the front door.

"Bloody good to see you, mate. Pleased you came. I see you brought your Sheila with you. Good on you."

Claude couldn't suppress his chuckle. He liked Barry.

"We didn't have anything planned today, so decided to take a drive and visit. This place is huge."

"It may be huge but it can't produce a good product in quantity. I'm trying to understand what's wrong here. Is it the soil or the vines. Both the red and white wines are bitter. They need to be doped with chemical treatment to be drinkable and I'm not in favor of that. If it doesn't get solved soon I suspect this place will be sold. The owners put a lot of money into it and it's not generating an income. I'm a bit worried ill end up back in Oz."

"I wonder if our vintner back home could offer any advice. Seems like it's a great location here. Have they done soil tests?"

"I've only been here a few months now. I'm still trying to work through what the previous owners had done. The records are a mess."

Claude thought about this for a while and about the work he had done in France examining the business affairs of the Berger Estate.

"Barry, I studied business at the Sorbonne in France and recently performed an analysis of a troubled vineyard and winery for my father and an investor. The deal was completed and they are now managing the business. I wonder if I could be of help here."

Barry looked at him for several minutes before he spoke.

"I'm fine with that, but I will need to talk with the owners. How long are you staying in Bodega Bay?"

"I have no schedule. Julia will need to return to LA to meet up with her flight crew soon. I can stay here for some time. I will need to find somewhere close to stay."

"There is a cottage on the property here. I think they would let you stay there."

While they stood talking two older silver-haired men approached. They shuffled toward Barry, Claude, and Julia.

Barry spoke quietly. "Here come the owners now. They are identical twins. Be careful. They are crusty old buggers."

Claude was somewhat shocked by their age and appearance.

"Claude and Julia, please meet Neville and Stanley Johnson. They own the winery and vineyards."

Claude stepped forward and extended his hand. The Johnsons looked at him suspiciously and ignored the extended hand.

"Who are you and what do you want here?"

"I am Claude de Passioné and this is my friend from France."

At the mention of France and his name, the Johnsons immediately became hostile. Barry spoke.

"Claude here has recently assisted with a troubled winery in France. I would like to hire him to help me with improving the operations here."

At that comment, the men's faces reddened with anger.

"Absolutely not. We are not going to have some dam Frenchman here trying to tell us our business. He's here to spy on us and get our secrets to making the best wine. I want him to leave now. Get off my property Frenchie."

The Johnsons turned and sauntered off into the nearby plantation of vines.

"Sorry about that, mate. See the shit I gotta put up with. If I can't get what I need I'm out of here and back to the

Barossa Valley where I can easily find a job. Australia's wines are booming."

"We will leave now. I would like to invite you as our guest tonight to join us for dinner and drinks. Will you come?"

"Anything to get away from those miserable old blokes. See you at your hotel around six then."

Claude and Julia returned to the car and started to drive off. Claude slowed the car and closely inspected the vineyard. He drove around the perimeter as far as the road would allow. It was an immense amount of land. He considered that Barry would have a formidable task to perform, especially with the attitude of the owners he had just met.

Chapter 47

Back at their hotel in Bodega Bay, Claude made his decision.

"Julia, Tomorrow I will drive back to San Francisco. You will be able to take the shuttle flight to Los Angeles and meet with your friends. I have enjoyed this week and your company.

She looked at him with a dejected look and exclaimed.

"Claude, I still have a few days left. Can I stay with you in San Francisco? We could go back to Fishermans Wharf and tour some other sights."

Claude sensed a possessive streak he had not noticed before. A long-term commitment was not in his plans.

"I won't be staying long in San Francisco. I intend to leave within a day or two for the South Pacific. I will fly first to Tahiti and from there visit other islands."

"That is good news, Claude. I can apply to crew on the Air France flight to Tahiti and meet you there. It will be glorious fun to be together on the islands."

Claude was now getting worried. He needed to escape from the situation he had created. He looked at her for a long while and then announced that he was going for a walk. He left the hotel and proceeded to the Tides restaurant and bar.

It was late afternoon, and already fishermen from the boats were generating a brisk business. Beer flowed freely and greetings and comments were shouted between the men. Claude found solace amongst them. He pushed Julia from his mind. After many drinks, Claude was feeling overconfident and returned to the hotel to tell Julia his final decision.

He went to their room. It was empty. He looked around. Her clothing was gone. He went to the bathroom. All her perfumes and accessories were gone. She had left him.

He sank onto the bed and immediately regret flooded through him. He was feeling sorry for himself and was surprised when tears welled in his eyes. He knew he had made a huge mistake.

Claude ran from the room to the reception desk to ask if she had stopped there or whether they knew where she was going. The matronly woman behind the desk had a snigger on her face.

"They come and go, lover boy. No idea where she went. Bad luck Romeo."

Claude was incensed at her arrogance and vowed to himself to take revenge. He intended to make her employment situation fragile.

He returned to his room and resigned himself to the fact he had lost a friend. He lay on the bed and dozed until Barry Jones arrived.

The phone in his room jangled and he answered it to a jovial Barry waiting in the lobby. He threw on a jacket and headed to meet him.

"Where's your Sheila? She not joining us?"

"It seems she has left. It was about time. I was growing bored of her."

Barry shot him a sideways glance. He could always tell when he was being bullshitted.

"Well, that's too bloody bad, mate. Still, plenty of trouble out there for a handsome guy like you. What are you going to do now?"

As they walked down to the dock and the restaurant, Claude told Barry of his planned trip and adventures.

"I will probably leave in a couple of days. I'm going back to San Francisco and making some travel arrangements. Then I will be off for a couple of years. I hope to visit your country on this trip. First I will be spending time around the islands and then going to New Zealand. I hear its beautiful there. I might try to get some seasonal work there."

Barry looked at him.

"I warn you, mate. You can't trust those bloody Kiwis. There a bad bunch. Fight all the time 'cause there's nothing else to do in that goddamm country." He laughed.

"Barry, you are not putting me off my dream. I hear that Australians are bad and that the Kiwis are good people. Very kind."

"Don't know who told you that nonsense. Anyway, have a good time there. I doubt you will because those Kiwi girls are the size of cows. They all got footballers legs too."

Claude knew that Barry was exaggerating and twisting the facts. He just laughed.
The special dinner at the restaurant that evening was crab. Claude was happy as it was one of his favorite seafood meals. Barry was less than enthusiastic and asked the waitress to get a meal that only Aussies liked. Steak and eggs.

"Claude I would like an address for you. Maybe the one in France. I'm sure that would be best as since you're traveling around it will be difficult to keep track of you."

Claude asked the waiter for a pen and paper and scribbled out the address for the Chateau in Bordeaux.

They continued to sit and talk for hours after the meal. They had moved from the table to a quiet location at the bar.

"I am very concerned Claude. I don't think Devil's Lair will survive. The Johnsons don't seem all that interested in the winery and there are rumors of them breaking up and selling the land. I may see you back in Australia before long. Got to look after me, you know."

"Is the situation with the vineyards that bad?"

"No. I think they just don't have the interest anymore. That winery used to win awards for the wines. Its that the business has not been managed well. I wish they would sell it to one of the other successful wineries before its too late."

"It's a pity. I'm certainly not interested. The de Passioné business has presented enough problems in my life."

He continued on and at length discussed the Marquis and bizarre Marie-France. When he was done talking Barry looked at him with an amused expression.

"They sound like a delightful couple of nuts. I guess that's where you're heading as well when you get to their age."

He slapped Claude on the shoulder and roared laughing.

"Ok, now sport. Time for me to start the long drive back. Got a busy day tomorrow. They have a bunch of Mexican migrant workers coming in. It's always a joy with them."

They returned to the hotel and Barry jumped into a rusting truck and fired it into life. The noise was deafening. The truck had lost its muffler long ago. He roared off in a hail of stones and dirt.

Claude watched the truck race down the driveway and thought how both the truck and the man had the same rough characteristics.

Chapter 48

The trip back to San Francisco was uneventful and boring. Claude was missing the companionship of Julia. He regretted how they had parted.

When he reached the city, he checked into the Fairmont Heritage Place, Ghirardelli Square. In his room, he called various airlines to book his flights. He discovered an itinerary that seemed to suit his plans perfectly. He called the airline. A representative from Air New Zealand answered.

After a long conversation, Claude had booked first class from Los Angeles to Tahiti and then onto Rarotonga, in the Cook Islands and finally through to Auckland, New Zealand. The fare was structured to allow up to a year to reach the final destination, and unrestricted stopovers were permitted. It was ideal, except for the fact the flight left from LA the next day. Claude booked a flight to LA for that day.

With his arrangements made, Claude decided to spend the afternoon walking around the city before taking an early meal.

After the meal, he started his way back to the hotel. He was on Folsom Street and passing a nightclub when he heard music from inside. It was early so he decided to stop for a drink and check out the club. He paid a cover charge and walked in and down a stairway to a cavernous basement. The club was crowded, smoky and loud. As he looked around, he realized he was in a gay leather club. Having paid the cover charge and somewhat amused he decided to stay a while. He forced his way to the bar past men of all ages and the occasional transvestite. The majority were dressed in black leather outfits with chains and other paraphernalia hanging from them.

Claude shouted his order to the tall skinny barman with shaved purple hair. As he stood to wait for his drink he felt a hard pressure against his thigh. He turned to find a bare-chested muscular man with a shaved head and several pierced pieces through his chin and nipple pressing against him.

"Hi, sweets. I saw you come in. I'm Bristol Dream. I've been watching you. You're a real honey. Want to join me and dance, then we can go for fun"

Claude was at a loss for words. He didn't want to start a fight in this club. He spoke in French and feigned not to know English. This only caused the man to become more forceful and excited. The man slid his hand around Claude's waist and southward. It was too much for Claude. He spun and kneed the man in his groin. He folded and collapsed to the floor. Claude hurriedly made his way to the exit. Once outside he hailed a cab to take him the short distance to his hotel. He was not going to loiter around the club.

The next morning he arose early and took a leisurely breakfast before heading to the airport. He returned the rental car and rode the shuttle bus to the international terminal. He entered the terminal and checked in at the counter before clearing through the security check. He took the elevator up to the departure level and was making his way to the gate when a flight crew appeared walking toward him. They were joking amongst themselves and laughing. Claude froze. There in the front was Julia. It was an Air France crew. She stopped and stared at him. He was unsure what to do. She briskly walked up to him.

"I knew we would have to part. I didn't want to make a scene. I guessed it would be hard on you. I'm sorry as I didn't mean to hurt you. I hope that one day we can meet again as friends."

Claude was dumbfounded. It wasn't him who left her…..she had left him. He felt a great relief. They hugged and she continued and ran to catch up with the others.

Claude turned and for a moment considered running after her. He was confused. Never before had a woman left him.

Chapter 49

Claude boarded the Air New Zealand flight and was immediately seated in the luxurious first class cabin The seats were large with ample leg room. He had no sooner sat when refreshments were offered. He was impressed with the courtesy and service the flight attendants provided.

The flight left LA late afternoon and arrived in Papeete, Tahiti at ten in the evening, local time, taking into account the time difference between the west coast and Tahiti.

Throughout the eight hour trip, Claude had read, watched a boring movie and slept.

Claude stood up from his seat and proceeded to the front exit of the plane. As he descended the stairs that had been rolled up to the plane, a warm fragrant air, perfumed with frangipani, caressed his face. His first impression of Tahiti was favorable.

He made his way to the customs and immigration clearance in the basic airport terminal. Beautiful Polynesian girls were placing leis around the necks of arriving passengers. Crowds were seated waiting for ongoing flights to various destinations. Claude immediately sensed the difference between Europe and North America. He was in the tropical islands and a different culture and life.

He believed he had never seen such beauty as that of the young Polynesian girls. He was in awe.
After clearing immigration, he was met by a young lady holding a sign with his name and the name of the beach villa he had rented.

"Welcome. Are you Claude de Passioné?"

"Yes, I am. What is your name? How do I address you?"

"I am your assistant for your stay. My name is Pearl Matapo. I will make your stay with us pleasant. How long will you be staying?"

"I haven't decided yet. Maybe a month or longer. Maybe less than that. What will you be doing for me as my assistant?"

"Our villas offer the finest service. I am here to assist you with anything you need. Rental cars, restaurant reservations, trips to the other islands. All you need to do is tell me and it will happen."

Claude studied her. She could not have been more than twenty-one. She had long black hair that hung down her back, a light tanned skin tone, and a cherubic face. She wore an apricot colored dress wrapped tightly around her. Claude was smitten. He was already liking Tahiti.

As they were leaving the airport terminal, Pearl waved and called out to a large, heavy and overweight gendarme standing near the exit doors. He smiled and waved back. The man was Tahitian and huge with rippling muscles.
She looked at Claude with a happy expression.

"That is my father. He protects me."

Claude had an immediate sinking feeling and his interest in a romantic encounter evaporated.

Pearl drove Claude a distance from the airport to a secluded area with a number of small villas dotting the shoreline of the property. She stopped in front of the nearest villa and jumped down from the old jeep. She opened the door to a majestically appointed space. Teak furniture was arranged throughout the living area and through the bathroom door, Claude could see the soft creamy brown marble counters and the sparkling glass doors of the shower. He turned and looked at the bedroom. An oversize king bed dominated the room. There was a flat screen TV facing the bed and a desk and chair at the window facing out to the beach. He was delighted with the accommodation.

"I will leave you now. If you require anything here is my information. What would you like to do tomorrow? Is there anything I can set up for you?"

"No thank you. Tomorrow I am going to rest and take some time on the beach and swim."

When the morning broke, Claude opened the shuttered doors to a wide white sand beach that ran all the way up to his doorway. He looked out at the calm turquoise waters. There were a couple of local men with spears fishing in the little lagoon. Already the temperatures were rising and the humidity building. Claude looked up at the sky and observed the high white mas of clouds. It didn't look like rain.

As he was taking in the view and the surrounds, a maid in a white uniform approached carrying a tray of fresh fruit, juice, and cereal. She greeted Claude by his name and entered the villa to set the tray down. Claude reached into his pocket and tipped the woman generously.

He spent the morning relaxing and swimming. By noon he had become bored and decided to call Pearl. She answered after several rings.

"Good afternoon Pearl. It is Claude. I am wondering if it is possible to rent a small sailboat this afternoon?"

Pearl called him back thirty minutes later with a confirmation for a sailboat rental at a nearby marina. Claude did not tell her he had never sailed or even been on a sailboat before. He thought it looked easy though.

She arrived at the villa to take Claude to the marina. He was dressed for sailing. He wore a bright yellow sleeveless shirt and a gaudy pair of purple board shorts with huge white hibiscus flowers embroidered on them and wore a white jungle pith helmet over his black mane of hair. On his feet, he wore red reef shoes. Pearl looked at him and suppressed a grin. Claude looked like a walking Technicolor cartoon character. He was the epitome of every badly dressed tourist.

She waited on the beach while the local boys pulled the little Hobie Cat sailboat into the water and Claude climbed in. He lied to the boys about his sailing experience.

The little boat was a pale sea green in color with a deep blue sail. It rocked up and down in the low surf. The boys pushed it out beyond the surf and Claude was on his way. The wind filled the sail and the yacht keeled to one side. Claude felt the exhilaration as it accelerated away from the beach. He decided that sailing was a simple task. Little did he know what lay ahead.

He sailed further out. The wake behind him bubbled and churned as he sped toward the horizon. Then it happened.

The bow of the Hobie Cat hit the coral reef hard. The bow dipped under the water and the stern of the boat rose in the air as the boat flipped over. Claude was thrown into the air and landed painfully on the coral. Instantly he started to bleed. The hull of the boat split and it slowly sank into the water. Claude was alone with a submerged boat on the coral reef. He looked to shore and barely made out the figures on the beach. He had not realized how far from shore he had sailed. He sat bleeding on the reef with the salt water stinging in his cuts.

He started to panic and his mind ran wild. He wondered if the blood from his cuts would attract sharks. He panicked more. For the first time in his life, he started to pray. He thought he was too young and attractive to become shark food.

He half sat and half floated on the reef. The sun was setting and the early dusk of the tropics was setting in. Soon it was dark. Claude sobbed. This was not what he had planned.

Chapter 50

The French Marines motored the rubber hulled zodiac in a search pattern but were unable to locate the sailboat or Claude. They had found debris that had washed in towards the shore. They shone a small searchlight across the dark waters looking for signs of him or the remains of the boat. The wind had started to increase and the waters became choppy. They decided it was pointless to continue and radioed back to the base in Papeete.

There was a beating sound as the search helicopter approached them. They watched as the high power searchlight beneath the helicopter scanned across the water. It was only a few minutes before it focused in on Claude who was hanging onto the reef in a semi-conscious state.

The Marines raced out to him and roughly pulled him aboard. Realizing he was injured they sped back to the marine base.

Chapter 51

At the base, they drove the zodiac in close to the shore where another couple of Marines ran to meet them and lift Claude out onto a stretcher. They carried him to a waiting ambulance to transport him to the infirmary. Photographers from the local newspaper snapped photos of the bedraggled Claude. At the infirmary, they cleaned his coral cuts and applied an antibiotic, gave him a sedative and placed him under observation.

Several hours passed by and finally, a nurse entered and provided a cup of hot soup to Claude which he quickly drank. A doctor returned to visit him and summoned for him to be taken back to his villa.

Two Marines escorted him into a military jeep and drove him to the villas. He thanked them and stumbled into his room where he quickly fell asleep.

He awoke early and decided to go to the outdoor patio where a breakfast was served each morning. As he walked in, he noticed people staring at him and some pointing. The patrons spoke in hushed tones as he passed by their tables.

He sat away from the other diners. He looked around and noticed a man reading a local paper. There on the front was

a half-page photo of Claude being carried ashore by the Marines. Large type headlines screamed out about the rescue. Claude shrank in his seat. Embarrassment engulfed him.
He ordered a strong coffee and pastries and ate quickly. He made his way back to his room and again called Pearl.

"Pearl, I have changed my plans. I need to leave for Rarotonga as soon as it can be arranged. I have a ticket to Auckland, New Zealand that is via The Cook Islands. Can you please arrange to get me on the first available flight. I can leave immediately."

It was later that morning when Pearl called.

"There is a flight this evening. It is direct and takes four hours. I have booked you on it. I will pick you up at five and take you to the airport. I am sorry your stay in Tahiti was not better."

Claude hung up and started packing the few clothes he had taken from his case. He decided to take a brief swim in the pool before taking a light lunch and a nap before leaving to the airport.

He was awakened by a gentle knocking at the door. He looked at his watch. He had fallen into a deep sleep. It was after five. He pushed himself off the bed and opened the door. A radiant Pearl stood in front of him.

"Claude are you sure you want to leave like this? I had plans. I was hoping that maybe we would become friends and maybe more."

They pulled away from the villas and drove to the airport. Claude thanked her and left the car with his luggage.

He was again conflicted but chose to stay with his plan. Tahiti was not somewhere he wished to stay.

"No it is best I leave now. I have not enjoyed my time here. It is possible I may return one day, but for now, I am leaving."

He lifted his case from the bed and carried it out to the car. He got into the car and sat on the front passenger seat waiting for Pearl.

As he entered the airport he saw Pearl's father standing and watching him closely. He followed Claude who walked to the check-in counter.

Claude finished his business at the counter and proceeded to the security check and the gate. He was followed by

Pearl's father until he exited the sliding door and walked out onto the tarmac and across to the waiting plane.

He climbed the stairs to the plane and found his seat in first class. He looked around at the other passengers. The flight was empty. He noticed a man and his wife staring at him. The husband had the local paper and nudged his wife as he turned back to the front page and showed her Claude's photo.

The cabin attendants closed the doors to the plane. There was a hiss as the airconditioning system kicked in. A mist expelled from the vents as the cool air mixed with the hot humid air that has penetrated the cabin interior.

Claude relaxed back in his seat and ordered a double scotch. Surely his luck would change in Rarotonga. He was beginning to doubt the wisdom of his decision to spend time in the South Pacific Islands.

The plane sped down the runway and banked sharply and out over the ocean. It leveled off and started the four-hour trip.

During the flight, Claude drank several more double scotches. He was feeling no pain and fell asleep. He was shaken awake by a flight attendant asking him to place his seat up as they were approaching the landing in Rarotonga.

Claude's mouth tasted horrible. He had never really been a scotch drinker and this reminded him why. He reached for the breath freshener he had bought at the airport and doused his tongue and roof of his mouth.

The plane banked and made sharp turns and quickly dropped before landing smoothly.

The captain came on the overhead speakers,

"Sorry about the acrobatics back there. The runway here is beside a huge mountain range and we had strong winds. There was nothing to worry about. Hope to see you all again. Enjoy your stay."

In the terminal, Claude retrieved his baggage and went outside where he waved to a local taxi…one of the few on the island. He gave the lady driver the address and she slowly drove toward his hotel. She was jovial and joked and chatted the whole way. Upon arrival, Claude was greeted by a young Cook Islander who offered to take his bags while he checked-in.

With the formalities performed, Claude was taken to his 'room'. It was a cabin on the beach. He was ecstatic. The doors opened toward the ocean and he could hear the breaking of the waves. Already he was feeling better.

After unpacking, he wandered around the grounds and finally to the reception desk. He asked about the availability of food and was advised there was none available at that hour, nor was there anywhere to buy food at that hour. In addition, the woman advised him it was a Friday night and on Saturday there was a local market he should attend.at Avarua. She gave him directions, but he looked confused.

"Don't worry. I am going with my kids. We will take you. Be here in the morning at seven. We will get local food there. Pork over charcoals, fruits, fresh juices. There are lots of pearls for sale. You can get some for your girlfriends. My name is Millie."

Claude raised his hand and explained he had none. The woman looked at him and shook her head.

"A piece like you with no girls? I think you aren't telling me the truth. I get you an island girl then."

Claude shuddered at the thought. He had found the Polynesian girls and women to be very assertive and aggressive.

"No, that won't be necessary. I am gay'" he lied.

She raised her hands to her face. "Lord have mercy, a pretty one like you. Oh, the shame."

Chapter 52

At seven the next morning, Claude waited at the reception area for his ride to the market at Avarua. A beat-up old white Chevrolet station wagon came to a noisy halt at the entrance. Claude could hear the yelling of the kids even though the windows and doors of the vehicle were closed. Millie moved her somewhat large frame from the front seat and marched towards the door to get Claude. He was unsure of what he was getting into.

She saw the look of trepidation in his eyes as he stared at the car with kids climbing over seats and loudly shouting.

"Don't worry about them. I'll make them quiet."

At the car, she opened the back door and shouted an admonishment to the kids. Her voice was loud and booming. It had the identical tone of a foghorn.

They continued driving towards the market for almost twenty minutes. On the way approaching cars would flash their lights and arms would fly out of the windows and wave enthusiastically. Some of the oncoming cars would stop in the middle of the road and Millie would stop for a brief chat. It was a scene unlike any that Claude had ever experienced.

Eventually, they arrived at the grassy park where stalls were set up and locals mingled. The air carried the spicy aroma from the foods cooking in steel barrels that had been cut in half and converted into grills. Pieces of chicken sizzled on the wire grills over the glowing coals. Large Cook Island men stood around under canopies drinking beer from a variety of glass half gallon jars.

It seemed more like a local social function than a market.

Claude walked through the market stalls enjoying looking at the items offered for sale by the various vendors. There were different fruits, fish, articles of homemade clothing, tools and other items he could not identify. At the end of a row of tables, he saw two girls sitting with an assortment of jewelry pieces spread out on a white tablecloth. He sauntered over to them and studied their display. At the rear of the display, there was a black pearl necklace and earring combination.

As he reached toward it, one of the girls snatched it from the table and held it out to him.

"You like? Buy it for your girlfriend or wife?"

"No, I'm not married and do not have a girlfriend. It is beautiful though."

On hearing his comment the girls giggled and immediately turned on their charm to attract him.

"What is the price of that? Maybe I will buy it for my mother."

"It too nice for an old lady. You buy for a young girl like me."

Claude recognized their clumsy attempt to flirt with him.

"Please just tell me how much you want for it."

"Not for sale to the old lady. Buy for pretty girl."

The haggling over price continued for some time. Finally, a price was agreed and Claude took the tissue paper wrapped necklace and earrings and securely put them in his pocket. As he was leaving the jewelry stall he looked up to see that Millie had been standing and watching the whole time. He smiled and waved to her.

"So you couldn't resist those pretty girls? Had to buy something. I think we need to take you back to your room. It's too dangerous here for you. Too many wahines."

She roared laughing and wandered off to a vendor selling roasted wild boar stacked on a slice of freshly baked homemade bread and smothered in a sweet tropical sauce. She handed one to Claude. He tasted it and was amazed. He had never tasted anything similar.

He and Millie sat on a rough stone wall that ran the length of the beachfront and enjoyed their treats.

"Who did you buy that necklace for? Must be someone special. Very expensive. Those black pearls are from here. They get sent to other islands and sold as Tahitian black pearl, but they are really from our islands."

It was then that Claude decided he would keep the jewelry himself until he found a special girl.

Millie's children arrived demanding treats and food. Millie looked at Claude.

"It's time to leave. Got plenty of food and drinks at home for these brats."

On the short drive back to the hotel, the kids fell asleep on the rear seat of the car.

"Finally I will have some peace. It is Saturday and this afternoon I will be busy with my sisters preparing for our traditional Sunday lunch and afternoon fun. Would you like to come and visit? We play music and sing. The men will dig a pit in the ground and line it with stones and flax leaves, then when the fire has burned and it is hot we will lower in a pig and baskets of vegetables to steam. They taste delicious with a flavor from the earth.

Claude accepted the invitation and she gave him instructions to her home.

Back at the hotel, he changed into swimming shorts and proceeded to the beach.

On the beach, he sat thinking about his trip and life on the islands. In some regards, he found it pleasant but simple. He recognized that he would soon become bored with the island life.

Sitting with his arms wrapped around his knees he absentmindedly twirled a small stick in his fingers. He was feeling lonely and missing Europe.

His silence was shattered by the shrill screams and laughter of some children who were running at the water's edge. As he watched them a couple appeared, walking behind them. Claude waved to them. The father called out to the children and turned to walk up to Claude.

"Hi. My name is Dave Mathews and this is my wife June. That's a real nice place you are staying at. Next time we plan a visit I will try to stay there. I haven't seen you on the beach here before. Did you just arrive?"

Claude introduced himself and confirmed he had only arrived the day before. He invited the couple to sit with him. For the next hour, they chatted about the island, their home countries, and business.

Claude was particularly intrigued when he found out that the Mathews were from New Zealand.

He asked many questions about the country.

"Claude, we don't live in one of the big cities. We own a farm in the North Island and farm sheep and dairy. June here breeds racehorses. Keeps us pretty busy. We come to the island a couple of times each year. What about you?"

He told them of the de Passioné vineyards and wineries. Dave Mathews was keenly interested.

"I've often wondered about that business. There's a lot of vineyards in New Zealand now and some are close to our farm. I'm tempted to try running a vineyard. It'll be a bit of learning curve though. Doesn't look too hard though."

Claude had listened and then spoke directly to Dave.

"It's a lot harder than many imagine. There is a lot to know about soil types, temperature, the direction of the vines for sunlight, the diseases to look for when to replant vines and many more things. In France, we have professional managers for the vineyards and experienced vintners in our wineries."

Dave nodded as he absorbed the information that Claude had shared on the issues with operating a vineyard. The sun was starting to set when Dave and June stood to leave.

"We need to go back and pack. We fly home tomorrow. If you get to New Zealand come and visit us. You are always welcome."

Dave scribbled their address and phone numbers onto a paper napkin that Claude tucked into his shirt pocket.

Chapter 53

The sound of raised voices singing to the accompaniment of an organ awoke Claude. He jumped from his bed and looked around. He was unable to locate the source of the music. Quickly he dressed and went out in search of the singing. He walked away from the hotel and noticed an old white church further down the narrow road. As he walked toward the voices were louder. He did not recognize the language. At the church, he opened the huge wooden door and walked in. There was row after row of women dressed in fine dresses and wearing large hats. They sang and clapped. The men were dressed in suits and would break into the singing of the hymns in rich baritone voices.

Claude was in amazement at finding this on a small South Pacific island. He had never expected to discover such a ceremony.

As the church service was ending, Claude hurried down the steps and away from the church. He was almost to the road when he heard his name being called. He turned to see Millie running toward him. Her huge frame was wrapped in a bright purple satin dress and she wore a wide-brimmed white hat decorated with plastic fruit. The fat on her torso wobbled like jelly as she awkwardly ran to Claude.

"Did you like our church? We sing and worship every Sunday, then return home for the family parties. Are you coming to my home? I want you to meet my brothers and sisters. You will enjoy."

"Yes, I will be coming."

Millie was delighted and bounced off to talk to other friends. Claude continued walking to the road when again he heard his name called. He turned to find a beautiful young Polynesian woman approaching him.

"Are you the Frenchman? I have heard about you. You bought jewelry from my sisters at the market yesterday. Can I walk and talk with you? My name is Atarangi. In English, it means Morning sky."

Claude was delighted to have company and thought her name was delightful.

"No please join me. I am walking back to my hotel. Please walk with me. I am happy to have someone to talk with."

"I want to ask you about France. I want to leave here and study. I don't want to study in New Zealand or Australia. I would like to attend university in Europe and become a doctor."

"It will be expensive to study in France. You will also have expenses to rent somewhere and to live. Are you sure you wish to do this?"

"It is my dream. I have some money saved. Please tell me what it is like to live in Paris."

Claude drifted back into his time at the Sorbonne and told Atarangi of student life. She soaked up every detail, asking many questions.

They chatted for hours. Claude looked at his watch.

"I am meant to visit Millie's this afternoon and join them for a family celebration. Maybe you would like to join me?"

"Yes. I know the family. We are related."

Together they left to walk to Millie's beachside Villa.

When they arrived, the men had already prepared the fire pit. The rocks glowed white from the burning wood above them. One of the men threw in green bunches of leaves to smother the flames. Two other men gently lowered a whole pig into the pit. It was then covered with branches and a layer of soil shoveled over it. Steam and smoke curled up from the edges of the firepit.

Claude was introduced to the family members and soon stood amongst the men with a large glass of beer in his hand. The men found the Frenchman amusing. It didn't take long before a guitar was produced along with a ukelele. The singing started.

Claude felt a sense of serenity as he listened to the women's soft voices singing traditional songs. He especially enjoyed it when Atarangi joined them and sung solo. Her voice was clear and carried the passion of the song she sang.

Darkness fell quickly in the islands. Claude had enjoyed the feast, the singing, and the drinking. He excused himself, and after making his farewells, returned to his room. Sleep came quickly.

For the next few days, Claude amused himself swimming and snorkeling. He visited the town and met with locals. He still felt a loneliness and was becoming bored with the beach and island life. He picked up the phone and called Air New Zealand. He reserved a flight for the next afternoon. It was a short four-hour flight.

When the arrangements were complete he settled his account and decided to find Atarangi and take her to dinner before he left.

He was told where he could find her. To reach her place of work he would need a car. Millie offered him her car for a small sum which Claude happily agreed with. He followed the directions he had been given and arrived at a low wooden building with a loose stone parking area at the front. The building had open windows and a wide porch. He parked and walked in through the front door. The aromas from inside rushed to greet him when he entered. He had walked into a native perfume factory. There were plants and cuttings piled high on tables. Bottles containing different colored ingredients sat on shelves.

Atarangi saw that Claude had arrived and ran to meet him.

"I am pleased to see you. Why did you come here? Surely you don't want to buy perfumes?"

"No. I will be leaving tomorrow and wished to spend the evening with you. We can go anywhere you like for a dinner. It is my invitation to you."

Atarangi beamed. She had silently hoped to spend time alone with Claude. She hugged him.

"I would like that. I will come and meet you at your hotel at seven. I will take you to a special place."

She arrived at the resort in an older convertible sports car. Claude sat in the passenger seat and they drove down the coastline until they reached some dense vegetation which appeared on the left side of the road. She slowed and spun the steering wheel and drove through a clearing in the trees. An almost invisible track leading down to the beach. They bounced along the dirt track before emerging at a Villa set on the beach. In the front, there were six tables set up on the beach. Each was draped with a white linen tablecloth and flickering candles. Overhead strings of white decorative lights were strung between the high palm trees.

"Atarangi. What is this place?"

It is a home of my friends. They serve meals to friends and guests. Her name is Panee and she is Maori and her husband is Carlo, an Italian. Come and I will introduce you."

They entered the home through the porch. Panee and Carlo were busy preparing foods in the large kitchen. Carlo turned and greeted them. With the introductions completed, he took them to a table beside the gently lapping waves.

"I will bring you drinks if you wish. We have a large selection of New Zealand wines. As you may know, The Cook Islands are a protectorate of New Zealand. We have many kiwi things here. Tonight we have a fresh shipment of lamb. It was flown in this afternoon. It is delicious. We use papaya to tenderize the meat. The flavor cannot be described. A piece of heaven in your mouth. We serve it with locally grown root vegetables. For dessert tonight, we offer our homemade pavlova cake with fresh peaches and kiwifruit slices floating on a bed of fresh whipped cream lightly flavored with vanilla. All of this is contained in a large meringue shell."

It did not take a minute for Claude to readily agree with the recommended meal. Carlo and Panee had each grinned at the formal attire that Claude had dressed in. He again wore a Regency shirt and his tight black trousers.

.As they ate, Atarangi spoke of her desires and wish to travel She was extremely interested in studying to become a doctor in Europe. Claude thought about this for a few minutes and then reached into his pocket and withdrew a small book. He thumbed through the pages and found the information he was looking for.

"While I was studying at the Sorbonne, I had two brothers as roommates. They studied and became doctors. Here is an address that you can contact them. Tell them I advised you to contact them. I am sure they will help you."

For hours Atarangi and Claude sat at the water's edge drinking and talking until she stood and offered to drive back to the resort.

The trip was short. Upon arriving, she parked her car near the beach and got out and went to the trunk from which she removed a bottle and 2 glasses.

"Let's finish our night here on the beach. We can sit on the sand and watch the moonlight reflecting off the waters of the lagoon."

Claude was happy and took her hand as they walked to a flat area on the sand.

"Claude, must you leave tomorrow? I was hoping we would share more time together. If you must go, then I hope we will meet in Europe. You can show me Paris."

It didn't take long before the couple moved from hand-holding to passionate kisses under the bright moonlight. Eventually, they made their way up the beach and into Claude's room.

She playfully pushed Claude by his chest and he feigned injury falling back into the bed. In seconds she was on top of him pulling away his clothing before stripping herself. Claude admired the tan skinned figure. He spun her over and thrust himself inside her. The lovemaking was fierce. She loudly screamed and Claude, concerned he had hurt her stopped.

"No don't stop," she cried as she reached up and pulled his head down to her chest by his long black hair. He collapsed onto her and she kissed his ears and nibbled his earlobe.

He lay beside her exhausted and drawing in the scent of her skin. It wasn't long before a repeat performance occurred. Not once but until dawn when they both fell into a deep sleep.

They were awakened by a loud knocking at the door. Claude threw a towel around himself and answered the door to find Millie standing with a huge grin on her face.

"You told me you were a gay boy. From the sounds coming from here last night, I don't think you told me the truth. Now its time for you to get up or you won't be on that plane."

She turned and laughing made her way back to the office.

Atarangi looked at the time.

It's too late for me to go to the factory now. I will take the day off and drive you to the airport."

"But, you will be in trouble with your work,"

"No. My family owns the business."

They embraced and decided to shower together, after which Claude dressed in jeans and an expensive Egyptian cotton white shirt. Atarangi went to her car and retrieved makeup and fresh clothing. She had planned the night.

Atarangi drove Claude to the airport and parked and assisted him to the counter. He was dismayed to find that his flight was severely delayed. An airline representative rebooked him on another flight at one the next morning. Claude was annoyed.

"Let us go back. I will go to the factory and you can meet my parents."

At the factory, Claude was introduced to an older, but good looking couple. They invited him into a cluttered office and spent the balance of the afternoon chatting. Atarangi spoke of her goal to study medicine and the information and contacts that he had provided. The parents thanked him and invited him to stay for dinner with the family before returning to the airport.

Claude graciously accepted.

Chapter 54

The four-hour flight to Auckland was uneventful. Most passengers slept in the aircraft darkened cabin. A few read or played cards. Claude was exhausted from the previous night's activities.

Shortly before dawn, the flight attendants walked through the cabin handing out hot facial towels, followed by a breakfast of tropical fruits.

The passengers stirred and activity started. Shuttered windows were opened and the dim light of the early morning flooded in. Claude stared from the aircraft window but all that was visible was the ocean below. It looked cold and menacing at that hour.

He was drifting into a sleep when he heard the jet engines slow and felt the plane dip as it started to descend. Looking from the window, Claude could now see land.

The aircraft continued to descend and approached Auckland airport. The flight entered Auckland from the Pacific Ocean on the west and swooped over the Waitemata Harbour. It crossed the city and farmland and continued out toward the Tasman Sea on the east until it banked in a sharp turn for the final approach.

The landing was smooth. They taxied to the terminal and the jets whined as power was cut to the turbines.

After deplaning, Claude gathered his luggage and was cleared through Customs and Immigration. Outside at the curb, he hailed a taxi to take him to his hotel. The taxi driver was particularly friendly and chatted to Claude throughout the thirty-minute trip. He discussed rugby, fishing, the terrible politicians, whether Claude was married and a whole barrage of other questions.

At the hotel, the driver jumped from his seat and assisted with the baggage. Claude tipped him well before entering the hotel.

Claude was delighted when he walked into the hotel. The whole interior was in the art deco period. The paintings, antiques, and furnishings were all from the 1920-1930 period.

The De Brett hotel was small with only twenty-eight rooms. Claude was shown a room in the rear area of the hotel which was furthest from the street and in a quiet location. The hotel was situated in the center of downtown Auckland.

Claude unbuttoned his shirt and collapsed back on the bed. The previous night's activities and the delayed flight had impacted him. He called down to the desk and requested he be woken around the noon hour, then fell into a deep sleep.

Shortly after noon, he was awakened by the tingling of bells from the old phone. He answered and thanked the operator for the call. He showered and decided to take a walk up Queen Street, Auckland's busy shopping scene. He browsed in the shop windows and again was surprised at the selection of items displayed. He had not expected to find this in such a small country. He continued his walk until the stores thinned out. He then crossed the road and walked back down toward his hotel. He decided to keep walking and soon arrived at the Ferry Buildings. He entered them and looked around at ships berthed and the old black and white ferries that crossed the harbor. Curious, he went to a ticket booth.

Good afternoon. I have just arrived in Auckland. Is it possible to buy a ride on one of the boats? Which would you recommend for a few hours?"

The ruddy-faced clerk thought for several minutes.

"Take the *Kestrel* across to Devonport and enjoy a walk around there. I sell you a return ticket. The ferry crosses back and forth almost every hour. You should plan a day trip to that extinct volcano you see, Rangitoto or take a longer trip out to the beautiful island of Waiheke."

Claude thanked the man and entered through the wrought iron gates to join the queue waiting to board. There were school kids in uniforms, young mothers with wailing babies, businessmen, construction workers, and others he couldn't place. He enjoyed the mix of passengers.

For the next two weeks, Claude visited many of the inner harbor beaches and took the advice and made a day trip to Waiheke. He found an advertisement posted at the hotel and called the number to join a hike through native bush in the Waitakere Ranges slightly northwest of Auckland.

Claude formed the opinion he had arrived in the perfect place. He was no longer missing Europe.

On Friday afternoon, Claude found the telephone number for Dave and June Mathews. He gave the hotel operator the number and the phoned rang at the other end.

A familiar strongly accented voice answered.

"Dave, here."

"Hello, Dave. It is Claude. We met in Rarotonga. Do you remember? I am in Auckland. Been here a couple of weeks and traveling to see some of the country."

"Good. Pleased you called. How long will you be here in New Zealand?"

"I am not sure yet. I want to see more, especially the South Island."

"Hold on mate, June is here. She wants to speak to you."

June's soft voice came on the line.

"Hello, Claude. It is good to hear from you. Where are you staying in Auckland?"

"I am staying at the De Brett hotel. A fine hotel. I am so happy here."

"Dave and I will be driving to Auckland in the morning. I have a meeting with some horse purchasers from the States. I have an idea. Why don't you come and stay with us for a while and see a different part of the country."

"I don't wish to impose myself on you. It is a very kind offer, but thank you I cannot accept."

Dave returned to the phone.

"Claude, its no problem. We have lots of space here. June has her meeting and I will be at loose ends so I will pick you up and we'll go and have some quality kiwi beers. I am not taking no for an answer. I will meet you at your hotel around eleven thirty."

Chapter 55

Dave Mathews arrived at the De Brett hotel at exactly eleven thirty. Claude was waiting in the lobby with his bags.

"Good to see you again, Claude. Let's get your bags in the car and we'll go find a pub for lunch."

Dave grabbed a bag and walked briskly from the hotel to his white Jaguar. He popped open the trunk and heaved the bags in. He started the Jaguar and they sped up Queen Street until Dave found the pub he desired.

The pub was crowded and noisy. They found seating on a long padded bench and Dave ordered a pitcher of beer. The lunch was a buffet containing fresh seafood, a roasted hip of beef, salads, beets, cold cuts and a variety of desserts. During lunch, they talked about life in France and New Zealand.

"We had better finish up here. It's time to pick up June. It'll take us a few hours to get back down to the farm."

Dave drove through Auckland until he reached iron gates leading to a grandstand with a sign announcing ' Ellerslie

Racecourse.' He pulled into a parking area and left Claude while he went to fetch June. They appeared back at the car in ten minutes.

"Claude, I am so happy you are coming to visit and stay a while with us. You will find the farm very different."

June couldn't contain her enthusiasm and talked about the farm, her horses and her children almost nonstop.

As they continued southward, Claude enjoyed the scenery. The highway cut through hills and climbed through densely forested areas. They continually were passing by brilliant green paddocks containing cattle and thousands of sheep.

Dave turned off the main highway onto a dirt road that twisted and turned its way down to a narrow bridge over a stream. They climbed up a steep incline and June proclaimed.

"There it is. This is our farm."

Ahead was a stately white house. There were sheds and a barn near it. Further back from the house was a track with white railings and a stable. Outside the stable two girls were brushing a beautiful black stallion. Claude took it all in….especially the girls. June was watching him.

"That's Lightning Prince. He's about to travel to the States for breeding and sale. He is a champion horse. Claude, I saw you looking at my stablehands. Don't get any ideas. It has taken me years to find good ones like those two, but there again love is sometimes too strong. As long as its love and not lust."

At that comment, Dave Mathews burst into laughter.

"June, he's French and he's young. Don't spoil his dreams."

Claude noticed the road continued past the house and beyond the stable to where a group of small cottages stood. He wondered what purpose they served.

They pulled up at the farmhouse next to a tractor and other pieces of farming equipment. Dave got out of the car and opened the door for June before he assisted Claude out from the rear seat.

Claude stepped out into a cooler air than he had experienced in Auckland. It was laced with the smell of the farm. He took his bags and followed June and Dave up the stairs. As he entered the house, a rich aroma of cooking greeted him. An older woman appeared and June introduced her to Claude.

"This is my mother, Abilene. She lives with us now. My father passed away about a year ago and the old house was too large and too much work. She loves it here and having the grandchildren around. That fantastic aroma you smell is one of her traditional roast lamb recipes. You are in for a treat. We have our evening meal early because Dave has to be at the cowshed to start the milking of the herd at five every morning. He has two hands to help him. The milking needs to be completed by eight for when the Co-operative milk tanker arrives."

Claude made a slight bow and stepped forward to shake Abilene's hand. He was then taken to a guest bedroom by June.

"I think you will find everything you need in here. There are towels and spare bedding should you need them. The bathroom is at the end of the corridor. Come to the kitchen after you are settled in."

Claude unpacked and changed into some casual clothing. He had decided to take a walk around the farm and had a particular interest in visiting the stables.

As he was leaving the house, Mathew's children decided to join him. They chatted and ran ahead of him, all the time asking questions and showing him things on the farm. He walked in the direction of the stables but noticed the black stallion was gone. He looked beyond the stable to the track and saw the stablehands exercising two horses.

They reached the railings surrounding the track and Claude leaned forward to watch. He found the horses to be magnificent. One of the girls waved to him as they passed by him. The kids called out to her.

"Sarah, can we pat them in the stables?"

"That's alright, but you will need to go home soon for your dinner."

"We want to say goodbye to them before they leave for America."

The children then started running toward the stable. Claude followed them.

Chapter 56

In the stables, Sarah led the horse to a pen. The children grabbed an apple from a bowl that was sitting on a table at the back area of the stables. They ran to Lightning Prince and the horse lowered it's head and took the apple. Claude stood watching. He found the agility of such a large horse astonishing. He introduced himself to Sarah.

"I am Claude de Passioné. I will be staying with the Mathews for a few days. That is a beautiful horse. He seems to obey you well. How old is he? He is huge."

"Hi, I'm Sarah. Yes, he is a well-behaved horse. He's two years and measures at seventeen hands. Later this week he will be shipped with some other horses to Kentucky in America. A horse like this costs a small fortune. June is an excellent breeder. She has bred and sent horses to Saudi Arabia and other countries. She is widely known for her prize-winning horses."

"I don't know much about horses or that business. I am from France and my family owns vineyards and wineries."

"That sounds very romantic. What are you doing here?"

"I have been studying for the past three years and have decided to do some traveling in order to experience different cultures. I am planning on staying here in New Zealand for a while. Maybe get a casual job."

"There is a lot to see in this small country. It is deceptive all that exists here. We have glaciers, alps, lakes and of course Rotorua with its geysers and boiling mud pools. I am sure you will find a lot to see and do. Have you ever ridden a horse before?"

Claude was concerned. He had never considered doing such a thing.

"No, I am a bit scared of them. I would like to try."

"I will talk with June. We have a very docile horse that is used to give riding lessons. I will see if she agrees for me to give you a lesson."

Claude looked closely at Sarah. He couldn't guess her age. Her hair was a ginger blonde and she had natural blush on her high cheeks. She appeared to be in remarkably fit condition.

"Sarah, thank you. I must go back to the house now. The children will be given their dinner soon."

As he turned to leave, he hesitated and turned back to Sarah.

"What are those little cottages over there?"

"The farm hires seasonal workers during hay season and at other times of the year. Those cottages are accommodation for the hired hands. I live here in the first one."

Claude nodded and called to the children to join him for the walk back to the farmhouse. The aroma of the roast lamb suddenly made him hungry. Abilene was setting the table and organizing plates and silverware. June was on the phone in the kitchen having, what he assumed, a business call. When she was finished she turned to Claude.

"Did you enjoy your walk. I saw you at the stables talking to Sarah. I'm sure she's trying to get you on a horse."

"Yes, but I'm not sure I want to do that. Always been terrified of them hurting or biting me. Sarah said that Lightning Prince is going to America. How are they shipped? By boat I imagine."

"No. The airline has converted a plane into a flying stable. They took an older freight plane and equipped it with pens and a veterinary clinic. The horses are given a mild sedative before they are loaded onto the plane. During the trip, they are accompanied by two vets. The horse breeding industry here is very active and our horses are in international demand. I will be going to the airport for the loading. Would you like to join us and see how it is done?"

"I would love to see how it's done. Thank you."

Moments later Dave Mathews arrived in the house with another tall, dark-haired man. June hurried over to greet him.

"Doc, you don't know how happy I am to see you. I was getting worried."

"Don't worry. Everything is done. The vaccination and International Health Certificates are done. The full medical file and check have been completed. All of the customs and export papers are with the shipping company. All that remains now is for you to get Lightning Prince trailered and to the airport for the Wednesday flight."

"Thank you. If we didn't have such a good vet like you I'm not sure we would be able to run our business."

Dave had watched the exchange. He grinned and slapped the vet on the shoulder.

"Now Doc, what will you have to drink. I remember you liked Guinness."

He turned to Claude and introduced him to the vet.

"Are you going to join us for a drink, Claude? You can come and hear all the Docs country vet tales of sick cows, sheep, dogs, and God knows what else."

The vet spoke to Claude.

"It's really not that exciting. I am sure I would prefer to hear about your trip and country. Dave has told me you are from a wine family in France."

Chapter 57

The next morning Claude joined Dave to go and watch the milking of the herd. Before they left the house, Dave threw a pair of worn gumboots to Claude.

"Better put them on. A lot of water and muck in the milking shed. Your shoes wouldn't survive."

Claude pulled on the boots and the pair walked the brief distance to the shed. The cows were standing in a pasture next to the milking shed. They seemed restless waiting to enter the shed. Dave pushed open a door and immediately two other men appeared from the shiny stainless railings that housed the cows during the milking.

Dave introduced Claude.

"These are my milking hands, George and Andy. They live in those little cottages you saw from the stables. They are good workers. Look after things when I'm away from the farm."

George threw open a wide door and the cows slowly walked in in a line. They seemed to automatically choose the stalls. Andy slapped the milking equipment onto their udders. A pump was running noisily. George returned and turned an old radio on. He turned the volume high.

"It soothes the cows. They love listening to heavy metal at five in the morning."

Claude was fascinated. He watched as milk flowed into the glass containment device before it pumped up and into a huge stainless holding tank.

He moved in the aisleway where the cows entered. He was standing close to the rear of a cow when the cow raised it's tail and dropped a cow cake at his feet. It hit the floor with a splatter and sprayed up and onto Claude's legs. Dave couldn't contain his laughter.

"Well, Claude. Welcome to milking. You are now officially part of the gang here."

Claude looked at the mess running down his jeans with disdain.

"Don't worry mate. June does a wash every day. We get pretty dirty working the farm. It's all part of it. Now come here and I will teach you how to milk one since you've been christened."

As the morning progressed, Claude found himself adept at attaching the suction caps to the cow's teats. Dave had been watching him and was impressed.

"You're just like a regular share milker. Those are the guys who go farm to farm and work milking and share the profits."

When the milking had finished, June arrived driving a tractor towing a trailer loaded with some wooden posts.

Dave looked over the items on the trailer and called to George and Andy to join him. June jumped down from the tractor. George and Andy leaped up onto the trailer and seated themselves. Dave turned to Claude.

"Go back with June. We're going to fix some posts where the fence has collapsed. Be about an hour. Going to be ready for a feast when we get back."

Black exhaust fumes spewed from the tractor as Dave accelerated away.

"Let's go back to the house. I think I am going to have to prepare a big meal for all you, men."

As they neared the house, the children were running toward them. The boy was carrying a tin bucket.

June called out to them.

"Be careful and don't take too long. I will be preparing a meal. Your father will be back with George and Andy in an hour. Get back in time to clean up."

She turned to Claude.

"They are going up to the paddock," she said pointing to a fence at the top of the hill. "They went to pick up the duck eggs. The ducks lay them in the grass up there. I also think you need to change and wash. Give me those dirty clothes and they will be washed with all the other laundry I have."

Even though Claude had only been at the farm a few hours he was enjoying it immensely.

While walking they encountered Sarah. She spoke with June and arranged for Claude to receive some riding lessons. He was petrified.

"Claude, the horse I will use is Jojo. She is almost twenty years old and very patient. I will teach you about the horse first before we even attempt riding. You must never let a horse sense your fear or they will take advantage."

"I am going to freshen up and change into clean clothing. It is eight. Can we meet at the stables at eleven? I wish to contact my family back in France. It will be eight at night now. I should be able to reach them at the Chateau."

June and Claude left Sarah and continued to the house.

"June, how did you start breeding horses?"

"My father was a professional racehorse breeder. I learned from him. It is in my blood."

"I never knew much about horses. They really scare me."

At the farmhouse, Claude made his call to the Chateau. The phone was answered by a male voice that he did not recognize. He asked to speak to Marie-France. Minutes ticked by until she came to the phone. When she found it was Claude she was ecstatic.

"Claude, where are you? What have you been doing? Have you made new friends? Have you met a future wife yet?"

The questions continued to pour out of her. Claude provided her with a report of his trip and where he was staying. He told her of how much he was enjoying the farm. She was surprised by this.

"Claude you never liked animals as a boy. This doesn't seem like you. Are you sure there is no woman at that farm who is trying to capture you? Can't trust farmer's wives."

Claude considered how nothing had changed with her. He inquired about the Marquis.

"Is my father there? May I speak to him?"

"No, since he got involved with those Italians he has spent a lot of time in Italy. It annoys me. He has never asked me to go there with him. It's very strange and he no longer wears that stupid sailor hat. I think he's going senile. I am left here and I'm lonely. Come back home please."

"I will come home when I finish the trip. It has been going well."

"Please come home to your loving mother."

Claude had never heard any words of kindness from her before. He was shocked.

"I must go now. Here is the telephone number to contact me. I will be here a few more days."

He hung up and joined the family and the workers for the steak and egg breakfast that Abilene had prepared. When he had finished, he left to meet Sarah at the stables.

She was waiting for him with a radiant smile on her face.

"Good morning, Claude. Are you ready for some lessons?"

Claude attempted to maintain his composure, though he was absolutely terrified.

"I am not certain that this is a good idea."

Sarah laughed at him.

"You will be fine. Come let's go inside and I will introduce you to Jojo."

Chapter 58

At the stables, Sarah waited for Claude. He was late arriving. It was obvious to Sarah that Claude was nervous.

"Claude, learning to ride is not easy., It is important that you don't let a horse sense that you are scared. They will know and take advantage. What is it that you are scared of?"

"They are so big. I worry they will trample me or bite. They could crush me as they are so heavy."

"Don't worry. Jojo is old and very mild mannered. She has never thrown a rider, but I guess there could be a first. I am of course just joking. Let me go and fetch her."

Moments later she emerged with Jojo, a grey mare. The horse dipped its head and snorted toward Claude. He started to back away.

"No Claude. You must stay. Don't let her frighten you. She is attempting to smell your body scent. Take a small step up to her."

Hesitantly, he moved to the horse. Sarah took his hand and raised it to stroke the horse She then handed the reins to

Claude and told him to start walking and lead the horse. Jojo followed gently behind him.

"Walk her around the perimeter of the paddock. That will calm her."
Back at the stable, Sarah handed him some carrots for the horse as a treat.

"I am trying to make her confident of you and quell your nervousness. You are doing well."
Centered in the stirrups.
Jojo crunched the carrots and nudged Claude for more. He was starting to like the old horse.

"See, she is accepting you. Soon I will get the saddle and tack her for you. I will lead the horse around once you are mounted and ready. It will be at a slow pace."

She led the horse over to a trough and watched as Jojo greedily drank. She returned and handed the reins to Claude.

"Here you hold these. I will go and get the tack."

Sarah returned with a saddle and rest if the tack. She prepared the horse for riding. When it was ready she fetched a mounting block to make it easier for Claude to mount the horse. He eased himself onto the horse. It slightly flexed under his weight and then settled down.

"It is important you sit straight and keep your toes forward and your heels down and the balls of your feet centered in the stirrups."

Sarah led the horse away from the stable and again they walked the perimeter of the paddock. They circled twice. Claude was amazed at the gentle rocking motion of the ride. He had assumed that riding would have been filled with a series of bumpy jolts.

"Claude, we will stop at the stables. I will fetch my horse and we will go on a serious ride. It seems you are a fast learner. Jojo seems very content. Are you still afraid?"

"I am still a little scared. What happens if the horse runs or rears up?"

"Keep a gentle contact with the reins on her mouth and relax your legs by her sides. Jojo has never thrown anyone."

Sarah brought a chestnut mare from the stable and saddled it up ready to ride. She hoisted herself onto the horse and stopped beside Claude.

"Now ride beside me. Let me go a little ahead and then give a gentle pull. Jojo will follow and then I will drop back beside you. Hold the reins as I showed you, through your hand but over the little fingerwith your thumbs on top.

They followed the road out to the main farm gate. Sarah turned her horse and led them down into a gully with a creek flowing through it. The small creek was bordered with high native trees that Claude could not identify. Bellbirds were chirping from low shrubs bordering the water. Claude listened to the unique song. He felt at peace on the farm.

They surfaced out of the gully onto wide fields of grazing sheep. Sarah decided to pick up the pace.

"Claude, do you feel confident that we can attempt a trot? It will be bumpy. You will need to rise up and down in the saddle. This is called posting."

"Yes, but not too fast. I never imagined that riding a horse could be so relaxing. I want to do this again."

"I will slowly give you some more advanced lessons. For now, just concentrate on controlling the horse. The rest will come easily.

Chapter 59

The horse lessons had gone well and Claude had discovered a new passion that he had never experienced. The life on the farm was teaching him many things.

The day for transporting Lightning Prince to the airport arrived. Dave backed the farm pickup truck with a horse trailer attached, up to the stable and June and Sarah led the magnificent horse out of the stable.

They took the horse into the adjoining paddock and walked it around. Doc, the vet, arrived to administer the sedative before the long drive up to Auckland airport.

Claude watched the proceedings with keen interest. He wasn't sure but thought he had seen tears in June's eyes as the horse was loaded into the trailer. He went to her and placed his hand on her shoulder.

"You seem to be upset. Is everything all right?"

"I get upset when they leave. Lightning Prince is special. He will win many races for the owners."

When the horse was secure in the trailer, Dave announced they were leaving. Claude crawled into the rear cabin of the pickup truck. June sat in the front seat next to Dave. They started the journey to the airport.

During the trip, Dave pointed out areas of interest to Claude. He was enjoying the trip and seeing the paddocks filled with sheep and cattle. As they approached Auckland, the rural landscape changed as they entered suburbia.

While driving to the cargo entrance, they all fell silent. Dave stopped at the entrance gate and was given directions where to drive and unload for the transport of the horse.

At the cargo shed, Claude noticed rows of individual small pens. He asked June about them.

"The horses are comfortably secured in these pens, which are then loaded into the plane. They stay in them until they reach there destination. Some are padded for horses that may become skittish during the trip. The flight always has some spare vacant pens in case of this. The horses are very expensive and valuable to the new owners. Great care is taken to keep them comfortable and relaxed for the flight."

Lightning Prince was taken from the trailer by Sarah. She led him quietly to some officials who checked the horse and the papers. When all was confirmed, the horse was taken to a pen for loading.

When all was complete, Dave started the drive back. He stopped at a small town for them to have a late lunch.

The return trip to the farm was uneventful. Claude found himself falling asleep. The early hour milking time was hitting him.

Back at the farm, Claude got out to assist Dave with unhitching the trailer.

"We're making you work for your stay. Better get some good sleep tonight. Tomorrow the shearers arrive to start shearing the lambs. I think we will teach you that as well. It's hard back-breaking work. You interested?"

"Yes, I am. I must start taking some photos of all this."
That evening as they were completing the meal, Dave looked over at Claude.

"This is a busy season here for us. It's late spring and we're moving into summer. I had an idea. How would you like to stay longer and do work on the farm? We can set you up in one of the cottages. There are lots of things to see and do close by, and if you decide to take longer trips away I am sure we can make that work for you."

Claude could not believe his luck or fully comprehend the words.

"That is a kind offer. Yes, I would like to stay. I enjoy the life here."

"Good, then tomorrow June can help you set up one of the cottages."

Claude thought of Sarah being his immediate neighbor. He appreciated her but in a different way to the others.

The next morning, June accompanied Claude to the cottages. Two were occupied by George and Andy, and the other by Sarah. They were basically all the same inside. Claude selected the one directly across from Sarah's. It was completely equipped with stove, bathroom, and shower and had a combined kitchen and living area. Claude found it perfect.

The days on the farm were busy and weeks flew by. On some weekends he and Sarah would spend time visiting towns and beaches or hiking in the mountains. His life had become settled. After spending two years at the farm, he wondered about France and how it would seem.

He was working with Dave repairing a shed when June sped toward them at high speed. She jumped from the car.

"Claude, there has been an urgent phone call for you at the house. It is from France. Somebody named Jacques said it was an emergency. He wants you to call him."

Dave frowned and told Claude to go and find out what the emergency was.

Claude dropped his tools and ran with June to the car.

At the house, he called the number for the servants quarters. Jacques answered.

"Mon Dieu. Thank God I have reached you. Something terrible has happened to the Marquis. Marie-France has relapsed and is in the hospital. We need you to return immediately. The police here are involved as well as the Carabinieri in Italy. Because I am not family they will tell me nothing. Can you return?"

"I will check and call you back. Please wait for my call."

Claude hung up the phone and tried to understand what could have happened that involved both the Italian and French police.

He found June waiting in the kitchen.

"What has happened?"

"There is an emergency. My father is involved. The police are not giving out information. I need to return to France immediately."

They sat and examined the best and fastest way for Claude to get back to Bordeaux. The best alternative was a flight that night on Air New Zealand from Auckland to Los Angeles and a connection with a direct Air France flight to Paris. Claude phoned the airline and made the arrangements.

Dave had returned and June had told him of the events,

"Claude, I will drive you up there. Let's get you packed. We don't have a lot of time."

June went to the cottage and helped Claude pack a small case. He decided to leave his other items as he intended to return.

They drove fast to get him to the airport in time for the flight that left just before midnight.

The airport terminal was busy. June and Dave stayed with Claude until he was boarding.

"Please contact us from France. We are concerned. Let us know what we can do to help."

He walked through to the gate feeling a combination of confusion and sadness at leaving.

Chapter 60

On the plane, Claude was seated in the first class cabin. The cabin crew fussed around preparing for the sixteen-hour flight to Los Angeles. He had settled into his seat when a tall striking blonde girl stopped beside him in the aisle.

"Excuse me. I think I'm in the seat beside you."

Claude quickly arose and assisted her to place some luggage in the overhead compartment. She thanked him and slid into her seat.

"Since we are going to be together for almost a day, I should introduce myself. I'm Claire Waters."

"And I'm Claude de Passioné from France. Pleased to meet you."

Claire smiled at Claude. He was struck by her natural charm and beauty.

A flight attendant stopped at their seats and offered refreshments. Claire ordered a Chablis and Claude asked for a Cabernet. After the drinks were delivered they sat talking.

The cabin lights flickered as the plane's engines were started. There was a jerk as the plane was pushed back for the terminal. The plane turned and in the darkness of night, lumbered down the runway before halting and turning. The jet engines whined louder as the plane started to roll for takeoff.

Claire turned to Claude.

"I am a really nervous flyer. Can I hold your hand? It calms me."

She reached across and firmly gripped his hand. Claude felt what seemed like an electric tingle pass through him. He had never experienced this before. She tightened her grip as the plane accelerated and lifted off. Even though they were airborne, she continued holding his hand.

Claude needed to visit the toilet and told Claire he needed to stand up. She released his hand. When he returned, he found a newspaper had been left on his seat by the attendant. He scanned the paper before dozing off into a deep sleep. The day had tired him.

Hours passed by until he felt the hand of a flight attendant gently shaking him awake. He awoke and found that Claire's head was resting on his other shoulder. Her long blonde hair was hanging down his chest.

"Sir, are you comfortable? We will be serving a light meal. Will your wife want a meal?"

"She isn't my wife. It is someone I've never met before."

The attendant frowned.

"Should I wake her. She is all over you."

"No, it is fine. Let her sleep. Bring her a meal. I am sure she will wake by herself."

Thirty minutes went by before the attendant returned with a menu of meals for first class passengers. As she handed them to Claude, Claire stirred from her sleep.

"Good early morning, Miss. Are you interested in a light meal?"

She sat up startled.

"I am so sorry. I must have dozed off and slumped onto you. I apologize."

"You were no problem. I hope you enjoyed your sleep."

Claire took the menu and selected a selection of cheeses, Paté on warm toastettes, and fresh grapes. Claude selected the warm chicken and cheese sandwich.

"Can I ask you where you are traveling to?"

"Yes. I am going home. There has been some emergency with my father. I do not have any details. I was called earlier in the day. This is a rushed trip for me. What about you?"

"I am traveling back to California. I have an apartment in Sausalito. I have been in New Zealand for the past three years studying veterinary science. My former boyfriend was from there. He encouraged me to study there. I thought we would marry, but it wasn't to be."

Her eyes misted over.

"I was a damn fool. He never told me he was already married. I could've killed him."

Not knowing what to say, he changed the subject.

"Were you born in California?"

"No, I am originally from Wisconsin. That is where my family has their business. What about you. Where are you from?"

"I am from Bordeaux. My father is a Marquis and we own wineries and vineyards there. I was taking a trip after graduating from the Sorbonne in Paris. Soon I will need to select a career. What business is your family in?"

"I'm sure you will know it. The business was started by my parents, Raine Waters and his wife Rose Waters. It's the world famous dog food company Woof Bites. The company makes the dog food and also cookies called Snack Bangers. The products are sold around the world."

After the meals were served, the cabin lights were dimmed and Claude settled back in the seat and arranged himself for a sleep. As they traveled east the skies lightened and the plane became alive with people talking and moving around. Passengers queued at the washroom doors. His sleep was finished and he decided to continue his chat with Claire.

He had noticed throughout the flight that Claire was often reaching into her bag and removing a cellophane wrapped treat of some kind. This seemed to happen every twenty minutes. He was curious.

"What are those that you are eating?"

"They are my favorite snack. They are called Twinkies, I am addicted to them."

Claude asked of her plans upon returning to The States.

"I intend to establish a clinic in Sausalito, but really wish to treat farm animals and other large animals. I have been invited for an interview at the San Francisco zoo. I will need to make that decision before too long. Tell me about your family's business."

He launched into a long description of the winemaking operations. She was entranced as he spoke.
Her interest in Claude was growing. She surprised herself at openly flirting with him. Soon they were making jokes and the barriers fell as they consumed more wine.

Shortly before the descent into Los Angeles airport, Claire took a notebook from her bag and tore out a page. She wrote her address and the telephone number to her apartment. Claude borrowed the pen and reciprocated.

The plane landed heavily and sat on the tarmac waiting for a gate to be available. Claude looked out the plane's window. The sky appeared hazy from the heavy smog. He wondered how anyone could live in that every day.

When the plane reached the terminal, they both exited together. She leaned forward to kiss him goodbye. Claude was expecting a normal kiss on the cheek but was shocked when she French kissed him. Now he knew it was more than just a chance meeting with a fellow passenger. He kissed her back with full force. She partially raised her leg and leaned into him. Passing passengers smiled and looked on.

Chapter 61

Claude found his way through the terminals for the Air France location. He checked in at the counter and was directed to the first class passenger lounge, where he sat reading the latest French newspapers until his flight was ready for boarding.

As he entered the aircraft, he noticed that Some of the cabin crew were the same he had flown with on his trip from France. A couple recognized him and gave waves.

He sat recalling the week he had spent with Julia touring the California coast. They were pleasant memories. He decided to ask one of the crew members about her. He drew no reaction and a somewhat negative response. Again, Claude was confused. It was a little while later that an older attendant approached him.

"I understand you were asking about Julia. Are you a friend of hers?"

"I spent time with her in California. We toured the coast. I have been away for over two years now. I have not had any contact with her."

"I'm sorry to say that after her last trip to California, two years ago, she returned to France and committed suicide."

The statement hit Claude hard. He was at a loss for words.

"She had a brief affair with a Frenchman on the last trip she took. Such a loss of a beautiful person."

Claude hoped she would not connect with the fact it was he that she had spent time with in California. He agreed.

"That truly is sad. I am sorry to hear this. It makes me sad."

The attendant nodded. Claude asked for a newspaper, hoping it would distract him. The attendant left and returned with a copy of Le Monde. Claude thanked her and sank back in his seat to read.

He scanned the front page. It was all the same news as he remembered. Politicians arguing, farmers complaining, strikes threatened…nothing seemed to have changed during his time away. He folded over the page and there on page 3 the bold headlines hit him.

'Prominent Marquis and famed French winemaker found dead in Italy.'

He rapidly read the story. It was scarce on details. No names were given. The police were withholding information pending family contact.

Claude felt a pit in his stomach. He recalled his father's involvement with Countess Cortelli. He was sure it must be his father.

The flight dragged on for what seemed endless hours. Claude was impatient and worried. He requested other newspapers and scanned them only to find no news of the death in them. He was becoming increasingly frustrated. He ordered a heavy red wine and after several glasses fell into a deep sleep.

It was late morning when the plane descended into the Paris airport. After clearing formalities, Claude made his way to the station to purchase a train ticket to Bordeaux. He next called Jacques at the Chateau and provided him with the arrival time of the train. Jacques would meet him and drive him to the Chateau.

Jacques was waiting at the station. He ran forward to help Claude with the luggage.

"Jacques, what is going on? I saw the news in Le Monde. Is that my father? No one is telling me anything."

"I really do not know. The police visited the Chateau and spoke to Mare-France. She was hysterical and collapsed she has been in the hospital for the last two days. From the police, I understand she is incoherent. I have tried to get answers. No one will speak with me. If you wish, we can go to the central police station here. I am sure they will tell you everything."

They made their way to the car and drove to the precinct.

Part 3

The reckoning

Chapter 62

Tuscany, Italy, 2 Days earlier

The Marquis escorted Countess Cortelli out of the "Teatro di Tradizione". They had enjoyed a fine evening of opera. The Countess wished to dine with a late meal before returning to her country castle with the Marquis.

They joined with friends and other theater patrons and headed to the Alle Terrazze restaurant in Palermo. The Marquis loved this establishment. It was old and only requested by those who could afford the expense. Most diners were either from high society or wealthy business owners. The Countess was well known and had a special table set aside for her.

At the restaurant, the Marquis ordered Beef fillet steak with cognac sauce, green and pink pepper berries, while the Countess ordered Ravioli stuffed with burrata cheese, shrimps and artichokes. To accompany the meal, the Marquis ordered a bottle of Chianti from the Countesses vineyard.

Over the past three years, the relationship between the Countess and Marquis Charles had developed way beyond business. They had become passionate lovers. The Countess had accepted a large investment from the Marquis in the Chianti producing vineyards. Her husband, the Count was less than happy with the French partner and showed his displeasure openly. The Countess enjoyed and appreciated the rivalry between them. She loved playing with fire, it excited her.

They ate leisurely and reviewed thoughts of the opera with their friends. Everyone agreed it had been a fine performance.

The Marquis and Countess remained while the others left. When they were alone, she spoke to him.

"Dear, you will come and be with me tonight at the castle. The Count has gone visiting friends in Austria. He will be gone for days. I want you to stay with me."

"I should return to France. I have business to look after. That new vineyard is just starting to produce some fine quality whites. I need to be there to promote them."

"I want you to stay here and promote me."

The Marquis laughed and agreed. He was tired of Marie-France and her eccentricities. He had been pondering ways to get rid of her. He wondered if it would be possible to manipulate a situation to free the Countess from the Count.

It was late when they started back to the castle. The night was extremely dark. There was no moon and the roads to her home were dimly lit. The Marquis took extreme care with his driving. They wound up through hills and came to the grey stone castle. It was surrounded by her vineyards. Rows of olive trees grew between the vines. Cypress cedars stood like sentries at her front entrance. It was a grand palace and reflected the wealth of their nobility.

They were barely up to the marble stairs at the entrance, when the Countess shed her coat and spun to the Marquis. She embraced him and engaged in long kisses.

"Let us have another drink and then we shall go to bed. I'm all yours tonight."

He went into the large parlor room while she went to fetch wine from the cellar. She returned with a Chianti Classico and two crystal glasses.

It was almost two in the morning before they retired to the huge bed in the Countesses room. Although it was late they engaged in ribald sex like horny teenagers. Eventually, they fell asleep.

The door to the room cracked open and the hinges creaked. The Marquis turned to look at the door. The Count stood there and leveled the pistol. Loud shots rang out. Bullets struck the Marquis through the neck and chest. Blood spurted from the severed jugular vein. The Count quickly turned the pistol on the Countess and fired. The shot went wild. Instead of hitting her in the chest it went high and removed the top of her scalp. Blood and brains splattered up the wall. The force of the bullets caused her to fall from the bed. The Count put the gun in his mouth and pulled the trigger. It was a scene of carnage.

Chapter 63

Central Police Station, Bordeaux. 2 days later.

Claude waited impatiently for the detective to arrive. It was a cold and inhospitable place. It reminded him of his misfortune years earlier. He had never forgotten the feeling of hopelessness that had engulfed him as he suffered in the cells. He looked at the dull grey walls of the office he had been escorted into. There was no personality or warmth. He wanted to leave but needed to stay and understand what had happened. The door finally opened and the detective entered accompanied by two men in tight-fitting suits.

"I am Inspector Geraud and these men are from our government. The situation is serious. It involves members of the nobility in Italy and we do not want a major problem with the Italians.

It seems your father, the Marquis had been having an affair with the Countess Cortelli. She had involved him in their businesses in a major way. The Italian government is angry. Your father had invested in some of the country's best wineries. They are concerned that control will be lost by the Italians.

Your father was shot and killed in bed with the Countess. The Count also killed himself. It is a major scandal. The Italians are trying to keep it all quiet.

It is complicated because the Carabinieri is causing problems. They will not allow the body of your father to be released without identification by a family member. You will need to go to Italy for the identification. I will have one of these men go with you.

There have been efforts by the newspapers to find out more details. I ask you not to speak to them at this time.

I am sorry for your loss. We attempted to resolve this with your mother but she is incapable of making any decisions at this time or having the ability to travel.

I suggest you come here in the morning and I will have arranged travel to Italy for you and one of these men."

There was little Claude could do but other than to agree. He left the police station and rejoined Jacques who had waited patiently for him at the car.

They were driving back to the Chateau when Claude changed his mind.

"Jacques, take me to the hospital. I wish to see my mother."

At the hospital, Claude met with the head nurse and a young doctor.

"I am sorry but the recent news she received has set affected her greatly. Her dementia seems to have progressed. At this stage, she is no longer capable of managing her affairs. I assume you will be responsible for her. We will need the authorization to start certain treatments."

"I have just arrived back in the country. I need to attend to the situation with my father. I will contact our legal advisors early tomorrow."

"We will await your instructions before we start any treatments. Please do not leave it for too long."

"May I visit her?"

"Yes, but she may not be lucid. I warn you it may be an unpredictable situation."

Claude was escorted to the room in which Marie-France lay. She was the only patient in the room. She was sleeping. He touched her arm and she sprang awake and stared up vacantly at him. Her forehead twitched as she tried to place his face.

"Marie-France. It is me, Claude."

She continued to look at him and in a croaking voice spoke to him.

"Did you say you know Claude? He is my son."

"I am your son. I am Claude."

She continued to stare at him, not comprehending what he was telling her. The doctor stepped forward.

"Claude, I think this is enough. She is on heavy medication. I don't want her to get agitated. She creates a lot of problems when that happens and that is why she is in this room alone. There are times we have to restrain her in the bed. I think we should leave. I will advise you of a better time to visit before she is medicated."

Claude returned to the car. He was depressed and wanted to drive home in silence and consider the situation he was in. He needed a friend to speak with.

At the Chateau, it was dark and quiet. Claude entered and decided to sit and devise a plan. He poured himself a large glass of wine and went to the salon. A servant entered.

"Is there anything I can get you or anything we, the staff can do to help."

"No thank you. I would like it if you can have the fire lit. I will be sitting here for a while and would enjoy that."

"I will have it done immediately."

As he sat beside the fire, he wondered about his role now his father was dead and his mother insane. He had never expected a situation like this. He started to have regrets for leaving on the trip. A lot had happened in the three years he had been gone and the additional four years he had studied at the Sorbonne. He was feeling guilty. The wine was not helping his mood or spirits. He checked the time in California. It was early afternoon. He took the phone and called the number that Claire had scribbled for him. The phone at the other end rang for a long time. There was no answering machine. After a long delay, the phone was answered. It was a female voice with a heavy southern accent. He did not recognize the voice and started to apologize. It dawned on him that Claire had given him the wrong number. He was about to hang up when the woman asked if he had called for Claire. He confirmed this.

"She's gone to the store. Should be back in ten minutes. Can I get her to call you?"

"No, I will call back. Please tell her that Claude called."

He returned to his chair beside the fire. He made some decisions.

Chapter 64

Again he phoned the number. This time it was Claire who answered.

"Claude, I am so happy to hear from you so soon. Is everything alright?"

"No Claire. I have returned to a bad situation. I am alone here and trying to decide what I should do."

He relayed the information regarding the Marquis death and the mental state of his mother. She listened attentively.

"Claude, I will come. I have the time I will make arrangements now and call you back."

He started to object but her word was final.

Hours went by before the phone jingled. He rushed to answer it.

"Claude, I have booked to Paris. I was able to get a flight for tonight."

"Good. When you arrive in Paris, call Jacques at the Chateau on this number. I am not sure if I will be here. I need to go with the police to Italy to identify my father. They will not release his body until then. I will need to make arrangements to bring him home."

He spent the rest of the night in a restless sleep. He dressed early and went to the police station as agreed. Detective Giraud was waiting.

"I will accompany you. We will take the short four-hour flight to Florence where they are keeping your father's body. I will advise the Carabinieri of our arrival."

At the airport, in Florence, they were met by uniformed offices and taken to a waiting police car. They drove erratically to a nondescript grey building and pulled in through old iron gates into an area to park beside the building.

One of the officers turned to Claude and spoke.

"We are here at the morgue. It is not a very nice place. I suggest you prepare for the worse. Here take this bag in case you need to vomit. There will be the strong smell of chemicals used on the corpses and the smell of death."

Claude felt his stomach involuntarily flip. Bile rose in his throat at the thought of identifying his father in such a place. He swallowed hard.

The officer held the door open for Claude and the detective. They entered the desolate looking building and were stopped at a desk in front of an old wooden swinging door. Claude tried to estimate the age of the building. It had formerly been a hospital.

A scruffy security guard sat at the desk. He recognized the Italian officers and stood to open the door and admit them. He nodded at Claude and Detective Giraud.

They continued down a narrow corridor and entered a small room, devoid of any furniture. A morgue attendant came in with papers and asked for Claude's identification in order to complete the identification process. He left to bring the Marquis body to the room. The large door at the rear of the room was pushed open to allow the attendant to wheel in a gurney with the body. As he did so the door stayed open exposing the autopsy room. Claude couldn't resist the urge to look. He regretted it immediately. An autopsy was in progress. A headless corpse lay on a stainless table. Its chest cavity was cut open and what appeared to be a liver hung in a silver scale hung above the table. An assortment of medical instruments, saws and knives were laid out on a bench beside the table. Blue coated technicians leaned over the body.

It was too much for Claude. As the attendant pulled back a sheet to expose the face of the Marquis, Claude projectile vomited. It flew across the gurney hitting the attendant and one of the officers. Claude turned and ran out to the corridor, where he painted the wall with a pink slime as a result of the red wine he had drunk on the flight. The corridor seemed to spin and he fainted to the floor.

He came to lying on a stretcher. The officers were seated at a table speaking with Detective Giraud. The officer who had been the recipient of Claude's vomit was draped in a towel.

They turned when Claude stirred and sat up.

"What happened? Where am I?"

Detective Giraud spoke.

"You are still at the morgue. You fainted. Many do, so don't worry. We are attempting to get the release papers for your father, so his body can be returned to France. There seems to be some complication. I have no power here to assist. You will need to deal with the authorities as you are immediate family."

Claude asked for water to rinse the acrid taste from his mouth. He was given a blue fluid to rinse his mouth and a kidney bowl to spit out the swill.

"We will wait outside. The coroner who authorizes the release will be here to speak with you about the arrangements for his return. I will wait with these officers outside."

Claude was hating every minute in the morgue. He was aware of the persistent smell of formaldehyde and disinfectant. He kept thinking of the corpse on the table. He shuddered and wanted to be away from the place.

There was a knock at the door and a swarthy middle-aged man entered. He had thick long black hair that was greased back, an oily olive skin and fierce beady eyes.

'I am Frederico, the Coroner. I will be preparing the necessary legal forms for you to take your father home. It will take some time. I am very busy. Maybe a week or two. Of course, there will be costs for the autopsy and storage."

This annoyed Claude, who didn't trust the man. There was something wrong. Why had the officers left him alone with the Coroner? Something was strange.

"I am unable to stay here. There are business matters that need to be looked after in France. Can the process not be quickened?"

"I am sorry. There is nothing I can do. Let me see. You are the famous de Passioné winemaking family are you not? Maybe we can come to some arrangement. Just you and me. It just might be possible to place your paperwork higher in priority, if you know what I mean. A well-placed investment for you."

Claude was astounded that he was being asked to offer a bribe to get the Marquis released, then he remembered that this was Italy."

"How much? He growled.

"I think maybe a thousand American dollars could start the process and another four thousand to get him to the airport."

Claude nodded. The Coroner stood and smiled.

"When can we complete this matter?"

"I will make arrangements immediately."

"It can only be in cash."

"I will leave here now and get the cash."

Chapter 65

Claude returned to the morgue with the cash. He asked the scruffy security guard to fetch Frederico. He was shown into an office and within minutes a smiling Frederico joined. Claude ignored the offered hand. He had no intention of shaking the crooks hand.

"Here is the full five thousand dollars you requested. I guess it would be stupid to ask for a receipt. Make the arrangements. Detective Giraud and I will be flying back to Bordeaux tomorrow morning. Here is the flight information. Just make sure my father's body is on that flight. I have already paid the airline and they will be contacting you regarding the transporting of the coffin. I have arranged with a local funeral director for the coffin and hearse. They are making the arrangements for transport in Bordeaux."

Later on the plane, he told Detective Giraud of the encounter with Frederico at the morgue and the extortion.

"I can not help you. It is the jurisdiction of the Italian police. I can send a report. It will mean you will need to return to Italy. It will be complicated and expensive. Maybe you should just leave it."

The return flight to Bordeaux was tedious and boring. Claude thought of how his life had changed. They arrived back in Bordeaux late afternoon. Claude noticed the black hearse waiting for the plane on the tarmac. For the first time ever he felt a sadness for the Marquis.

It was early evening when he returned to the estate. Lights shone from the salon. He entered to find his new friend Jacques sitting and talking with Claire.

She rushed to him and wrapped him in an embrace.

"Claude, how are you? You look exhausted."

He felt a sudden relaxation ripple through his body. The tiredness of the travel and stress seemed to melt away. He was happy Claire was now with him but didn't understand the effect she had on him. He had never experienced this with any other woman. It confused him. He sank back onto a couch. Jacques left them and went to the wine cellar to select a wine to relax with.

For hours they sat discussing events and how to proceed. Claude advised them that he would be visiting The Cathedral of St. Andrew of Bordeaux to make funeral arrangements. Claire offered to join him.

"Claire, I need to speak privately to Jacques. Have you been settled into a guest room?"

"Yes, Jacques has been a gentleman and arranged everything. He even had my Twinkies taken to the room. In fact, he tried one and loved it."

Claude shot Jacques a look of amazement. He went to Claire and kissed her goodnight.

When she had left, Claude addressed Jacques.

"Jacques, things are going to be different here. Until the legal aspects of the estate are settled, I will be unable to assist here. I remember your desire to work at the winery. I am prepared to make that happen. After the funeral, I will arrange for you to join the vintners and learn the business."

Jacques was speechless.

"Thank you. This is what I have always wanted. I will learn quickly and work toward making the best wines."

His enthusiasm caused Claude to smile.

"I am tired and have a busy few days ahead. I will now retire for the night."

For a few moments, he thought of joining Claire but decided against it. He was too drained.

In the morning he dressed and joined Claire for a breakfast of coffee, croissants, cheese, and fruit before leaving for the Cathedral.

At the Cathedral, he was greeted by the Archbishop who expressed sympathy and extolled all of the Marquis virtues. Claude sat patiently listening to the lies. The Archbishop was obviously worried the large donations the family had made to the church would cease. At least the Marquis had bought himself an extravagant funeral.

Arrangements were finalized. The church would also announce the passing of the Marquis to the parishioners, though no mention would ever be made as to the circumstances under which he died.

Claude then drove to the hospital to visit Marie-France. He was pleased to find her coherent and cheerful upon his arrival.

She seemed to be unaware of the passing of the Marquis. She had forgotten.

Claude was about to remind her of the events when two doctors entered the room.

"Good morning Marie-France. How are you this morning? It seems the new medications have worked. You seem very happy today, in fact, it is good that Claude is here as we have decided to release you and you can go home."

At this news, she gasped and hugged Claude.

"We will arrange for a nurse to take you to the car. In the meantime, I need to spend some time speaking to Claude."

The doctors directed Claude to an office area by the nurse's station, while a nurse went to assist with Marie-France.

"Claude, she is now on very heavy medication. It is important that she take the recommended dosage at the times we have suggested. She is responding well. I suspect the impact of the Marquis death will be blunted by the drugs. It is important she remains calm. Try to avoid situations where she is exposed to anything upsetting. We are available by phone should you need to contact us."

Claude politely thanked them and left to join her at the car, where the nurse stood waiting with Marie-France in a wheelchair.

On the drive to the Chateau, she chattered away continually. Claude decided to announce that he had a friend staying.

"There is someone special I want you to meet. She is American and staying at the Chateau. I think you will like her. She is a veterinary doctor. A very smart and kind girl."

"This is a surprise. Have you finally met someone good enough for us? What is the family's business in America?"

Claude sensed the clouds gathering.

"Her family is in the dog food business. The biggest dog food company in the world. They process the meat, package it and distribute around the world."

Marie-France was shocked.

"The daughter of a dog food canner. How could you get involved with such a person? Go and find a person of our status. The very thought of you with a low-class American. I did not bring you up to waste your life. Get rid of her or I will."

"I think you should not make any comments until you meet her and get to know her. She is lovely."

"Claude, I am not having a dog food princess stay in my house. Get rid of her today."

"I will not. We will discuss this with you later. For now please be calm."

The rest of the trip was driven in silence.

Chapter 66

At the Chateau, Marie- France was escorted inside by two of the servants. Claude advised them to take her to the salon. Claude was curious. He had noticed several cars near the front gates. He looked back down the long driveway. Press reporters were at the gates. The news of the Marquis had leaked. Claude decided to face the reporters.

As he approached the gates, questions were shouted at him constantly. He held up his hand to silence them.

"I am Claude de Passioné, the son of Marquis Charles and Marie-France. I will make a statement regarding the passing of my father and then I ask you to leave us.

My father was on a trip to Italy where he had invested in some winery operations with the Cortelli family. During the night an intruder broke into their home and shot my father, Countess Cortelli and the Count, Italian police are investigating. I have no further information. A funeral service for the Marquis will be held soon at The Cathedral of St Andrew of Bordeaux. Should more information become available, I suggest you contact the local authorities here.

Thank you."

He turned his back and returned to the Chateau where he found Marie-France holding court with several of the female maids. They skeltered when Claude arrived.

"Claude, do you know when the Marquis will be home. I need to plan our dinner. It will just be our family. Have you told Miss dogfood to leave?"

"I have no intention of asking her to leave. I ask you to behave and be the lady I know you can be. Remember that you are French Aristocracy after all."

That comment seemed to register with her.

"Of course and I am beyond such pettiness. Please bring her to meet me."

Claire was dressed elegantly. Her long blonde hair was draped forward over her shoulder and she wore a conservative dress. She went to Marie-France and took her hand while making a slight curtsy.

"I am pleased to meet you. Claude has said such nice things about you," she lied.

Marie-France was flattered. It had been a long time since anyone curtsied her.

"Yes, he is such a wonderful boy. I am so proud of him. He is a brilliant man. Now tell me about you and your family."

Claude excused himself and left them talking. There were a number of phone calls and messages he needed to attend to.

There was an urgent message from the family avocat requesting Claude contact him immediately. He picked up the phone and dialed the number. The avocat answered himself. Claude introduced himself and listened intently to the information the avocat relayed. He was shaking when he hung up. Though he did not drink spirits he found a bottle of scotch on the office shelves and poured himself several glasses before sitting and contemplating his next move. He was now facing matters in which he had no experience or knowledge. Things were happening too fast for him to comprehend.

He returned to the salon to find the women engaged in a discussion about animals and life in America. It seemed that for all her airs, Marie-France had decided to accept Claire.

He joined them and decided to remind her of the death of the Marquis. To his amazement, she didn't say a word but just stared at him as if she didn't understand. Claude remembered the words of the doctors regarding the effects of the medicine. Finally, she spoke.

"Well, that's nice. I hope he enjoys it."

Claude looked over hopelessly at Claire. She nodded.

"Marie-France. You must be tired. Can I assist you to your room for a rest."

"Yes dear. I would like that. Claude, you have brought me a nice new friend."

Claire assisted her to her feet and wrapped an arm around her waist and escorted her to her room.

After fifteen minutes she returned to Claude in the salon.

"I see what you have told me. She is in a very fragile state. I don't think she really understands a lot. You looked very worried when you returned to join us. Is everything alright?

"I don't know yet. I have been asked to visit with our family's legal firm tomorrow. They say it is very urgent"

Chapter 67

While they sat talking, one of the servants knocked then entered.

"Sir, there is a phone call for you from California."

Claude and Claire exchanged startled glances. Claude shot to his feet and rushed out to the phone.

He was relieved to hear the voice on the other end.

"Gidday mate. Barry here. What are you doing Frenchy? Need to talk to you."

Claude told Barry of the recent happenings.

"Well, that's too bad mate. I guess the old fella would have to go at some point. We all do. Better to die in his sheila's bed I reckon."

Claude couldn't help but help smile. Only his Aussie pal could make light of the black situation.

"Barry, what is so important that you are calling me here in France. Is everything alright in California?"

"No mate. It isn't. The owners, those Johnson brothers you met will not invest in the winery or undertake to do the work I recommend. The place is going bust. I think it'll be over in a few weeks. Nothings getting fixed. Men are leaving because of arguments about pay. It's a bloody mess here. You got any jobs up there in France for me. I can teach all those guys how to speak real English when I get there."

"It is possible now that the Marquis has died. Things here will change, but until I know what is happening with the estate I cannot tell you. Tomorrow I will meet with the lawyers. Call me tomorrow at the same time."

Claude was deep in thought when he hung up the phone.

He needed to find a distraction and decided to take Claire for a tour around Bordeaux. She was delighted at the prospect. They drove through surrounding vineyards and into the town. Claire was excited to visit a number of stores selling ladies fashion. Claude was amused and tagged along. It was late when they had finished, so Claude decided to dine in the town.

There were a number of messages marked urgent when they returned to the Chateau. Claude examined them and decided to wait until morning to return calls. The exception he made was to call the Archbishop who wished to confirm funeral arrangements.

That night, Claude and Claire slept together for the first time. They shared gentle passion and pleasure. There was something about Claire that had enraptured Claude. He was convinced he had finally found the right woman.

The next day, he arose and dressed appropriately for the meeting with the avocat. He wondered why the importance and urgency of the meeting.

The receptionist quickly arose from her desk and walked rapidly to a conference room. She knocked at the door and opened it. She leaned in and announced that Claude had arrived. A young lawyer emerged from the room and hurried towards Claude.
"Good morning. My deepest condolences on the death of your father. I had many dealings with him. A fine man. I am Carlo de Vine and I am the official executor for the family estate. There are important matters for us to discuss. My colleagues are waiting."

He found six austere looking lawyers seated around the table. Each one stood, offered their condolences and introduced themselves.

Carlo addressed the assembled legal minds.

"I am sure everyone knows why we are here this morning. As executor of the estate for Marquis Charles de Passioné, it is my duty to carry out his last wishes as written in his will. There are, however, some complications and that is why Signore Bartelli from Florence is here with us. I asked him yesterday to come so I could deal with the complications.

Claude, Marie-France has been declared incompetent and therefore you are the sole heir to the estate, including all businesses, investments, and other assets. There is a provision for the care of Marie-France that I am sure you will find more than satisfactory.

The complication is best explained by Signore Bartelli.
The tall dark handsome lawyer directed his words at Claude.

"In some ways it is simple and in other ways it is complex. The death of the Cortellis is unfortunate and sad. The Countess was the wealthy one. The Count was more a social and convenience toy for her. Your father, the Marquis, had made significant investments into the wine operations she owned. There is a shareholder agreement between the Countess and the Marquis. In the event of her demise, the business passes to the Marquis. The other assets were to pass to the Count if he survived her. He has not. There are no other immediate family members to inherit. The Countess had foreseen the possibility and there modified her will to leave everything to the Marquis. It seems the relationship was one that surpassed just business. Because the Marquis is dead I am advised it will, therefore, pass to you. You are a very wealthy man now, but there are many things to address. There will be taxes, transfer of property titles, and many more details will require attention. I am here to offer you my services in this matter."

Claude was in a state of disbelief.

"I would like time alone with Carlo. I need to consult with him."

The assembled lawyers stood and filed from the room

Chapter 68

Back at the Chateau, he told Claire of the situation. She was at a loss for words and did not know how to react to the news. They talked for hours until he was interrupted with the phone call from Barry Jones.

"Barry, I am unable to speak at present. I will call you back shortly."

He took the phone number and returned to Claire.

"Claude, I must return to California after the funeral. I wish I could stay longer but I have the business of the clinic I am starting. I have to meet with banks and investors. I will leave the day after the funeral. Maybe soon you will come and visit me.."

"I have a better idea. I will fly to California with you. I need to see Barry Jones."

She was thrilled to have him accompany her on the return and agreed wholeheartedly.

The morning of the funeral rolled around. Claude dressed in a formal black suit. Marie-France dressed in somber clothing and Claire wore a dark dress and hat.

At the cathedral, they stood at the entrance to greet mourners and friends. For Marie-France, it was like the social event of the year. People stopped and hugged her.

Some cried openly while others were unsure what to say or do.

As people flowed into the church, Marie-France observed some women arriving that she did not know. They were all in the forty age range. She turned and asked Claude if he knew them. He had never seen them before.

The Archbishop started the formal ceremony. There were hymns sung, incense burned and then a fiery sermon from the pulpit on life and sacrifices. It ended up with a tribute to the life of the Marquis and all the good he had done for the underprivileged.

Claude could barely suppress his smirk at the hypocrisy he was hearing. In his mind, the Marquis was a major sinner and cheat.

After the funeral proceedings were over and the pallbearers carried the coffin down the aisle, people left the pews and started to stream out of the church. Marie-France had counted the number of the women she did not know. Maybe they were from one of the companies the Marquis did business with. He was well known and respected.

When the church was empty, Marie-France, Claire, and Claude walked down the steps and toward a waiting car to take them to the cemetery. As they approached the car, one of the women came to speak with them. She was young with long curling red hair.

"I am Edith. I was the mistress of the Marquis. I am sad he is dead. I came to respect him and to meet you. The Marquis told me he had provided money for me in his will."

Claude was shocked. He looked across and saw the other women had congregated and were watching. It dawned on Marie-France and Claude at the same time. All eighteen of the Marquis mistresses had come to pay their respects and get their money.
Claude was incensed.

"There will be no money for you or anyone else. I will see to that."

He growled at her and then guided Marie-France and Claire into the car. They drove to the cemetery in silence. The day was grey and bleak. Claude was impatient for the service to be completed and for him to escape back to California away from all the madness.

When they returned to the Chateau, he went to the office and called Barry Jones. The now familiar Australian accent answered the phone.

"Claude boy. It's great you've called back. Things here are hectic. They have declared the place insolvent. Now I've got a bunch of bean counters pouring through all the records. Crazy bunch of bastards. You tell them something they asked about and they stand looking at ya like a stunned fish. Real dopey bastards and not nice. I think I'll need that job now. Not staying here with this bunch."

"Barry be patient. I am flying back to California tomorrow with Claire. I will drive up to see you and we will talk about this."

"Crikey, mate. Didn't take you long now did it?"

Claude was confused.

"What do you mean?"

"She's caught you like a big red snapper."

Claude laughed. He told Barry where he would be staying in San Francisco and hung up.

Claude called Jacques to join him and Claire. Minutes later they all sat together in the salon.

"Jacques, something has come up in California. It is business. I am going to fly back with Claire. I am asking you to ensure that Marie-France is looked after. Here are the phone numbers for the doctors at the hospital if you need to contact them. It is most important she receives the medication on time and with the correct dosage. Can you promise me this?"

"Yes of course. The new maid we hired last month has studied nursing. I will ask her to help."

Claude felt relieved. He knew she would be looked after.

After checking the weather conditions in California, he packed lightly for the trip.

Chapter 69

For the majority of the flight, they slept. It was dusk when the Air France flight touched down. After they cleared customs and immigration, Claude said farewell to Claire and was about to proceed to the taxi stand. Claire called after him.

"Claude. There is no need for you to go and stay at a hotel. Please come and stay in my apartment in Sausalito."

He hesitated and then remembered the night they had spent together. The appeal of her drew him to a quick conclusion. He turned and went back to her. They hugged and were soon in a taxi and on their way to her home.

The taxi wound its way through the Golden Gate Park and across the bridge. It took the sharp turning exit for Sausalito. Claire gave the driver instructions and soon they stopped in front of her apartment.

They dropped their baggage and walked down the waterfront to a restaurant on the pier. The wind off the bay was cold. Claire shivered and Claude removed his jacket and placed it around her shoulders. She looked up at him and smiled. He seemed perfect.

After a light dinner, they returned to her place and retired early, though sleep was delayed due to the amorous actions.

Claude awoke early. A beam of sunlight streamed through the window and danced on his face. The beveled glass caused a prismatic effect with blues, reds, and yellows shining on the walls. He looked at Claire. She was in a deep sleep.

Quietly, he left the bedroom and showered and dressed. He decided to take a stroll along the waterfront and think of what he had planned for that day. Lost in thought, Claude was oblivious to the surroundings. He sat on a bench and looked across the bay to San Francisco. The sky was a brilliant blue, except over the city where a brownish haze hung from the pollution caused by the early commuters.

He returned to find Claire sitting at her kitchen table sipping a coffee. There was a plate of Twinkies on the table and she had a half eaten one in her hand. Claude pretended to frown at her early morning snack. He was convinced now that she really was addicted to them.

"Come Claude. I have made some fine Colombian coffee. Can I prepare you a breakfast?"

"No. I will just have coffee thank you. I have a busy day ahead. I need to rent a car and drive to meet with Barry."

"I have to meet with the realtors and sign the lease for space for my clinic. Will you be back tonight?"

"No, I doubt it. I have a lot to do and discuss with Barry. I will call you this evening."

After arranging a rental car, Claude left to make his trip to the Devil's Lair.

Traffic on the northbound highways was light. Claude enjoyed the drive through the countryside. He used the time to review the details of his plan, during the two-hour drive.

It was late morning when he stopped outside the office of the Devil's Lair winery. He was surprised to see a number of cars parked there.

He entered the office and saw Barry sitting behind a desk with a mound of papers in front of him. Standing in front of him were several men in ill-fitting suits. Claude decided they were obviously accountants.

Barry looked up as Claude entered.

"Bloody hell, mate. Didn't expect to see you so soon. These bloodsuckers are demanding all sorts of reports. Be pleased to get the hell out of here for a while. Time for some tucker anyhow. There's a great little place in the town. They make their own homemade food. Let's go get some lunch."

He scrapped his chair back from the desk and ignoring the accountants proceeded to walk to Claude. They exited and Claude followed Barry's instructions until they reached the little restaurant. It was located on the ground floor of an old stately home.

"Barry I have a lot to discuss with you. We will probably not finish now. Are you busy tonight or can we meet again later?"

"What's on your mind?"

Claude explained the death of the Marquis and the Countess and how he had inherited. Barry listened and said nothing.

"Barry you had told me that Devil's Lair had produced excellent wines in the past. Could it be saved and produce them again?"

"It would take a lot. It's not impossible but it would require replanting of vines and some serious treatment of the soils. The equipment in the winery is old and unreliable. Whoever buys this place will need to invest heavily. The orientation of the land is excellent for growing the grapes. These stupid buggers wouldn't listen to me when I told them they need to install a system to protect the vines from all the birds around here. That has cost them plenty. The birds have decimated the grape yields. They still think shotguns with birdshot are the best deterrent."

"Barry, I am thinking of buying the place. Are you prepared to stay on and help?"

Barry mulled over the question for several minutes.

"I can't guarantee that the production will be able to start for maybe a year. There is so much work to do. I think the wines will be superior to many. Will I have the ability to recommend and purchase the type of vines that are suited to here, especially to make fine wines."

"It would be my plan to rename the winery and rebrand all of the wines. New name, new labels, and new product. I have yet to review the financials and any outstanding liabilities. I would like to obtain that information and have our people in France review them."

"I will introduce you to the head bean counter when we return. He seems to have a lot of power over the Johnsons. He will be critical to your being able to bid and purchase the winery."
"I don't intend to bid. We will negotiate a price and that will be it."

Barry listened intently.

"After I own it, we will establish good relations with the neighboring vineyards. I will have some of our vintners from France come to work with you at the beginning. In addition, I want to make you a partner."

Barry couldn't believe what he was hearing. His jaw dropped open.

"In that case, the place bloody well will work out."

He thrust his hand across the table and shook Claude's hand with force.

"Beauty, mate. What do we do next?"

"Introduce me to the Johnsons first, then the accountant. I will convince them to sell to me."

Claude and Barry left the little restaurant and returned to the winery.

Chapter 70

Back at the winery, Claude met the Johnsons. He explained his offer to them. Initially, they resisted. The thought of a Frenchman running the winery in the Napa Valley was not acceptable to them.

Claude was frustrated by them and about to leave when the head accountant knocked at the door. He was welcomed in and the Johnsons spoke with him regarding Claude's interest in purchasing the vineyard and winery. The accountant listened and made notes. He addressed the Johnsons.

"The records show that the losses are far more serious than we had first estimated. I suspect that finding a buyer is going to be a long and difficult task. You both are indebted to the banks and have guarantees in your names. You both have a lot to lose. I suggest you take Mr. de Passioné's offer very seriously."

Claude carefully watched as they whispered together. They were certainly an eccentric pair. He thought how in some ways they reminded him of Marie-France.

It was Stanley Johnson who spoke.

"How do you expect to finance this purchase? We are not interested in waiting for you to go and find the money. We will accept a good offer at a fair price but without conditions attached."

"I personally have more than enough money to buy this place today."

Claude was getting annoyed at the Johnsons and started to understand why the business had not succeeded. Barry Jones had been correct about the cantankerous pair.

"Gentlemen, I have other business to attend to. I will contact you in the morning. If you choose to continue negotiations, I will need a complete information package to take back to my advisors in France. I intend to return in three days from now. I hope that is adequate time to prepare the documents."

The accountant stepped forward and spoke.

"It is possible. It will be up to the Johnsons if they wish to go ahead and authorize the release of the papers. I hope for their sake they are rational and entertain your kind offer."

The Johnsons looked at the accountant with venomous eyes.

Claude wished them the best and left to stop and briefly visit Barry Jones before leaving.

In the office, he found Barry with the other employees of the accounting firm.

"Barry, I am about to leave. Can you see me outside please."

Barry quickly stood and joined Claude as he walked to his car.

"Well, Claude. Arent they a special pair. Real dumb shits. Stubborn, mean and stupid. How far did you get with them?"

"I don't know for sure but suspect they were playing a bit of a game. Can you meet me later? I am going to stay tonight. I think they will want to continue talking. I will be staying at a lodge I saw driving here. It is named '**The Cedar Inn**.' I would like to have dinner with you. I have many questions you can answer about this place. I need that information before I meet them again."

"I'll be there at six. I know the Inn."

At precisely six, Barry Jones arrived at the Inn. He found Claude sitting alone in the expansive lobby area. After drinks, they went to the dining room for dinner. Over dinner, Claude peppered Barry with questions about the yields of the vineyard and other aspects of the winery operation. They spoke for hours. It was late when they finished and Barry left. Claude checked the time. It was eleven and he calculated it would be eight in the morning in Bordeaux. He placed a call to the Chateau and was pleased when it was Marie-France who answered. Her voice sounded strong and she enthusiastically greeted Claude. They chatted for minutes before he hung up. The next call was to the de Passioné lawyers.

Claude briefed them on his plan. The lawyer called other partners into his office and held a conference call. They listened to Claude's plan and strategy. One of the senior lawyers advised Claude to contact the law firm of Biggar and Biggar in San Francisco. He gave Claude the name of the Managing Partner. Claude took the information and promised to call back when he knew if the deal was to proceed.

The next morning he called the Johnsons.

"We are prepared to accept an offer from you. There will be a dossier prepared by this afternoon."

"That is good. I will come by at two thirty. I was tired and stayed in the area overnight. That is perfect. I will see you both then."

His next call was to Biggar and Biggar. He asked to speak with the Managing Partner. He was connected.

"Mr. de Passioné. I was hoping you would call. My colleagues in France contacted me and advised you may be calling. I think we should meet. Where are you staying?"

"I am in Sausalito, but can visit your offices in the morning."

"Good. I will schedule some other people here. How about ten in the morning?"

"That will be fine. I will see you then."

Claude drove back toward the Devil's Lair. He slowed and took note of the neighboring vineyards. They all appeared healthy and in good shape. He was encouraged and believed Devil's Lair could be reinvigorated with the right management.

He arrived at the winery prior to the two thirty meeting. He wanted to speak with Barry Jones. He found him standing and looking down through the rows of vines that sloped to a ravine. Claude looked around at the land and studied its contour. Far back from the main entrance was a large flat expanse and a stand of tall eucalyptus trees and redwoods. Claude thought it the ideal location for a house. His thoughts were interrupted by Barry who was returning to the office.

"Hi, Claude. I was looking over the vines and the layout. I believe we will need to do some replanting here. I am going to prepare a plan and discuss it with the others here. I believe we can produce more grapes than we currently harvest from these vines."

"Have you had any conversations with the Johnsons today? I am curious to see what valuation they have placed on the property. I have contacted a law firm in San Francisco and in France. If the price is reasonable, I intend to move ahead very quickly."

"No, but there have been many cars coming and going this morning, including some of the neighbors who own the adjacent vineyards. I'm not sure what those two old crafty buggers are up to. Be very careful in your dealings with them."

Back in the office, they found the Johnsons seated with several accountants from the insolvency team. On the desk lay a thick dossier of reports and financials.

Neville Johnson spoke.

"The documents you requested are available. You will need to sign a confidentiality agreement before we will release them.."

"That will not be a problem. I expected that."

He took the offered document and read it carefully before scratching his signature across the bottom of the page. A copy was made and the original passed to Stanley.
"Here is the valuation report. The price we ask and a description of the assets and land survey are included. You will find the price on the first page. Please consider it. If you agree, then we will continue this meeting. If not, then we have no further business and you can leave without the dossier."

Claude flipped open the folder and read the opening paragraph. There in bold print was the requested amount. He showed no emotion. He found the price a little high.

"I will need to have the supporting materials examined, but it is in the range I expected. I am prepared to continue. I would like time to have these reviewed. I will be returning to France and will be in contact from there. I have spoken with the law firm, Biggar and Biggar in San Francisco to represent me for assistance with this deal."

At the mention of the law firm's name, the Johnsons exchanged looks. It was not lost on Claude. He sensed their hesitation.

He stood to leave.

"I will be in contact before I leave for France. Good day gentlemen."

Chapter 71

On the return drive to Sausalito, Claude wondered why the Johnsons had reacted to the mention of the law firm. He decided to call his lawyers in France. Something was strange. They should have been happy to have a prospective buyer, given the state of their affairs.

The traffic southbound was heavy. Several accidents had snarled the traffic to a stop. It took three hours to complete the short trip to Sausalito.

Claire was seated at her desk beneath the window in the front room of the second floor. There was a magnificent view across the water to San Francisco. She turned and rose to greet and hug Claude.

"I have signed a lease for space and have received some resumes of other vets who are interested in joining a new practice. I am so excited. Tonight we will celebrate. Now tell me about your day, but first, let's go downstairs and get us a drink. Its been a long day so far."

They sat in the tiny kitchen while Claude told her of the past two days and the strange reaction of the Johnsons. She listened and frowned when told of how they had reacted.

"They don't sound like nice men and why would they act like that. Something is being hidden. Be careful Claude. I have an uncle here who is a lead investigator with a private detective agency. I should call him and ask what he knows about the Johnsons."

Claude agreed. The more he knew about them the easier it would be to deal with them.
Claire called her uncle at his home. After pleasantries were exchanged she lead right into the topic of the Johnsons. She remained quiet as the uncle spoke at length. She spoke to him briefly and handed the phone to Claude.

"Hello. Claire has spoken about you. Nice to speak with you. I understand you want to know about those Johnson brothers up there in Napa. They have a somewhat dubious past. Why are you asking?"

As he explained his interest, the uncle listened. There was a pause before he spoke.

"If I was you, Claude, I would walk away. The Johnsons have been watched by the FBI and IRS for years now. They barely escaped imprisonment for a sophisticated investment scam using the winery. The business is tainted. You will find many people will not deal with Devil's Lair or the Johnsons. They will have a terrible time trying to find a buyer. If you think anyone will deal with you after the purchase you will need to do a lot of convincing."

Claude explained their reaction to the law firm. The uncle laughed.

"That was the firm who handled the litigation against them. They won't be happy to see them again. I suggest you hire a forensic accounting firm before you make an offer. I am sure any documents they have provided are probably fraudulent."

Claude thanked him and hung up. His enthusiasm for the deal had waned.

"Thank you, Claire. That was an invaluable call. I need to carefully consider whether to continue with the purchase. There may be some hidden liabilities."

"Don't give up. Tomorrow when you meet the lawyers, tell them what he advised you. I am sure they can recommend a good honest forensic accounting firm. Now let's go and enjoy the evening. I have a special place to take you."

They drove south and over the Golden Gate bridge. Instead of turning into the city, they continued down the coast until they arrived at a restaurant the protruded out from the cliff and was supported by heavy cantilevered beams sunk into the rock.

Claude was a little nervous about the structure but his concerns diminished when he looked out from the wall of glass over the Pacific.

They dined on fresh crab and enjoyed watching the magnificent sunset as the sun sunk below the horizon. It was a magical place she had taken Claude for dinner.

As he went to order dessert, she stopped him.

"No, I will take you to Ondines of Sausalito. They are world famous for the Gran Marnier Souffle they make. Once you try it you will never forget it."

The trip back was fast as the traffic was light. They parked at her apartment and walked along the path beside the water until they reached Ondines. The building reminded Claude of a ship as it was perched over the water. The décor was unique.

It was clear that Claire frequented the restaurant often as the staff welcomed her by name.

They were seated at a table beside a window. As the night grew darker, Claude watched the continual stream of lights from the aircraft approaching to land at San Francisco airport.

He was growing to like California more and more.

Chapter 72

At the law firm of Biggar and Biggar, Claude waited patiently in the mahogany-lined reception area. He sunk into the luxurious leather club chair and waited. He did not have to wait long. A pleasant looking silver-haired gentleman arrived from inside the offices. He briskly walked to Claude with an extended hand.

"Welcome, Claude. I am Al Pine. I am the senior managing partner here. It is a pleasure to meet you. I have requested several of my fellow lawyers to join us in the conference room. I trust you are having an enjoyable time here in California."

Claude confirmed this and followed as he was lead into the conference room. It was huge. A long wooden table occupied most of the room. There were more leather chairs arranged around the table. Off to the side, another smaller table was set with coffee pots and plates of cakes and sandwiches.

As they entered the other lawyers stood and introduced themselves. Claude was pleased to see that they had nameplates in front of them. He was worried he would be unable to remember all their names.

When the introductions were completed, Claude was asked to address his particular legal requirements. He stood and addressed the group.

"I thank you all for seeing me this morning on such short notice. My family, the de Passioné s have been involved in winemaking in France for many years. We have produced wines for nobility and other foreign royals. Our reputation in France is well known. Several years ago, my father, Marquis Charles, invested in an Italian winery.

It is unfortunate that he was recently killed on a trip to Italy. The estates in Italy and France were inherited by me, along with significant investments.

I became aware of an opportunity here in California just recently. It was only late yesterday that I learned information that is making me reconsider the wisdom of going ahead with the deal. I am advised that this law firm is well aware of the individuals who own the business. They are the Johnson brothers in Napa."

There was a marked increase in the attention of the lawyers at this point.

"I have been told of some past history and the negativity that now surrounds their business dealings. I am concerned that if I was to purchase the Devil's Lair business I would end up with untold problems and liabilities. I will only move forward if the information they have provided me is examined by a forensic accounting company. I do not know one here in the States. I need assurance that they are an honest and credible firm. If the information is true, then I will need the services of your firm to assist with the purchase. You will be working with our French legal firm and banks."

When Claude stopped the room was deathly quiet. Claude sat. Al Pine gestured to a lawyer on his left. The lawyer spoke.

"You are right to be concerned. The Johnson brothers have been operating on the thin border of the law. There is a forensics group we work with on a daily basis. I can vouch for their professionalism and honesty. I can assure you that if you decide to go ahead, we will be in contact with our friends in both the IRS and FBI. We will guarantee there are no issues that will come back on you.

Are we able to review whatever documentation the Johnsons have provided you?"

"Yes, but I need to take a copy with me when I return to France tomorrow."

One of the lawyers took the dossier to have it copied.

"In order for us to commence, we will need to request the payment of a retainer. I think fifteen thousand to start will do it."

"if you provide bank information, I will contact our bank to initiate a transfer."

The meeting concluded and Claude took the elevator down to the lobby. As he was leaving the building he caught a glimpse of a face he thought was familiar rushing into the building. He was sure it was Lise Victor from the art gallery in Paris. Before he could turn and run after her, she had disappeared. Claude thought to himself it was crazy and just someone who looked like her. There was something that convinced him it was her.

He returned to Sausalito and spent the afternoon on the phone to his legal and financial people in France. The meeting at Biggar and Biggar had restored his confidence in making the purchase.

It was late afternoon and Claire had not yet returned. The phone rang. Claude disputed whether to answer it. It continued to ring. He answered and was shocked to hear Barry Jones' accent booming through.

"Barry, what's happening? Why are you calling?"

"I've had it with these Johnson blokes. Had enough so I quit. The other guys are about to walk as well. I suspect they are trying to fool you. I overheard them instructing those accountants to change some of that information. They are trying to make things look better than they are. Some of the receipts for equipment are fake. They have included leased equipment and claimed they own it. The information they gave you is a minefield."

"Barry, I met with the lawyers and they have a forensic accounting firm who will be auditing that dossier. Don't worry. We will deal a blow to those Johnsons."

"I'm thinking of going back to Australia next weekend. I'm not convinced you will get to buy the Devil's Lair. No point in my waiting around."

"Don't do that. Drive down here tonight. I have an idea."

As he was talking, Claire returned bubbling with enthusiasm. Claude quickly told her of the new development.

"Tell Barry he can stay here with us. We have a guest room. What time will he be here? I will prepare a supper."

Claude coaxed Barry to accept the offer. Barry estimated he would arrive at six that evening.

Claude was eager to hear Claire's good news.
"I received my license to open the clinic and I found a vet to work with me. I can't wait to start. Tomorrow I will meet with contractors for the design and building of the clinic. I have yet to think of a name."

Claude hugged her. It was no ordinary hug. He was going to miss her back in France. He led her to the bedroom. She willingly let him strip her clothing and with the ferocity of wild animals engaged in lengthy lovemaking.

They arose late and showered together. Claire realized she had little time to prepare their meal. She playfully told Claude off for distracting her. He just laughed at her and gave her a playful pat on her behind. They were truly in love.

As she breezed around the kitchen humming, Claude relaxed and happily watched her until loud knocking and front doorbell ringing snapped him back to reality. Barry Jones had arrived.

"Bloody hell, mate. This is one posh place here. You know how to pick em Frenchie."

Claude's like of the man was growing at each encounter.

"Come and drink some real wine. First, come and meet Claire. This is her apartment."

Barry turned on his most exaggerated manners for Claire. Claude guffawed at his feigned politeness.

"Claire, don't be fooled by this ruffian."

There was no doubt that Claire had also taken a liking to Barry."
Claude took Barry into Claire's office area. He wanted to speak with Barry before the dinner.

"Barry, I am meant to leave tomorrow for France. I want you to come with me. We can arrange a ticket tonight for you. I want you with me during the efforts to buy that business from the Johnsons. You worked for them and I am sure you will be able to assist."

"I'd love to mate. Problem is though I don't have that kind of money."

"You will be my guest. I will buy your ticket. I'm sure you have a passport. What else is there to keep you here or make you want to return to Australia?"

Barry considered this.

"I'll come then. I am hoping we can buy Devil's Lair. It does have the potential to produce award-winning wines. Id love to have that chance."

"Its agreed then. I will make the call and get your ticket. While I do this, go and keep Claire company."

He found the number for Air France. Twenty minutes later Barry Frederick Jones was booked first class to Paris.

Chapter 73

The flight was scheduled to leave in the afternoon. In the morning, Claude contacted Al Pine, who confirmed the receipt of the retainer.

"Claude we are checking some new information we received through one of the partners late yesterday. It seems there are some recent developments with the Johnson brothers. I do not have enough information yet or know if it is accurate. We are having it checked. If it is true your position will be strengthened. I don't wish to create false hope, but the source of this information is impeccable. As soon as I hear more I will be in contact. I will phone my colleagues in France."

Claude wondered what information could have come to light in such a short time. He called Barry to inform him.

"Mate, I wouldn't be surprised by anything those two may be involved with. I saw enough when I was there."

It was the lunch hour when Claire called. She advised Claude she would drive them to San Francisco airport.

Barry had packed all his worldly possessions into a small case. Claude wondered if he had other things stored in Australia or if that case represented everything he owned.

Claire arrived at the apartment to drive them. Again she was chewing a Twinkie. Claude tried to estimate how many she ate each day.

She drove them over the Golden Gate bridge and down Highway 101 to the airport. At the airport, she held Claude tightly and he noticed her eyes misted.

"Don't worry. I expect to return very soon. I am determined to buy that business."

Barry and Claude took their baggage and headed to check in with Air France.

The trip was long. During the flight, they slept and ate or discussed the planned purchase. Barry was brimming with ideas.

It was mid-morning in Paris when they landed. Claude had booked a commuter flight to Bordeaux. During the wait, he called Jacques at the Chateau.

"I am in Paris with an associate. I will be in Bordeaux in three hours. Please arrange to meet us."

Even though he was tired from the trip, Barry was keenly observing all the French girls passing them at the airport.

"Jezz Claude. You Frenchies kept all the good ones for your selves. Not the same as those ones built like trucks in Australia. Reckon I could move here and be very happy."

Claude shook his head at the comment. Barry kept him amused.

The short flight got them to Bordeaux at one in the afternoon. Claude decided against stopping for lunch. He was eager to get back to the Chateau and learn of any new developments.

Jacques advised him there were a number of important phone calls from California and his French lawyers. He was curious and asked Claude to explain why. Claude deferred.

"I am looking at some investments in America. I guess they have details for me. I will call them when we arrive home."

Throughout the drive, Jacques asked Barry questions about Australia. Barry was only too happy to oblige and inflated every story. By the time they reached the Chateau, Jacques wondered how anyone could live in a land infested with so many wild beasts and poisonous critters. He decided he would never go there.

Once inside the Chateau, Claude spent time with Marie-France before leaving to return the urgent calls. He left Barry with her. She was flirting with Barry like a teenager. Claude had not noticed her overt advances.

In the office, he first phoned Claire. She was happy and filled him in on details regarding the progress on setting up her clinic. While talking, he thumbed through the messages. There were several marked urgent from Al Pine.

He hung up with Claire and placed the call. It was still early morning in California, but Al Pine was at the office.

"Claude, I hope you had a good trip home. There has been a dramatic development. Our firm acts for several banks here in San Francisco, including an investment bank. What I am about to tell you is public knowledge so I will not be violating any confidentiality here. Our firm was called on by representatives from the bank with respect to the Johnson brothers. There is a huge problem. The financials they have been releasing to the banks and investors are inaccurate. They have manipulated them to present a better situation than really exists. Last night the FBI arrested both men. There are many charges against them. The banks have moved to seize the vineyard and winery. The actual Devil's Lair company is a front and a fraud. I am sorry to tell you this but your deal to purchase is dead.

I do have a suggestion for you and if you agree, my firm will pursue it. Instead of buying the business, structure an offer to buy the land for the vineyard and the winery from the banks. I am sure we could negotiate that for you. It will be better than buying the whole business. There are too many problems with it. You will be exposed to hidden liabilities. The FBI is talking of a Federal jail term for the Johnsons. If they are convicted of this fraud they will be guests of Uncle Sam for many years. In fact, they may die in there."

Claude was at a total loss for words. He considered Al Pine's advice.

"Yes. I like your idea and ask you to approach the banks. I am interested to get that property."

It was a turn of events he had not foreseen. He considered it to be a good omen. He would not have to deal with the Johnsons or any of their problems. He was actually relieved.

He returned to the salon to update Barry on the situation and was annoyed to find Marie-France openly attempting to seduce Barry, who looked very uncomfortable.

"Please leave us. I have important business to discuss with Barry. You can join us later for drinks."

Barry heaved a sigh of relief when she waltzed from the room.

"God almighty. What the hell drugs is she taking. One old horny broad there my friend. A regular bloody man-eater."

"I am sorry. She has severe mental problems. Why would any respectable woman want you anyway, Barry."

"I'll tell you what, mate. I was the hottest stuff at school. The sheilas couldn't keep away from me. Bees to honey."

Claude just laughed at his exaggerated claims.

"Barry there has been a change in plans."

He told Barry of the call with Al Pine and the new approach to purchasing the vineyard and winery. Barry was pleased not to be dealing with the Johnsons.

Bary slept lightly that night. He was awakened by a click from the door. He glanced across the room and saw Marie-France standing naked in the shadows. He bolted towards the door and ran out into the corridor and shouted to Claude. Marie-France chased after Barry calling his name. Claude thundered up the stairs carrying a piece of pipe. He was startled by all the commotion and worried that the chateau had been broken into.

He stopped when he saw Marie-France running after Barry in the nude. He rushed to catch her and pulled her into her room where he wrapped her in a sheet. It seemed she was not awake. He waited and held her until she was quiet, then lowered her back to her bed.
He went back downstairs and found Barry cowering behind a large antique chair.

"I tell you mate. She's bloody crazy."

Chapter 74

Next morning, Claude introduced Barry to the manager responsible for the vineyard and left to meet with his bankers to brief them on his plan to purchase the California vineyard. He provided instructions with respect to drawing funds from certain investments when the deal was to close.

With the arrangements made, he prepared to drive back to the Chateau, but changed his mind and decided to visit the avocat's office. He remembered that there were still legal papers to sign related to taxes and the Marquis death.

He was welcomed warmly and sat with Carlos and chatted as they drank coffee. The documents were explained to him and he signed without questioning them. When the business was complete, Claude told Carlos of the Johnson arrests. Carlos replied that Al Pine had already forwarded details of the arrest and status of the legal proceedings against the business by the banks in California.

"I think you are a lucky man, Claude. The banks are looking to dispose of the property and recover their investments. Al Pine advises this will be significantly less than the Johnsons had asked. I understand you will not take over the company, just the vineyard, and winery. That is smart."

As he was leaving, he invited Carlos to visit the Chateau for drinks later that night and meet with Barry Jones.

Back at the Chateau, Claude huddled with Barry and prepared plans for the reworking of the vineyard. Both were optimistic about the prospect of turning Devil's Lair into a world-class winery.

"After we take it over, I intend to rename it. In honor of our family, I intend to call it 'Passion Fields'. All the wines will be renamed and new labels will be used. Devil's Lair will go with the Johnsons."

"Claude, I am impressed with the men you have working here. I met your vintner from the Spanish winery. He has great ideas. I think we should consider using the vintners from your other wineries in Spain and Italy during the redevelopment. They have a lot to offer and can contribute to assisting in producing some unique but excellent wines."

It was late when Carlos arrived at the estate. He was taken to the salon to meet with Claude and Barry Jones.

"I am excited for you. I received a message from Al Pine that the banks were successful in court and now have the control of the land and winery. They are eager to proceed with a sale, however, you will not be the only bidder. They have a bid from Fairylight Wineries of California already. I suggest we don't delay if you are serious."

"Do you know any details of the other bidders offer?"

"No, but Al Pine hinted it was not a strong bid and he is well informed."

The trio continued discussions into the small hours of the morning. When they had finished, the structure and amount for the bid were agreed.

"I will contact Al Pine with the details. I will contact your lawyers here and within days we will have our offer to the banks."

"Barry and I will travel to California and meet with the bankers and present the offer. Carlos, I will need you and a partner from our lawyers to accompany us. There will be complexities to resolve. We are a French company. We will need to handle any issues that arise because of that. It may be necessary to set up an American company. I see a lot of work ahead for us."

For the next week, Claude and Barry traveled between the Chateau and town for meetings. The following week the group left for California.

Claude did not wish to be distracted. He did not advise Claire of his arrival. He wanted to complete the takeover before contacting her. He found it difficult and occasionally his mind filled with thoughts of her.

Another week passed. They were occupied with meetings involving the banks, the state government, lawyers and other authorities. It was the third week before the deal was accepted and Claude and Barry Jones were the new owners. That afternoon Claude called Claire with the news. She was dumbfounded and cried at the news.

"Tonight I will come and we will celebrate. Just the two of us. Barry can go and celebrate with Carlos and the team. I have missed you so much and I am horny. This weekend I am going to the vineyard. Will you come?"

"Yes, of course. I too have missed you. I will close early and be ready for you. I have a lot to tell you about the clinic. It has been a success."

Claude hung up and in anticipation of the evening ahead ordered a huge bouquet of flowers for delivery to her home for that evening.

Chapter 75

The weekend arrived and Claude, along with Barry picked up Claire for the trip to the winery. They arrived shortly before noon and entered the house that had formerly been occupied by the Johnsons. It had been kept neatly but lacked any character.

"Claire, we will go and find some furnishings. This place is depressing. I want color and life in here. There is no feeling of joy. We will go into the town and search out some things. Hopefully, we can get some delivered for tonight. I will pay them well."

Barry decided he would stay and start looking at details for the start of the rebuilding of the winery.

On the way into town, Claude stopped at a burger joint. He loved the greasy no class American hamburgers and oversalted fries. Claire playfully admonished him.

"Claude you live in a country with some of the best foods in the world. How can you eat these unhealthy things?"

"I need all the energy. You wear me out at night. You are a little vixen. I think we will need to buy a very strong bed."

They both laughed and devoured the huge hamburgers. Ketchup and bright yellow mustard oozed out and dribbled down their chins. Claude was in high spirits and wiped

Claire's chin with his finger. She almost choked when he dropped his hand down onto her breasts and gently squeezed them.

"Later my lover. We have a task ahead of us."

The afternoon was spent selecting furnishings. Claude joked about how many of the American items were tasteless. He preferred the older antique furniture of France.

They selected linens, beds, dressers, and other items. Claude spoke to the store manager and offered an inducement that guaranteed the delivery of the goods immediately. Claire was thrilled and set about trying to organize the house after the delivery was made.

Even with the new furnishings, the house still lacked the atmosphere that Claude hoped for. He decided that he would worry about that at a later time. His priority was to restore the vineyard and re-equip the winery with up to date winemaking equipment.

On Sunday, Claude, Barry, and Claire toured around the vineyard. Barry made copious notes of problems he observed. That evening, they devised a plan to start the work. Claude decided to return to France to tend to business there. He needed to visit the Italian operations. Things had been going well and he was looking forward to spending some time in Italy alone.

Six months went by with Barry running Passion Fields. He was pleased when he received the call advising him that

Claude was returning the next week. He was proud of what had been achieved in the short timeframe.

Claude returned, accompanied by a tall olive-skinned somewhat gaunt man with slicked back greasy black hair and piercing dark eyes.

"Barry, meet Lorenzo Carducci. He is one of Italy's leading architects. I have made some serious decisions. I have decided to move with Marie-France to California. My future is here. I will maintain control of the wine business in Europe but wish to make this one the premier winery. I have decided to build a replica of the Chateau in France on the land here. Lorenzo has been working on plans. He will be selecting contractors. The replica will not be as big as the Chateau but will be my mansion. I have some other plans too. During my trip to New Zealand, I was introduced to horse riding. I have decided I will have horses here. I am going to contact Dave Mathews in New Zealand and arrange for assistance in selecting them. I am going to invite his trainer and assistant, Sarah for a working vacation here to help Lorenzo with the design of the stables. It is time for me to enjoy some new things in life."

Barry was concerned. He wondered whether this meant his relationship with Claude had changed. He asked Claude.

"No Barry. I am going to build down by the ravine where there is that little forest of trees. It will afford us privacy. I will have the existing house renovated for you. It is yours."

Barry sensed that something had drastically changed in Claude's life. He was not looking forward to the return of Marie-France. He shuddered as he recalled the now infamous night she had visited him naked.

"When will you start building?"

"I anticipate in about a month we will start. I will return to France and Lorenzo will be supervising the project. I have arranged to meet Claire in San Francisco this evening. Her parents are visiting and she would like me to meet them. Tonight I will dine with the royalty of dog food."

Chapter 76

During the construction of the mansion, Claude commuted frequently between California, France, and Italy. The Spanish vineyards had been managed by reliable workers for years and required the least attention. Claude had considered selling them but decided against doing so.

The day finally arrived for Claude to take Marie-France to California. At the Chateau, she had packed suitcases full of clothing and personal items. She acted like a queen about to embark on a Royal tour.

She had arranged for a photographer to record her departure from France and sent invitations to politicians and members of society to attend her farewell party. The attendance was meager.

On the flight to San Francisco, Marie-France kept the flight attendants busy with constant questions, requests, and stories of her privileged past. Claude was embarrassed and attempted to apologize for her. There was no stopping her.

"You are my son and should remember that. You were delivered by me into nobility. I expect you to act appropriately instead of telling those common people I am not well. Shame on you."

Approximately four hours into the flight she fell into a deep sleep. Claude left his seat and joined the staff at the front of the plane.

"I am so sorry my mother has been treating you all the way she has. She was diagnosed with a deteriorating mental condition. She is medicated and sometimes acts strangely."
"You need not worry. We are trained to deal with many situations. She is your mother and we do understand. If you require anything that will make her trip more comfortable, please let us know."

The plane flew on for what seemed endless hours to Claude. He attempted to watch the movie and quickly lost interest. Claude reached over and held her arm in reassurance. He tried reading but was not comprehending the words or story. He put his head back and drifted into a sleep.

He was shaken awake by one of the attendants.

"We will be starting our descent into San Francisco. Can I get anything for you or your mother before we land?"

"Yes, I would like a strong coffee and could you bring a gin and tonic for my mother. Need her to be relaxed when we clear US Customs and Immigration."

The plane touched down heavily. Marie-France let out a shriek as the huge aircraft lurched to the side and snapped back. The plane braked sharply. Loose items shot along the aisle and under seats to the front of the cabin. It was the roughest landing Claude had ever experienced.

When the plane slowed and taxied, Marie-France exploded.

"That man isn't the right person to drive this contraption. I will complain."

"Marie-France, he doesn't drive a plane. A pilot will fly a plane. Sometimes landing here is difficult because of winds off the bay. We are here and soon you will be at your new home."
In the terminal, they were met by Barry Jones.

"Good to see ya, mate. The old girl's looking just fine. Hope she's got her hormones under control. I'm a bit worried having her in the car on the way up to the winery. Don't feel like getting attacked."

Claude laughed. It seemed Barry had a way to create humor in any situation.

Barry had driven down to meet them in an old Mercedes and had one of the workers follow him in a van to transport their luggage back to the winery.

During the drive, he asked Claude about the European vineyards and then updated him on the latest developments at Passion Fields.

"We just produced our first Chardonnays for the Passion Fields label. It's an amazing drop, a real beauty, soft and smooth. Just like a mother's milk from the breast."

Claude shook his head. He had never heard wine referred to in that manner. The talk continued and he asked Barry about the completion of the construction of the mansion.

"All the major construction is complete. A few little things. We got a message from that Sarah babe in New Zealand. She is delighted to visit and help design and manage the construction of the stables. Lorenzo Carducci, your strange architect friend has been in contact with her. They have many questions for you, like how many horses will you keep. Dave Mathews wants you to contact him. He says they have some new horses he thinks you will be interested in."

As they turned onto the drive leading to the new mansion, Marie-France could barely contain her excitement.

"It is beautiful. It is just like the Chateau. I am going to be happy here. Claude, you are a good boy and make me proud that you are my son."

Claude wondered what had come over her. She had never expressed acceptance of his ideas and decisions.

Marie-France was happy when she entered the mansion and found it to be exactly the same as the Chateau in France. Even her room was duplicated. It was then that she decided her life in California would be new and fulfilling. She wondered about local motorbike gangs and if they would let her join.

Life was calm and together, they all settled into the mansion. There was a calmness in Marie-France that Claude had never seen before.

Weeks passed and a normal life evolved until Sarah arrived to supervise the design and building of the stables. She exerted herself immediately upon arrival.

"Claude, I thank you for the opportunity you have given me. I look forward to a vacation here and at the same time having the stables built for your equestrian venture. I must say though that Lorenzo knows nothing about horses. They are not just animals. They have needs that require comfort and serenity. He thinks they are just like cows or bulls. They are not. If you want this done right you will put me in control here. He is an idiot when it comes to animals. In fact, he is more stupid than most animals I know."

"He is famous. I hired him to duplicate to intricacies of our Chateau in France. I agree that he is not an expert in animals. I am sure you can assist him. He will work with you to build the finest stables according to the requirements you give him. I think you are too serious. I will find you a nice French lover. Maybe then you will smile."

Sarah scowled. The last thing she wanted was a temperamental French lover.

"Claude, I want you to set up a meeting with Lorenzo. I want to discuss the issues of designing a good stable."

"I will ask him to visit this afternoon. Surely it is not that complicated to build a stable?"

"There are many things to consider. It's not so simple."

Chapter 77

That afternoon Claude, Lorenzo, and Sarah met in the private office that he had constructed for him. Lorenzo was annoyed. He had planned an afternoon of golf and considered the meeting a subordination of his architectural authority.

Claude addressed them in an effort to diffuse the apparent hostility.

"Lorenzo, my friend has extensive experience with horses in New Zealand she works for a racehorse breeder whose horses are in demand internationally. She is here to help us build my stables. I am not an expert and neither are you. Sarah can provide us with valuable information. I intend to have a modern stable and not just some old barn."

"In my opinion, a stable is just a place for the horses to stay inside in winter and somewhere to sleep."

Sarah bristled.

"You are wrong, Lorenzo. There is much more to an efficient modern stable. Firstly, Claude must decide on the location. It should be away from the main part of the mansion, and in a quiet area so the horses do not get spooked. Then there is the design and the amenities. While it may cost a little more, it is safer to build now for a larger number of horses that Claude will initially have. The stalls should be larger than typically found and the aisles to walk the horses out wider. The floor of each stall needs to be comfortable for the horses. There are new carpet products. I strongly urge you, Claude, to include an inside horse wash stall and a separate space for a tack room to keep bridles, blankets, saddles, and brushes. I do not believe that hay or food should be stored in the stable. There have been many incidents of fire in barns caused by hay igniting. Please, Claude, build a separate storage area away from the main stable to store their feed in."

Claude had listened intently and now realized the importance of Sarah's advice.

"Lorenzo, can you prepare plans? I am considering the stables down toward the raven behind the mansion. Now you see the value of Sarah. I trust you will both be able to work together to make the stables the best in California."

Lorenzo agreed and smiled. He stood and went to hug Sarah.

"I am sorry. I did not know such things. I always thought that a barn with stalls could be a stable. I was wrong. I am eager to work with you and learn more."

"I will ask Dave Mathews to send photos of the stables we built in New Zealand."

The meeting ended and Claude was happy that the two had agreed to work together. He had poured a wine and was about to sit and complete paperwork when Marie-France came bounding into the room.

"I am so happy here. I like the house and the nice people here. I don't want to go back to France."

Claude had noticed the change in her. She was no longer fainting or acting irrationally.

"I am sure you will want to go back and visit the Chateau and your friends there."
"I will visit but this is going to be my home. When are you going to bring my nice friend Claire to see me?"

"I have invited her to stay with us this weekend."

Marie-France did a little hop and rubbed her hands together like an excited child. Her mood soured when Claude told her that Claire's parents would also be visiting.

"They have no class. She is nice. They didn't deserve a beautiful daughter like that. Couldn't you have found someone whose parents don't make dog food? Low-class people. You always found tramps. Where did I go wrong? I tried to teach you. You are from nobility and now dragging the de Passioné name down. We don't slaughter and put animals in cans."

"You like Claire and when you meet her parents I am sure you will like them too."

"Is the mother fat? Is he elegant or a pig? I'm not sure I want to meet them."

"I think you need to understand that I may possibly marry Claire. You have no choice in that matter."

At those words, Marie-France feigned a fainting attack. Claude was not fooled. He left her crumpled on the floor and went to the salon, where he found Barry Jones.

"Barry, what are you doing here? I did not know you were waiting."

"Well, it's a bit embarrassing, but I guess I should tell you. You will probably find out anyway. I'm having an affair with Sarah. She's a real goer that one. A bit feisty but nothing a red-blooded Aussie can't handle. I reckon she just might be the one. Can't get her loins out of my mind."

Claude was both shocked and amazed. He had never seen Sarah that way.

"Barry that's great news. Don't let it interfere with our business here. Thank you for being honest and telling me. I guess if it gets serious you will go to New Zealand."

"No bloody way that's happening. She'll be coming here. I told her I was going to let you know. She was concerned."

"Barry we all have our jobs to do. If the two of you are happy and this works I am fine with it. Now let's celebrate. Go and get Sarah."

Chapter 78

Life on the vineyard settled into a pattern. Claude would take trips to France and Italy to the wineries. At Passion Fields, Barry played a major role in the redevelopment of the winery. Business was good. Barry and Sarah got engaged.

Claude handed more control of the daily operations to Barry. He was taking more time alone and riding the recently imported horses. His life seemed settled. He had Claire, Marie-France was calmer then in past years, Barry had a firm grip on the business. In France, Spain, and Italy the hired managers and staff were managing well. Claude ensured their loyalty and paid them handsomely. The neighboring vineyards had accepted Claude and were pleased that the Johnson brothers were gone.

The portfolio of investments that Claude had inherited continued to grow. He was determined to use the money for something different than the wine business. He thought of the perfume factory in Rarotonga that Atarangi's parents owned. He wondered if the perfumes would succeed in Europe and decided to hire experts in France to assist him in determining the possibility. Although he loved Claire, he had never forgotten the directness of Atarangi.

Claude had become restless and wanted a change. He decided to spend time in Europe on his next trip traveling and exploring. He called Claire and proposed making combined business and vacation trip. She wasn't sure.

"Claude, I have the clinic to be concerned with. I am not sure I can leave it now."

"You have told me about the great team you have assembled. Surely they can look after the clinic for a few weeks. I am not going to take no for an answer."

Minutes ticked by until she answered.

"I will join you. When will we leave? I will need some time to arrange this with my staff."

"There is no hurry. Make your arrangements and then we can plan."

"Claude, I love you so much. I can't believe our chance meeting on that plane ride. I hope one day we will be together always."

"I will drive down to see you tonight. I have some business in San Francisco tomorrow."

They talked for a while and made dinner arrangements. Claude was looking forward to a change from the mansion and the wine business. He planned to stay several days with Claire.

That evening over dinner he discussed the idea he had for the tropical perfume business. He omitted the intricate details of Atarangi however. Claire listened but didn't seem convinced.

"Where would you produce the perfumes? Will there be enough to make it successful? It is a small island."

"We will make it a unique and prestigious brand. It will be a luxury product from the South Pacific."

"Claude, I think you are crazy."

Part 4

The Decision

Chapter 79

Present day, Bodega Bay, California

They drove from Sausalito up to the Napa Valley and continued on to Bodega Bay. During the drive, Claude was tempted several times to tell her of his plan to marry her but resisted.

He looked across at her. She had opened the window of the Ferrari and the wind was tossing her hair. He thought how beautiful she looked. He had decided to accept her passion for Twinkies and in fact had a special surprise for her at The Tides restaurant. Claude was friends with the chef and had asked them to conceal the wedding ring in a specially decorated Twinkie. The chef and staff were happy to oblige and had decorated the ring bearing Twinkie with pink icing.

As they approached the bay, a swirling mist from the ocean blew a cool air into the car. Claire shuddered and closed the window, that made the roar of the Ferrari's powerful engine louder. They drove down an incline and around the sweeping righthand corner. Claude slowed and stopped the Ferrari across from The Tides. He opened the door for Claire and with his arm around her, they walked to the restaurant's entrance where they were welcomed. The staff had been told of Claudes plan to propose but made no indication of any special event.

They were seated by a window that afforded them a magnificent view of the bay and the fishing boats moored at the dock. Fishermen went about their work storing nets and generally preparing for the days work.

Claire loved Bodega Bay and the rugged atmosphere of it. Claire was not a huge fan of seafood but chose a crab salad. Claude ordered pan-fried scallops.

A bottle of champagne was delivered to their table and the chef also appeared carrying a white plate with the special Twinkie on it.

"Claude has told us how you love Twinkies. We have made this special one for you."

She beamed a smile and thanked the chef and Claude.

They ate leisurely and Claude worked up his courage to ask Claire to marry him. As he was about to propose, the adjacent table guest dropped her purse. The contents scattered under Claude's table. He pushed back his chair and bent down to assist the woman in picking up the articles.

She thanked Claude profusely. Claude looked at the table in horror. The Twinkie with the 3-carat diamond ring in it was gone. He stared across at Claire. She had pink icing around her lips. She had eaten the ring. He did not know what to say or do. He was appalled that she had eaten the whole Twinkie so quickly.

"Are you alright Claire? I think we should leave now. I need to take you to the mansion. There is something special I have planned."

They left the restaurant and started to cross to where the Ferrari was parked. A Volkswagon Kombi van sped around the corner and was headed toward them The young pigtailed, gum-chewing girl had her earphones on and did not see them until it was too late.

The Volkswagon hit them hard. Claire was thrown into the air for thirty feet. Her sneakers were ripped from her feet and flew down the road, landing much further away. She crashed down onto the curb and edge of the wooden planked dock. Her head split open like a watermelon. She was dead. Undigested Twinkie sprayed from her mouth. The 3-carat diamond ring from inside the Twinkie rolled across the planks and with a muffled plop fell into the rising tide.

Claude was thrown onto a grassy embankment. He lay unconscious. Blood streamed from his head and soaked the back of his shirt.

People rushed to their sides. Blankets appeared and covered them. Ten minutes passed before the police vehicles arrived. An ambulance and other emergency vehicles arrived shortly thereafter.

Claude was transported to the hospital. At the hospital, he was rushed through the Emergency Department. Xrays were taken. Throughout the procedures, Claude never regained consciousness.

At the accident scene, an older Police Sargent and a younger officer were interviewing the distraught driver and collecting information. The younger cop took her drivers license and other ID. He couldn't suppress his grin and called to his superior.

"Joe, come and look at this one. It cant be for real. If it is then her parents were either cruel or had a real sense of humor. Look at her name. Eileen Dover."

The senior cop chuckled and walked back to the sobbing Eileen.
"It doesn't look good for you Miss Dover. I am going to need to take you to the station for a detailed statement. Have you been drinking or taking any drugs? We will be testing you so tell the truth now."

She sobbed and pleaded her innocence, as she was lowered into the back seat of the police cruiser.

The young cop walked over to the group of employees who had run from the restaurant when they heard the screech of brakes and the sickening thud as the van hit Claude and Claire.

"Does anyone know these people?"

The chef shakily responded.

"It is Claude de Passioné, the owner of Passion Fields Estate and his fiance. They had just eaten lunch with us. He was proposing to her."

"I will need to get a statement from you. Do you know any of the family members?"

"No. His mother lives with him in their mansion on the vineyard. He has a business partner there as well."

"Will you come with me and guide me to the home?"

"Yes, let me change out of my chef's uniform and I will assist you."

With siren wailing, the young cop sped away with the chef in the direction of the mansion.

Chapter 80

At the mansion, Barry was horrified when told of the accident. He and Sarah immediately wanted to leave and be with Claude. Barry thought for a few moments and made a decision. He called the staff together and told them of the accident.

"There has been a terrible accident. Claude has been injured and Claire is dead. It is important that Marie-France not be advised of this yet. It will trigger her illness and add to the problems we now have. I need all of your support and ask you to keep this matter from her. If she asks, Claude and Claire had to leave. Claude was called away on a business trip and Claire needed to return to her business. It is crucial Mare-France not be told the real situation yet."

The staff was shocked. No one spoke or moved.

Barry and Sarah left and followed the young cop to the hospital where Claude was being treated.

At the hospital, Barry introduced himself as Claude's business partner. He explained that there were no sane next-of-kin that could deal with the situation. He asked the nurse about Claude's condition.

"It is very serious. I will get Dr. Keene to explain the extent of the injuries. We are still assessing Claude for any additional problems."

Dr.Keene was a jovial man with a permanent smile.

"The good news is that he is still alive. He is very fortunate. Had the injury to his back been over by an inch he would have a destroyed kidney and ruptured spleen. He is a lucky man. Now the injuries we have diagnosed are a broken right leg, severe bruising and contusions on his back, and, dare I say this in front of the lady, a damaged penis. He is going to need surgery on his leg, treatment by a urologist and some time to recover. We suspect he may have a head injury and are performing tests at present. He is in a coma.

The bruising on his back is unique. Where the van hit him he has a blood bruise that is part of the Volkswagon insignia. I think we will photograph that for him. Never seen that before.

I suggest you do not wait here. It will be hours before you will be able to see him. Go and rest. There is nothing you can do for him here. Please leave a telephone number where we can contact you."

Barry was about to object until Sarah took control.

"It is the best advice, Barry. Now I am sure the hospital will contact us when there is a change in Claude's condition. Let us go home now. I will contact Dave Mathews in New Zealand and also Claire's parents. We have a lot to do now and need to keep things controlled."

Unhappily Barry agreed and swore violently about the situation. Claude's first shipment of horses was due in a few days and bottling was planned the following week.

Barry was worried. He was concerned about how Claude had arranged for a situation like this. He wondered if he alone had the authority to operate the business with Claude incapacitated. He decided to phone Al Pine at Biggar and Biggar.

He reached Al Pine in his office and explained all that had happened. Al Pine offered to immediately drive up to Passion Fields but Barry advised him to wait until they had an update from the hospital. Al Pine agreed.

"To answer your questions, Barry, he did have an agreement drawn up whereby you are in control in an event like this. It is best I explain your authority and responsibilities when we meet. We should do that soon. Please call me when you get the update. If it is tonight then please call me. Here is my home number."

The night turned to dawn and still, there was no call from the hospital. Barry was impatient and decided to drive to the hospital. Sarah asked him not to leave, but nothing would stop Barry, especially in the mood he was in.

He found Dr. Keene at the nursing station in deep conversation with another doctor. When he saw Barry he smiled.

"Good you have saved us a phone call. We were about to contact you. This is Dr. Mendez, he is a neurosurgeon. He has been examing Claude it is too early to have a conclusive diagnosis. Claude is still in a coma. The Xrays are disturbing. We see bleeding and it appears there is some trauma, possibly bruising. It is going to be some time before he can go home."

Barry felt lonely and panicked. He wondered if he was capable of operating Passion Fields.

Marie-France was looking for Claude and Claire when he returned. Sarah was consoling her and explaining there had been an accident and Claude was in the hospital. She omitted the fact that Claire was dead. Marie-France seemed to be calm as she absorbed the news.

"Barry, I am unsure how to explain to her that Claire's parents are arriving here this evening to arrange to take her home to Wisconsin. I am concerned they may say something to set her off. She liked Claire and believed she was her best friend."

"I will meet them and explain everything. I am sure they will understand. How long will they stay?"

"Just tonight. They have a service planned in Wisconsin. How is Claude?"

"There has been no change he is still in a coma. The doctors said we can see him later this afternoon, though he may still be in that coma."

"I don't care. I want to go and see him. He has been kind to both of us. We must now do what we can to help. Do you know what is happening to that girl who hit them?"

"No. I believe she has been charged. I am sure we will get more details from the police."

"The staff are very upset. I suggest you call them all together and assure them. Some are thinking about what will happen if Claude dies."

In the early afternoon, Barry met the assembled staff and provided them with the reassurance that Claude would be fine and that he had made legal arrangements for Barry to operate Passion Fields."

The staff asked many questions and Barry was able to answer most of them. He realized the affection the staff had for both Claude and Claire. Many asked about the arrangements for Claire's funeral. Sarah explained that her parents would be staying at the mansion that night. Some staff volunteered to work late to ensure all was well for them.

Chapter 81

Claude lay in the hospital bed with his right leg in a plaster cast. It was elevated and held high by a pulley and wires. His head was bandaged like a mummy. Intravenous tubes were taped into the veins of his arms and a monitor blipped his heart rate and measured his blood pressure.

While Barry and Sarah stood beside the bed Dr. Keene entered.

"Good afternoon. We have some progress. A little while ago he was trying to murmur something. It was in French we think. He was still in the coma and it was strange he could do that. We are encouraged by it."

"Why is his head bandaged?"

"There was a deep cut that required many stitches. He lost a lot of blood and we had to do a transfusion. That is now under control. The Xrays show the break of the bone in his leg is clean and will heal nicely. The other matter, his damaged penis, I cannot comment on. It is under the care of Dr. Stanley Stubbs. He is the urologist here."

Barry was confused.

"Ok then. What's exactly the problem with his willy?"

"It seems the soft bone was snapped when he fell. Very painful. He won't be able to keep the girls happy for a while."

Sarah sighed at that comment.

"You men are all the same. It doesn't seem to matter if you're a doctor or a ditch digger. All the bloody same. What about poor Claire? He was about to marry his love and now she's dead. You all are insensitive and piss me off!"

Sarah stomped her foot and marched off leaving Barry with the doctor.

"I swear horses are more sensible than men," she called to a passing nurse.

Barry remained with Dr. Keene who was discussing the treatments Claude would need if he was to regain consciousness. They were joined by a short plump red-faced man with wild hair pointing in all directions.

"I am Dr. Stanley Stump. Here at the hospital, they call me Stumpy. I will be looking after your friend here. He is going to need some very special care to overcome the trauma he has suffered. I will need to wait for him to come out of the coma before I can operate on him. After the operation, he will be in some pain for weeks. I am going to arrange a nurse and a physiotherapist to assist him. The nurse can help with the pain reduction and the physio will help him as his leg mends. I have already discussed this with Dr. Keene. Now, if I can ask for privacy I need to examine his private member."

The doctor and Barry left the room and walked towards the exit where they found a still fuming Sarah.

"I promise that either I or the hospital will be in contact if Claude regains consciousness."

"Sarah, why are you acting this way?"
"I feel sorry for Claude. He has lost a friend and future wife. He has serious injuries. He is going to suffer and you men make jokes. What has happened to him was not his fault and now he will be unable to enjoy his life for God knows how long. Yes, I am angry about the whole thing. I am sorry, it has deeply affected me."

He moved toward her and took her in an embrace. Sarah started to cry.

"He is a good man and has helped many of the workers. He has been kind and funny. Why do these things always happen to good people?"

"There is no easy answer to that question. Now come and I will take you to a little café for fresh cream buns and tea."

They were barely back at the mansion when the phone rang. It was the hospital to advise that Claude was out of the coma.

That news cheered Sarah up.

"We will go back and see him in the morning. Will you be able to take the time Barry?"

"Bloody hell, I'll make the time for my mate."

Chapter 82

Ten weeks after being admitted to the hospital, Claude was informed he would be able to return home in another week or two. He was happy. The lengthy stay at the hospital had become boring and Claude was eager to experience life again. The blow came when he was told of Claire's demise.

His joy slipped to deep despair. He had truly believed that Claire was the perfect woman for him. He had known many women, but she was the only one who possessed a special flair he had loved. He questioned why his dream had been shattered and doubted he would ever meet someone like Claire again.

There was excitement on the morning Barry was to bring Claude home. It seemed as if a dark mood had been lifted from the mansion. A celebration was planned. Marie-France dressed formally for the occasion and wore almost every piece from her vast jewelry collection.

At the hospital, Barry and Sarah made arrangements with the administration department for Claude's release and then went to take him to the car in a wheelchair. On entering the room, they found Claude and Dr. Stubbs speaking with an extremely attractive Asian woman.

"Good morning, Barry and Sarah. I'm just introducing Misty Moon to Claude. Misty has helped numerous former patients through her physiotherapy clinic. He is going to need some unique treatments that Misty can provide. Her clinic is one of the best in San Francisco."

Barry eyed her. There was something he sensed that he didn't quite trust.
"That's a bloody long way to drive just to get physio treatment. Isn't there somewhere closer?"

"There is, but only Misty can give Claude the treatment he will require. I suggest he works with her. The treatments can start in a week or two and she will perform the work at his home. Misty also has attendants who can assist him in other areas."

Barry's instincts bristled. There was something wrong and he couldn't identify what it was. Her appearance was nice and she exuded an over friendliness. He tried to focus on why he was unsettled with her but gave up. He vowed to find out more about Misty Moon.

Outside of Claude's room, Barry spoke to Sarah.

"I don't feel good about her or Dr. Stanley Stubbs. I cannot say why. There seems to be some sort of a relationship between those two. Did you sense it?"

"Yes, there is something strange. I don't trust her. I will speak to Claude back at the house. I think we should find out more about the Misty Moon if that's even her real name."

"When she comes to the house I will be watching her. I sense trouble with her."

A nurse arrived in the lobby of the hospital pushing Claude in a wheelchair. He held a pair of crutches and was smiling, eager to be away from the hospital and back at the mansion.

With some assistance, they lowered him into the car and drove carefully home.

The staff welcomed Claude home. Decked out in all her jewelry, Marie-France jangled over to hug him as he awkwardly maneuvered up the front entrance steps on his crutches.

"Please don't hug me. I am still very sore."

She stopped in front of him and leaned to kiss him on both cheeks. Claude sneezed. She was wearing a perfume that reminded him of fly spray.

Sarah had arranged a special welcoming lunch for Claude and all the loyal staff. There was a distinct party atmosphere.

It was early afternoon when Claude retired to his room to rest. He was still weak and tired easily.

Barry sat alone with Sarah in the salon.

"I am going to call Al Pine at the law firm. I will ask his assistance to help me find out more about Misty Moon."

Sarah nodded in agreement and Barry placed the call. After telling Al Pine of Claude's progress, he stated the reason for the call. Al noted the information and advised Barry that the firm did perform investigations into people. He would assign a private investigator immediately and have him in contact with Barry.

The visits by Misty commenced the next day and lasted hours. After several weeks, Claude was taken to the clinic to make use of the specialized equipment.

Barry grew more concerned. He had noticed that Claude had started speaking fondly of her and spending more time at the sessions. He wished to tell Claude of his dislike and suspicions of her but refrained. Claude had experienced enough disturbance in his life.

He was growing impatient and called Al Pine to check whether any information had been found on her. None had.

After several months, Claude shocked Barry and Sarah by announcing that he was planning on taking a vacation with Misty. He had recovered well enough to walk without crutches and his manhood was again intact.

Barry objected strongly. He decided to tell Claude of his concerns.

Claude was furious when he was told Al Pine had a private investigator looking into her background.

"Nothing has been found now after several months. I guess nothing will be found. I will call him."

"I could have told you that. She is an educated, charming and witty woman. I am back in love."

Sarah rolled her eyes.

Chapter 83

While Claude was at one of his physio sessions, Barry received an unexpected call from Al Pine.

"Barry, the private investigator, James Fitzroy, has just received information on Misty Moon from his sources. I would rather have you come to our offices and meet him. Your suspicions were correct. She is major trouble for Claude."

"I am going to be in San Francisco on Saturday to meet with some friends visiting from Australia. Can we meet then?"

"Yes. We will meet for a lunch. I will advise James."

Barry hung up the phone and wondered what had been uncovered that was so serious he wanted to meet rather than discuss over the phone. He only had a day to wait before the mystery would be revealed.

Mid-afternoon, Claude returned with Misty Moon. He took her to the stables to view his recently acquired horses, then invited her to stay for an early dinner and drinks. Barry declined an invitation on the grounds that he and Sarah had a reservation for dinner at a local restaurant. Barry could not stand the thought of sharing a meal with her.

When Barry and Sarah returned late that night from dinner, they were surprised to find Misty Moon still at the mansion.

Claude called to them as they entered.

"Come and join us for a drink. Misty will be staying the night here."

"Thank you, but Sarah is not feeling well and I have an early morning meeting. Another time perhaps. Good night."

Their avoidance was not missed by Claude. He wondered what the issue was and what had triggered such a strong reaction from Barry.

The next morning Claude confronted Barry.

"What is your problem with Misty? I have not seen anything strange or untoward. Until last night, all our sessions have been a strictly patient and professional service provider. Today that has ended. I have decided to pursue a romantic relationship with her. I am no longer needing the services of a physiotherapist."

"Claude, you had better listen to me and take some advice. I received a call from Al Pine. I had asked the investigation be stopped weeks ago when you requested that. He called yesterday to tell me that something serious was found. I am meeting him tomorrow for lunch with the investigator. I think you should come and hear things first hand. Al Pine sounded very serious and worried for you. I am your partner and friend. Please listen to what the investigator has to say."

"I'm sure it is something minor. I am not worried. I never thought I would ever find anyone after Claire. I still miss her."

"She was a special person. I too miss her."

"I don't like it but I will come with you tomorrow to meet with Al Pine and that investigator."

"I need to leave now. I have a meeting with a new distributor who wishes to carry the Passion Fields wine in Europe."

Claude was now concerned. He phoned the hospital to speak with Dr. Stanley Stubbs. He needed to know more about the doctor's relationship with Misty Moon. He was disappointed to learn the doctor had gone on vacation for a month. It seemed too coincidental that Misty was traveling to see family for several weeks at the same time. He started to wonder if Barry had been right about her.

On Saturday morning they drove down to San Francisco. Sarah accompanied them as she wished to visit certain stores. Claude and Barry agreed on a time and location to meet Sarah after the meeting and continued onto the law offices of Biggar and Biggar. Al Pine was waiting for them. He was with a wiry grey-haired man.

"This is James Fitzroy. He was formerly with the FBI and has extensive experience tracking down missing people and performing background checks. I believe what he is about to tell you both will both shock and upset you."

Al motioned to a long redwood table and asked them to sit. There was a slide projector set up and aimed at a silver-colored screen.

"Gentlemen, before I start I should explain that there are other authorities investigating the women and several others here in California and in Hong Kong. Some information has been shared with me. The authorities have demanded that we do nothing to interfere with there investigation and plans. I must get that commitment from you before we proceed. Al has prepared an agreement to keep all information confidential. Those agreements must be signed and Al will provide them to the appropriate people. Is that satisfactory?"

Both Claude and Barry were intrigued by the cloak and dagger approach the simple background check on Misty Moon had taken.

"Yes of course it is. Barry and I will sign and agree to keep all this confidential."

After the documents were signed, James commenced and explained his findings.

"I know you will find this hard to accept Claude. This woman you know as Misty Moon is, in fact, someone called Wendy Wong. She assumed the identity of the real Misty Moon years ago when the real Misty died under unusual circumstances that are still under investigation. She has had facial surgery done to make her appearance more like that of Misty Moon. She was born in China and she and her husband are active members of a Chinese triad here in San Francisco. Her physiotherapy practice is a front for illegal activities including money laundering, drugs, smuggling, bogus immigration processing and she is a fence for the stolen antiques and art from collections here in America and in Europe. She is part of a notorious Chinese gang that Interpol is investigating, hence the reason for the confidentiality. I traveled to Hong Kong and with the help of my local partner there, we were able to monitor her for days. I have photos that I will now show you."

Al Pine dimmed the lights in the conference room and the bright light of the projector reflected back off the screen. James started flipping through various pictures taken in Hong Kong. Most showed the woman with different men, some of who James identified as gang members and provided a little information about each of them.

Claude gasped out loud when a slide was selected that showed Wendy Wong with a short-haired blonde woman.

"Where is that? What is happening in that photo?"

"Claude that is one of the art smugglers that Interpol is after. Why are you so interested in this picture?"

"When I was studying at the Sorbonne, I had a part-time job at a gallery in Paris. She was the daughter of the owner. That is Lise Victor. She disappeared when the gallery was raided for dealing in stolen art and antiques. Because I worked at the gallery I was arrested and jailed until the police found out that I was not involved."

"You say that her name is Lise Victor, but she is operating under the name Michelin Fournier. If you are sure that Lise Victor is her correct name I will advise my friends in Interpol."

"It is her real name. What other information do you have? Barry told me that you have uncovered something that is serious and puts me in danger. What is it?"

James paused and looked at Al Pine.

"Al, I think it is best for you to tell Claude of the rest."

"Claude, the woman you know as Misty Moon has been operating that physiotherapy clinic for a number of years. She has befriended a number of male patients referred by Dr. Stanley Stubbs. In each case, the men have died. The police suspect a form of poisoning but have been unable to verify it. They believe it is a poison from China that they are unable to test for. In every case, the men left estates to Misty Moon. All died when traveling on vacations with her. We are concerned you will be her next victim."

Claude's face was ashen. He sat in silence. Barry reached over and shook him.

"OK now, Claude boy. Time for you to make a decision. Seems you were about to go deep six."

Even in this serious situation, Claude's Aussie partner and friend was able to make light of it.

"I thank you for this. If I can assist in the investigation, I will. Lise is an evil force. She has caused many to suffer. Al, are you available for lunch with me. Barry has friends visiting and I will be alone for a while."

"Yes, of course. Would you like James to join us?"

"Yes."

Chapter 84

At the mansion, Claude was despondent. It seemed as if all his romances had ended in tragedy or just collapsed in strange ways. His extreme wealth couldn't compensate for the emotional distress he had experienced in his life.

He thought of all the women he had known and loved. Only one still was firmly in his mind. Atarangi. There were qualities she possessed that the others didn't He wondered whether that was because of the culture of the Cook Islands.

In the morning, Claude decided to walk in the vineyards and reflect on his life and decide whether he should abandon the relationship with 'Misty Moon' or try to work it out. He visited Barry in the winery. Barry was furious when Claude expressed his concern and idea.

"You are a bloody idiot. You have been told she is a fraud and involved with international crime. She is married and has lied to you. Do you have a death wish? Look at all those other blokes she might have bumped off. Do you want to be the next one? Bloody great, mate. Just sign the papers and give me everything before you go then."

"I am in love with her. Maybe I can change her."

"You can't change the crap she's involved in. Chinese gangs, smuggling, drugs. Jesus Claude, wake up."

"I'm going for a walk. I am really upset. I hear the workers have bee having trouble with those blackbirds attacking the new vines. I'll take the shotgun and some birdshot and go help them."

Claude picked a long-barreled shotgun from the gun case and placed it behind his neck and put his arms over it. He strolled off down towards the ravine. Barry watched as his figure grew distant and then returned to check a new fermentation of grapes from the newer vines.

He left the office and was walking back to his house when the loud gunshot echoed up from the ravine. Barry turned and looked in the direction of the gunshot. It was where Claude had been walking.

As he looked down to the ravine he noticed the curling greyish-blue smoke from the weapons discharge swirling into the air.

He ran towards the area and found Claude on the ground with the discharged shotgun still in his hand.

Fin

www.ingramcontent.com/pod-product-compliance
Lightning Source LLC
Chambersburg PA
CBHW030429010526
44118CB00011B/557